What hope is there for a man so desperate for money to support his drug addiction that he drove the girl he loved to prostitution—and, ultimately, to suicide? Or another man, who frustrated the attempts of some of America's top psychiatrists to halt his ten year run of dope addiction and crime? Synanon.

This book about Synanon, a highly controversial organization dedicated to curing drug addiction, explains, among other things, why it makes newspaper headlines. Its non-orthodox methods of handling addicts, its outspoken attitude toward traditional treatments, and its all-addict administration have made it a target for sharp criticism and bitter persecution.

Each year of Synanon's existence has been a struggle for survival. Money is

(continued on back flap)

methods, the questions of why and how it works become relatively unimportant—it *does* work.

SYNANON

SYNANON

Guy Endore

1968

DOUBLEDAY & COMPANY, INC., GARDEN CITY, NEW YORK

To all the friends and members
of Synanon, past and present,
named and unnamed, who gave me
their opinions, their feelings,
their memories for the writing
of this book

SYNANON

Prologue

I've often thought that the story of Synanon—the story of that unique society of ex-dope addicts, ex-criminals, and ex-prostitutes —a society which these former felons now proudly hold up before the world as a model of sanity for all to copy (surely the most colossal piece of impudence in the history of man)—I've often thought this story worth recording.

The world—at any rate most of it—knows little or nothing of Synanon. Such ignorance cannot last much longer, however, to judge by a talk that Chuck Dederich, the ex-alcoholic founder of the organization, gave not so long ago before a general meeting of these one-time outcasts now banded together to lead lives free of drugs and crime.

Chuck declared that the membership was then verging on the eight hundred mark, and he went on to make the following forecast: "During the coming year Synanon will do exactly what it has been doing every one of the nine years since it was incorporated as a non-profit foundation. That is to say it will once again double the number of its resident members. And it will more than double its turnover in goods and in cash which together are now reaching towards a total of three million."

The gathering responded to these ambitious words with warm applause but with none of the frenzy or fanaticism that it seemed to me such a shattering statement ought to have evoked. Was it possible, I asked myself, that no one in that audience recalled the story of the inventor of the game of chess and the reward that he asked for?

The reader may remember that all the inventor asked from his grateful monarch was the modest sum of one grain of wheat for the first square of the board, two grains for the second, four for the third, and so on, doubling the number of grains with each succeeding square. A request that the king considered both silly and trifling until the mathematics of it struck home and he realized that not all the wheat his kingdom could raise in a million years would meet his obligation for those sixty-four squares!

Obviously if Synanon can actually keep up its present rate of growth, then in less than a quarter of a century this "only sane society in the world" must blanket the earth!

Is it conceivable that a simple "togetherness cure" for dope addiction can seriously pose such a challenge? And pride itself on being the salvation of man?

"Synanon," so Chuck has explained on innumerable occasions, "is like a six-and-one-half-sided peg. There are no slots in existence for such pegs. Absolutely none. Neither in our minds, nor in our language, nor in our institutions. So there can be no convenient pigeonhole into which you can slip Synanon and consider the question of where Synanon fits a settled matter.

"Because Synanon doesn't fit in anywhere. Not anywhere.

"If Synanon were a prison—if it were an asylum or a hospital or a halfway house," so Chuck has said, "it would constitute no problem for our citizens or their authorities. But since we're none of those usual places where crime and dope addiction can continue to remain unsolved and out of sight, with everyone complacently convinced that the issue is being taken care of according to the latest scientific methods, nobody quite knows what to do with us.

"Those who know a little about Synanon are often under the misapprehension that we are in the business of 'curing' dope addiction. Of course that isn't so. Synanon just happens to be a better way for people to live together, both with themselves and with others. Here criminals stop committing crimes. Dope addicts stop

shooting dope. Whores become ladies. And squares stop taking tranquilizers. And this is something that cities, counties, states, ruling
bodies of all kinds, prison boards, bureaus of rehabilitation, boards
of medical examiners, and all the usual official groups who have to
cope with civilization's misfits are totally unprepared to face. They
have—as yet—no slot for such a thing. And their impulse at present
is either to destroy us or pretend we don't exist."

I ask the reader to consider once more Chuck's statement, because,
if true, it is epoch-making: "Synanon just happens to be a better
way for people to live together, both with themselves and with
others." What else is this if not an open challenge to the world—
to a world forever poised on the brink of riot and nuclear war? Where
people certainly seem to have a long way to go before they can be
described as living comfortably with themselves and with others.

Exactly what is this Synanon?

I cannot think of a better answer to that difficult question than
to say that Synanon is an idea. An idea that is struggling to be
born, and that is being born. Slowly at the moment, but perhaps
explosively in the future.

Synanon, furthermore, is also the increasing numbers of people
that this idea is gathering around itself in its efforts to make itself
manifest in a world that obviously needs such an idea desperately.

Historically Synanon is something that began to happen to a handful of people, all of them former alcoholics, some nine years ago,
first in a cheap apartment, and then in a couple of rundown storefronts in Ocean Park, and subsequently at various addresses in Santa
Monica and elsewhere.

Not all of those who took part in these very early gropings could
see that something big was trying to happen on the human plane,
something important and new.

Some saw only the excitement of being part of a novel and more
powerful form of group interaction that was taking shape among
them, and the help that they, as individuals, were personally deriving from it. And when they had had what they needed out of this,
these people left.

And later, when dope addicts began to join the group there were others who saw only the startling results that could be achieved with these almost hopeless cases. And again, there were some who felt that this was achievement enough. And it is due largely to the numbers of these drug addicts who have been helped that Synanon is known as a self-staffing association of addicts who wish to cure themselves—and that's it. Nothing more. Nothing more.

One former alcoholic, however, Chuck Dederich, has consistently stuck to his belief that the Synanon idea was to be a continuing revelation and that it was therefore his task and that of as many of his associates as he could persuade to remain on indefinitely, to watch this process, follow it wherever it might lead, while trying to understand it and assist it in its efforts to achieve reality on earth.

Thus the two aspects of Synanon, the Synanon idea and the Synanon people who live by it, have had to grow by trial and error, under a leadership that faced the necessity of being both visionary and practical.

Practical because this leadership had in its care fifteen, twenty, thirty, fifty, a hundred and now close to a thousand people, all of whom had to be fed, housed, clothed, instructed, and amused, to say nothing of being helped toward physical and spiritual restoration, a task that required Synanon to constitute itself as a tax-exempt non-profit foundation, as well as a business of getting money through donations, through the operation of gas stations, through the sale of advertising specialties, and so forth.

Visionary because there was this other Synanon, the Synanon of fresh ideas as to how people should live and function together, a task that required the members to constitute themselves into an experimental laboratory in sociology and psychology, guided by executives who were themselves also guinea pigs in the same laboratory, but who had the patience to study something still largely unknown, and the strength to make decisions in the dark, and accept failure when their decisions turned out to be wrong—and meanwhile put up with the accusation of not being qualified professionals. As if one could become a qualified Synanon specialist at any other place than Synanon.

It is because of the newness of all this mélange of drug addiction and sociology that Chuck keeps saying: "We can't explain what we're doing because we still haven't got a language for it." And he ruffles his lips with his fingers making a sound like bibbily-bibbily-bibbily. "You see, we haven't yet got the noises that go with it. We haven't got those noises yet." And he will reach for a piece of chalk to illustrate on the blackboard what he feels Synanon is trying to do that cannot yet be expressed in any of our usual mouth-noises.

He will generally start with a horizontal line and affix a letter to each end. This line will serve to represent the world as it is at present, made up of all the dichotomies—all the polarities—that either imprison people away from each other or else drive them at each other in headlong collision. He will write at one end the letter G to stand for good, and B at the opposite end to stand for bad. Or the letter N for Negro against W for white. Or else R for rich and P for poor, or the letter H for Hippie and S for square. And with arrows pointing this way or that, Chuck will illustrate the tension or the conflict that keeps these opposites forever locked to each other along the base line.

"This is not the line of Synanon," Chuck will say. "This is not us."

And then he will draw a vertical line up from the center of that horizontal base. A line going up through "space-time," a line that will be shown reaching toward a point that Chuck will variously label G for God, or R for Reality, or any one of the many attempts that man keeps making to overcome his dichotomies and get himself out of his mess.

"Here is our line, the line of Synanon," Chuck will say, and he will label the point which that vertical line is reaching toward with the letters C.P., which stands for the Conciliatory Principle, that point where it will no longer matter to an individual whether he is white or black, rich or poor, Siberian or Mexican, a former criminal or not. Just so long as he is human. In other words: is there such a thing as mankind, or isn't there?

The vertical climb of Synanon toward the C.P. is not easy. It is a march through the unexplored, holding steadfast through a world that continues to fight along that base line: reactionaries against progressives, doves against hawks, Communists against capitalists, Black Power against white supremacy, atheists against believers, under the permanent illusion that something can be solved by this struggle. The list of dichotomies is enormous. And their tug and clash are endless. And all the religions, all the arts, all the sciences of man seem unable to prevent that base line from moving ever closer to a final conflict where all differences are likely to end by incineration.

That diagram illustrates better than words why Chuck and the people around him are convinced that Synanon must go its own way, however obscure and difficult. A quotation from Henry David Thoreau's *Essay on Civil Disobedience* that Chuck keeps framed on his wall long ago explained that necessity and that difficulty. Thoreau said:

"Action from principle, the performance of right, changes things and relations; it is essentially revolutionary, and does not consist wholly with anything which was."

Thus, with one foot planted squarely in the Synanon of the here and now, and the other groping for a secure spot out in the dense fog where lies the Synanon of the future, the organization moves toward the end of the man of today who is his own worst enemy and the beginning of the human race.

1

It is of these ex-outlaws perhaps for the first time in history gathered in a group that is neither a prison nor a mafia, that I now propose to write.

"What I'd like to do," I said to Chuck one day, "isn't anything of a theoretical nature. I'd be afraid to tackle that. But just the story of Synanon's birth and development. Nothing profound."

"Not the story of Synanon," Chuck corrected me. "The saga of Synanon." The difference was a question of reverence, of something hallowed, which Chuck conveyed to me not only by his choice of the word "saga," but by a certain inflection of his voice.

I resisted for a moment. But then I agreed. Yes, a saga. Because a book about Synanon would be more of a saga than a story. Because events that happened only yesterday in the scant eight or nine years of Synanon, have nevertheless already ripened into legends—legends that the older residents love to tell and retell. This is one of the distinguishing marks of groups that from their origin feel themselves heavily pregnant with importance and one of the best demonstrations of the richness of the human material and human experience out of which these legends have sprung.

But for me, personally, the saga of Synanon did not begin until the organization was over two years old—until Elaine Brandchaft (whose husband, Dr. Brandchaft, had been among Synanon's earliest supporters) took me down to the old armory building on the beach at Santa Monica. (That was a year or more after the group had moved out of their original location a mile or so to the south, where they had occupied a couple of crummy stores that were scheduled to be bulldozed into a parking lot.)

And the moment I entered the place I was captivated.

There's something about the fascination that Synanon exerts on some people that defies analysis. I was not immediately aware that other visitors were puzzled and disturbed by this same curious magnetism until Ed Spiegel—who made the earliest documentary film about the place—said to me one evening: "Don't you see? This place is a microcosm."

I recall pretending for a moment that I was now seeing Synanon in this new light for the first time. "Oh, so that's what it is!" I exclaimed.

"Well, look around you," he argued. "The whole world is here in a thimble. The good and the bad. Crooks and philosophers, mothers and prostitutes . . ."

"Former prostitutes," I corrected.

". . . Negro and white. Jews and Christians," he went on. "Everything. In miniature. Why bother to roam the world? Just come down to Synanon in Santa Monica. It's all here."

Yes, that was certainly true. And no doubt one of the reasons why people took to the place.

"Best coffeehouse in Los Angeles," Ed Spiegel used to say flatly. "Bar none."

There was a little combo at work in the next room. Some couples were dancing. Others were at the tables playing cards. Everywhere groups of people drinking coffee, talking of this and that. Former addicts and visitors totally indistinguishable.

Really a wonderfully congenial place. Except that none of this could possibly explain what I was doing there. I had never had any desire to visit even the best of coffeehouses. I have no special predilection for microcosms. Combo music is something I've managed to live without. To me it's nothing but a certain kind of noise that interferes with conversation. I don't dance. And I'm not a coffee addict.

And yet there I was, totally captivated.

"Of course you were captivated," a fellow named Frank something-or-other pointed out to me. "Synanon is actually a very cleverly compounded addictive. All these fantastic characters with their prison records and their suicide attempts. And the whole aura of drug addiction with its macabre details. And then old Chuck himself, the gravel-voiced spellbinder, with his chunky stance and his bulldog determination to put this thing across. This place is really a more powerful fix than heroin. You get hooked here. I don't know about you, but I'm hooked. I'm really hooked."

He was indeed. And Frank was to be seen at Synanon almost every night. Until one evening Chuck turned his gravel-voice on him, asking him what the hell he thought he was doing here, drinking up Synanon coffee, listening up Synanon music, and never once writing a check for the foundation, never so much as bothering to empty his ashtrays or return his soiled cups to the kitchen. If he wanted to live free in Synanon, fine! crazy! he could get right to work in the dishpan and they'd find a cot for him upstairs in the men's dorm.

Frank something-or-other wasn't hooked after that. In fact I never saw him in Synanon again.

But I stayed hooked, continuing to wonder what it was that held me. Me, a writer, already addicted to a twenty-four-hour-a-day job: keeping myself alive in the most fiercely competitive field in the world: the literary arena. No live doctor need fear any competition from a dead one. No lawyer in the United States need be concerned about lawyers in Italy cutting into his business. Only in the arts is the competition on a worldwide basis and with the dead still holding their own or even increasing their share.

Of course writers who exploit the criminal area for their literary material might find some valid reason for frequenting the Synanon coffeehouse in search of characters and plots, which are endless there. But that was not my field. I tend to take my material from books. I haunt the library stacks where I find my most congenial subjects in the great men of the past.

So what was there for me in Synanon? Nothing but a bunch of former addicts, former thieves and streetwalkers, people who had never earned an honest dime in their lives and who were now taking it easy, living off the charity of hard-working, responsible citizens whom addicts scornfully called squares.

"Such as yourself?" Chuck suggested.

"Yes," I said. "Such as myself." Not that I overestimated my occasional little checks. But I did contribute. Without me and my kind there would be no Synanon.

I can still remember that conversation—and others like it. Held in the "room across the hall" from the main room, a darkish sort of place, with ugly time-ravished couches and chairs surrounding a huge coffee table, and Chuck lolling back, puffing a cigarette, his bare feet, sometimes clad in Japanese flip-flops, resting on the coffee table amidst a confusion of old magazines, dated newspapers, and correspondence still unanswered. He is dressed as always in baggy bargain-counter trousers with his ample belly lapping over the belt, and a thin short-sleeved shirt doing its best to cover a bulky torso. A defiant crop of short stand-up bristles crowns a misshapen face that you admire without knowing why, a right side dished in from a penetrating ear operation that has deafened and partially paralyzed it, but with plenty of life still in a glinting eye that stabs at you from between folds of unresponding muscle that almost close it off and a left side that is whole and more than makes up for the repose of the right by its electric animation.

It's the head of a latter-day Socrates: ugly and wise, complex and simple. A face that repels and attracts, refusing to leave you indifferent.

"Think of it this way," Chuck argues with me. "You'd be supporting these animals in any case, wouldn't you? Well, wouldn't you? Wouldn't they be living off your taxes while in jail? And even when out of jail and on the streets, wouldn't you still be supporting them? Because they'd be stealing from stores to buy their dope. And merchants have a percentage that they slap onto all their costs to cover theft insurance. And you know to whom they pass off that cost?"

"To me," I admit, "as a consumer."

"That's right," Chuck says. "To you. So you can't escape it, can you? Well, can you?" he challenges.

All right. But just the shabby appearance of the old armory in those days—before endless remodelings had managed to eliminate some of its original ugliness and even lend it considerable beauty— ought to have driven me off the premises. Those huge, crudely furnished rooms with their miserably carpeted floors, and the walls where pictures and photographs fought a losing war against the corrupted plaster and paint . . . I could well understand why so many dope addicts came into Synanon and then left almost immediately. In fact I often wondered why anyone ever elected to stay in that frightful place.

I remember when I first met Morris Hodges and asked him what had brought him to Synanon and whether he intended to stay. He looked at me for a moment, and then said—with a candor that overwhelmed me: "I'm a three-time loser, Guy. One more conviction and I'm in jail for good. I'm fighting for my life here."

Yes of course. That certainly explained poor Morris. But what about me? I wasn't fighting for my life. Synanon wasn't about to save me. Why then should I go on putting up with this endless cigarette-smoking that the members were addicted to, a legal habit that obviously helped some of them overcome the loss of their forbidden one. The smoking at Synanon was so general and consistent that I would have to take a shower when I came home late at night, because I, as a non-smoker, couldn't stand my own body odor, couldn't sleep with myself, so drenched was my skin with tobacco fumes.

Really, to come right down to it—or "gut-level," as the Synanon people love to say—I hated Synanon. I really did. And I shuddered when I was invited to eat there and saw the kind of food the members were forced to consume because in those early days they were unable to be choosy and had to accept whatever ready-to-spoil stuff charitable grocers consented to dump on them. A condition that is still only partially corrected.

Why then did I keep on going to Synanon? And when I went, why was I so pleased to be asked to stay for lunch? And late at night, my body and clothes reeking from smoke, why did I nevertheless leave with reluctance?

It must be said that there was something homey about the place, though at the time I could never understand precisely what made it so. Something genuinely warm and homey. So that I felt accepted on a level I had never before experienced. Thus I will always remember with a feeling close to tears how I introduced myself one evening to a man who sat alone at a large oilcloth covered table. And how after some exchange of courtesies he lit up one of those inevitable cigarettes and said quietly: "There's nothing much to say about me, Guy. I'm just an old con. Been in and out of jail all my life for just about every crime you can think of."

Whereupon, for some crazy reason, I liked this gentle soft-spoken man at once. And I think he liked me. And that was curiously comforting. I remember he talked to me about opium, a form of addiction now almost extinct. He recalled the little cans that opium came in, cans weighing from fifty to five hundred fun, an oriental measure of weight, and the various brands of it, the Rose being the best. And he told me about the ritual of smoking and eating opium, a habit that has practically disappeared in the States.

"It was the apparatus," he explained, "the lamp and the pipe and so forth. And especially the sickeningly sweet odor. After the Harrison Act made narcotics—unless medically prescribed—a federal offense, opium had to go. That odor was a dead giveaway. The narcotics officers couldn't miss it. Morphine, cocaine, and then heroin, took the place of opium. Quicker and safer."

Charlie Hamer and I have remained friends ever since. After an interval of several years during which I somehow never bumped into him, I saw him again recently at the new Tomales Bay branch of Synanon where he is in charge of the corral. He gave me a cheerful handshake and I watched him for a while busy medicating a mare that had been ganged up on by the other horses.

"I was born on a ranch," he said to me. "In Oklahoma. Long time ago."

Charlie Hamer had obviously come home to something. In Synanon. Could that be true of me?

Perhaps the crisp sparkle of the sea, the wind and the sky coming in through the tall windows of the Santa Monica building had something to do with my love for the place. Or the many battered couches strewn about the rooms. Couches covered with disintegrating pieces of terry cloth whose color was beyond redemption, couches where one's buttocks sank comfortably deep between the broken springs, and one felt welcome to come or to go, to stay or not to stay, to take potluck or turn it down. . . .

And where, for all those reasons that I have tried to define but haven't, I chose to linger and make friends with people whose former lives I could not possibly have shared, and to whose present lives I had some difficulty accommodating myself. . . .

Perhaps it roused in me long-dead emotions of a portion of my childhood spent in an Ohio orphanage. Just such an ancient building with huge bare rooms, a place I hated violently, and yet now, across nearly sixty years, often think back to fondly.

In any case I kept returning to Synanon in Santa Monica again and again. Invited and reinvited, to become partly or wholly involved, however much I pleased. And no one ever questioning me as to why I hung around incessantly, and then disappeared for weeks or months at a time. I was made to feel accepted. And I was inexplicably grateful.

Except once, when fat Melanie . . .

Which was partly my own fault. Because I should never have opened my mouth. Actually I spoke little. I was never sure I had anything of value to contribute, not even to those group interactions that everyone insisted on labeling "group therapy" but which Synanon stubbornly declared were not group therapy at all but synanons with a small "s," and which, much later, in order to differentiate them from all connection to psychiatry were baptized "games."

At that time these games were played every Monday, Wednesday, and Friday nights, when the whole membership, plus a couple of squares such as myself, would be divided up into groups of about ten to fifteen and sent to the various rooms of the building, there to sit on beds or chairs or on the floor and to say whatever they pleased to each other. There were no rules as to the kind of language that might be employed—cross-examination, tirade, ridicule—only physical violence, or even the threat of it—being strictly forbidden.

I joined—but never quite became a member of these varying groups. I somehow remained outside. A spectator. Trying not to look too wide-eyed. Just drinking it all in. The most frightful tales. For example one that was torn from the cupid lips of a sweet young thing whose only emotion was revealed in a soft flow of tears from eyes of the most innocent blue: how every weekend when her father came home late at night, in a drunken rage, she had to submit to his incestuous fornication. And if she dared complain to her mother the next morning, she was slapped for having lewd dreams.

And another about a Negro who while in prison was brutally beaten up by white convicts for having dared to drink from the tin cup reserved at the pump for whites only. . . .

But once I did open my mouth and said something to fat Melanie, I can't remember what, only that it caused her to turn on me viciously.

"You!" she screamed. "What the hell are you doing here? Who the fuck let you in? What are you sucking around here for?"

I remember mumbling something or other about all of us being here for pretty much the same reason, namely to help and be helped. "Isn't that the essence of Synanon?" I asked.

I guess this early effort of mine to pin down that elusive essence of Synanon was just too sanctimonious for Melanie. And I myself would have been glad to withdraw it, because this search for the secret attraction of Synanon was really my private concern. All I succeeded in doing was make her roar with merriment. Her stout body, sleek as a German bratwurst, looked as if it would pop open its skin from the explosiveness of her laughter.

I must admit that there was something darkly beautiful about Melanie that made her name, which means "black," singularly appropriate: a dusky complexion but so silken-smooth that a movie star might have envied it, hair like a great black cloud, teeth as if freshly carved from the whitest part of a raw potato, her tongue as clean and pink as a cat's. Ungainly, yes, because of her fat, but exuding such waves of vitality that my eyes often followed her bursting thighs as far up as they could see. Wondering . . .

Oh yes. She definitely attracted me. The girls at Synanon generally exerted considerable fascination on me. And repelled me too —at the same time. Just as almost everything else in Synanon cut both ways. Melanie certainly had her share of these strong provocative characteristics, otherwise she would not have been pregnant at the time, and trailing a string of abandoned children all over the United States. This was in truth the dark part of her.

She flashed her sparkling and scornful eyes at me: "Help and be helped? Haha! You help me? Why you're nothing but a baby with your diaper full of shit. You don't know the first fucking thing about life!"

Oh, that obscene language of Synanon! How difficult it was for me to reconcile it to the lofty aims of the organization. Not that I never used any dirty words myself. Nor that I had any rigid objections to their use by others. Indeed I thought I knew the value of such words for arousing passion and energy, and I thought I knew their purpose here at Synanon where they were supposedly restricted to these therapy sessions and served as a lubricant for the outlet of hostilities which if repressed might explode into physical violence. . . .

"Do you suppose," Chuck asked me once, "if diplomats were not so careful about their language and got down to such words as fuck and shit we might have considerably less etiquette and also considerably less warfare? And might not the same thing apply to theologians and politicians. . . . Maybe war is a visceral problem, and not to be solved by cerebration alone."

I agreed. I agreed wholeheartedly. And indeed I was all for the liberation of both the cerebral and the visceral in man. But somehow to have this foul avalanche perpetually pouring into one's ears at these synanons, as if there were no other aspect to life except that of the gut. . . .

I'm recalling right now a long and heated argument with Barry. It seemed to me that he, with his literary talent and ambition, ought to have sided with me, and agreed that these obscene expletives ought to be reserved for a forceful underlining of our language and not be forever dissipated by being used where our brains were too lazy to find more pertinent and meaningful expressions. Wasn't it the tendency of unrestricted obscenity to reduce our vast English language to this one dirty fragment?

How many of these obscene words were there anyhow? A couple of dozen or so? And didn't they tend to become boring if used indiscriminately? While thousands of other striking and descriptive words of our tongue remained unused simply because people were too lazy to reach for anything else but obscenity to color and power their talk.

I remember saying at one moment during my dispute with Barry: "Why, for example, do I never hear the word 'love' at Synanon? Doesn't anyone in this place ever fall in love?"

And Barry snorting back at me: "Love? What kind of shit is that? I never love. I fuck!"

I think I retorted: "In that case I'm sorry for you." Or more likely I never said it. Because I have this failing, that is of thinking of bright replies but too late to use them as repartee. And then, later, my mind will make up for my lack of verbal skill by letting me imagine that I didn't really muff my chance so ingloriously.

For instance in this case with Melanie. Without a doubt I should have roared right back at her. Using against her all those wild curse words that she so generously flung at me. I should have told her that it was not my diaper that was full of shit but her fucking head.

24

After all who the hell was she? Whereas me—I was somebody! I was in *Who's Who*. Books of mine could be found in libraries from Tel Aviv to Tokyo. I had money in the bank, too. Which I hadn't earned lying on my back getting screwed. Nor was I forever shuttling back and forth between jail, hospital, and asylum. Or perpetually struggling to feed a stupid drug habit that never gave one anything but a greater need for more. And what the hell did she have to look forward to in her crazy existence unless she snapped to it soon, except whorehouse or prison or death from an overdose?

I could think this way—yes—but I couldn't talk it. In any case not fast enough to have ever won a verbal battle against Melanie. Never could I have equaled her flow of language. Much less topped it. In a duel of obscenities she would soon have smashed me against the wall with her "mother-fuckers" and God only knows what other bombshell words that she had in her vocabulary and which she could explode against me with burp-gun rapidity.

While my poor wits and my halting tongue would be occupied with logic and coherence, with the choice of *le mot juste*, with all the hampering baggage resulting from an over-education that had unfitted me for the tug-of-war of life. In those early days—and even now to a large extent—I resisted what I ought to have accepted, namely the gut-level language of the Synanon game, somehow imagining that I could go swimming without getting wet.

"Have you ever had a fix?" Melanie screamed at me. "Just one little chippy of a fix?" And she went through a whole list of her crimes and misdemeanors, asking me whether I had ever been picked up for marks, or for shoplifting, or for soliciting. Whether my door had ever been broken down by narcotics officers looking for paraphernalia . . . "Why you've never even been in jail. Never been busted in your whole piddling life!"

And then she hit on a solution and greeted it with the joy of discovery. "Why you're just jealous! That's all. You come down here like you were slumming. To get a smell of the life you've never lived—and never will. And you know why? You know why? Because all you squares are just people who've never had the guts to live it up! Scared! That's what you are. Scared out of your sensitive skins!"

These may not have been her exact words. But they will do as a sample.

And meanwhile I had nothing to say.

"Why you poor stupid square!" she finally spat at me with a mixture of disgust and pity. And I just sat there and took it. In silence. With a silly little smile on my face that I wanted to correct but somehow couldn't. Because I was shaken. I felt suddenly how far away I was from all these people. That I was in fact a stranger. That they were bound together in some sort of club, a secret society of the gutter that had broken all the rules and then contemptuously flung their problem at mankind, their insoluble problem of drug addiction, daring anyone to heal them.

And here I was, an interloper. An outsider. My arms, for instance, completely bare of tattoo marks. Whereas in this house almost everyone had enormous dark tattoos. The darker and more complex the pattern the better, since that obscured those telltale marks that the narco bulls were always looking for. Even some of the girls had tattoo marks—or did until they got Synanon's volunteer doctor, Bernie Casselman, to excise them delicately.

This was the first time I felt myself unwelcome at Synanon. And that hurt. I realized suddenly that I didn't belong here—and never really would. I was a square. A very square square. And Synanon wasn't made for the likes of me. It was a home for people who could drink cough medicine by the pint, and even by the quart, in order to accumulate in their bodies a real dosage of narcotics. People like Chester Stern, now a director of Synanon, who during his trumpet-playing days never went anywhere without his drugstore suitcase filled with bottles of cough medicine, his hypnotic pills of carbromal, his supply of chloral hydrate knockout drops, and his caps of heroin whenever he could get hold of any, and whatever other drugs he could lay his hands on, thus devoting his whole existence to making the money he needed in order to wipe himself out of existence.

And me? To this day I can't take so much as an aspirin without trepidation.

Reid Kimball, now director emeritus of Synanon, once told me of a group of addicts locked up in the hype tank, and so maddened by their craving for dope, that when a new prisoner appeared and it was learned that he had stashed away a supply of the stuff in a fingerstall shoved up his rectum, or else had swallowed some caps wrapped up in a condom, I really can't recall the ugly details, but in any case the others had got him to void his gut over some newspapers and then Reid had described to me how these addicts had fought and scrambled in the excrement, each struggling to get the greatest share of the glycerine caps containing the precious dope.

Reid roared with laughter as he told this story. And then, seeing my face frozen with disgust and horror, he stopped his laughter and expostulated. "Well, that's why we call ourselves fiends. Sax Rohmer invented that name for us in his Fu-Manchu stories. You don't expect dope fiends to behave like Little Lord Fauntleroys, do you?"

He even went into a well-argued defense of the practice of using one's gut to conceal dope. "Look at it this way, Guy," he said. "Isn't it really a very sensible solution to the problem of bringing dope into jail? That is to say if you can bring yourself to look at it for just a second from the standpoint of a dope-crazed addict. Can you imagine a hype, out on bail, who knows that he must eventually appear before the judge, and will then most likely be taken straight to prison, can you imagine him giving no thought whatsoever to the pain of withdrawal that he will have to suffer from lack of his drug? Wouldn't that be totally illogical? Of course it would! And obviously he can't conceal the drug on the outside of his body because he'll be undressed for sure. So what's left? He must conceal it inside.

"Now let's take it one step further. If this hype has done his share of bringing drugs into prison and distributing them, has he not got the right, as a prisoner, to expect that others coming in will do the same for him? And since prisoners are being constantly released and new convicts constantly coming in, a small, but fairly steady flow of drugs can be maintained.

"Wouldn't all concerned be justifiably indignant if anyone failed to follow this simple 'do-unto-others-what-you-want-others-to-do-unto-you' rule? Wouldn't prisoners be entitled to scream at a new-comer: 'Why you dirty ass-hole you! You knew you were going to be sentenced and you didn't have brains enough to bring with you at least one cap of shit? We would have done as much for you!'

"I remember once when I had been fighting a charge, with Maxie for my lawyer—he was the best and the most expensive in that line—and he certainly kept me out of jail for six months—but when I knew that I had to appear before the judge I stuffed at least seventy of those little number-four glycerin caps into a fingerstall. They're usually about five dollars apiece, but when you buy them by the gram you can get ten of them for twenty-five or less.

"So when I finally landed in the hype tank for a ninety-day jolt I was ready to do something for the guys already there. Naturally I wasn't dividing up my stash among all of them. There were about thirty of us in the tank. I limited myself to the elite of the gang. Some six or seven fellows. And of course the trustee. We had to take care of him. We gave the mail-runner a buck or two to bring us a hypodermic and I had no trouble squeezing the stuff out, and then we all fixed.

"Afterwards I still had about twenty caps left and I was figuring on doling them out to myself day by day. But I noticed that all the guys who had fixed must have been clean too long, and now they were so obviously loaded, rubbing their noses and beginning to nod, that I panicked, thinking that any passing bull would realize what had just happened here and would give the place an imme-diate shakedown. So I decided to shoot the whole twenty caps into my arm even if it killed me. Which it didn't."

Reid's story flabbergasted me. I didn't know whether to be-lieve him or not. But I couldn't find any flaws in it. "Suppose the mail-runner couldn't have gotten a hypodermic for you. What could you have done with your supply?"

"Oh there's bound to be a hypodermic around. Always is, in jail. Some of the guys may have brought their own. Like Herman used to do."

"Don't tell me that this Herman—whoever he was—could conceal a hypodermic in his rectum," I said. "What about the needle?"

"There are lots of ways to take care of that," Reid explained. "For example. With the top of a Murine bottle. You know it's capped with a heavy little eyedropper. It'll hold one of those baby hypodermics. The cover of a book of matches can be wrapped around the needle so that the point doesn't protrude, then it can all be stuffed into this eyedropper and rubber bands can be tightened around it so that nothing will slip out. Grease it well and shove it up. And later—in jail—you've got your hypodermic. No problem."

No. No problem at all. For addicts. But insurmountable—even as a thought—for a square. Certainly for me. There I was, already well into my sixties and still unable to smoke a cigarette or down a cocktail. Truly I did not belong here. I just didn't. And yet I was filled with a most painful desire to belong. Why? And did not that desire betray precisely what Melanie had accused me of, namely jealousy.

Was it really possible that I who had never granted myself any excuses from the straight and narrow, I who was always pushing myself to greater and ever greater endeavor, forever rejecting all signs of exhaustion and all fears of failure, convinced that a life of constant effort must have some meaning and that a struggle never relinquished must have some reward, was it possible that I now envied these people their self-indulgence, regretting all my own years of devotion to the rational and the real, while they had escaped into the fanciful and the absurd?

All because their way of life had eventually landed them in Synanon, while mine hadn't? So I now found myself with neither the reward of their life of crime, nor any reward for my life of virtue. While they had had one and now were taking the other.

Of course this was not the first time in my life that I had felt all the structure of my existence disintegrating. It was not the first time that I had questioned all my values. It was not the first time that I had cried upon all the great framers of the world's commandments to come to my aid, that I had screamed for help to all those compilers of copybook maxims, to all those writers of mottoes and of precepts from whom I had taken the guidelines of my life.

But I suppose I had never before felt how unstable were the quicksands on which I had built my life as I did that evening when Melanie attacked me. And it was no doubt at that time, while I watched Melanie cracking a match and setting fire to a fresh cigarette, that I was first conscious of a still obscure urge to kick her kind out of Synanon and take over the club for decent people. And when she blew a fat puff of smoke at my face, expressing both her pride in herself and her contempt for me, I thought: "Wait, you bitch. Just you wait. Squares will some day own this place! And it will be your kind who will just be tolerated."

I remember we were sitting down in the basement. A couple of huge naked electric bulbs gave the place a glaring brightness while leaving large areas around in darkness. Some of the members had quickly grabbed whatever upholstered seats there were. Others had hiked themselves up on the edge of a huge snooker table, letting their legs dangle. And the rest of us were doing the best we could with hard and uncomfortable chairs that had long been ready to be smashed into firewood.

How and where Synanon had got hold of that immense snooker table I haven't the remotest idea. The strangest contraptions used to appear suddenly at Synanon in those early days, when the whole house sometimes seemed like some sort of way-station on the world's drain down which all the broken and useless articles of Los Angeles were sewered out to some final dumping ground.

I remember for example endless bottles of ketchup of some unknown cheaper brand looking far too red to be real. And an

enormous stockpile of canned soup. What wholesale house had un-
loaded these unsalable items on Synanon I have no idea, but it was
obviously a matter of clearing space in one's warehouse at the expense of Synanon's basement. And Synanon still too poor to refuse
anything.

In those now remote days the people of Synanon sometimes went
hungry. No. Not actually hungry. A great effort was made to keep
the place always supplied with bread and peanut butter. Also jam.
And coffee. But there were periods when that was about all that
was available.

It was at times like this that violent altercations would rouse the
entire membership. Perhaps because someone had dared to go into
the kitchen and fry himself two eggs. The enormity of it! Two
eggs! I recall walking into the house one evening and finding the
place filled with indignation, and finally tracking down the cause
to this little omelet that had been cooked and eaten some forty-
eight hours before.

This, too, of course, was something the members had shared and
that I now somehow included in my jealousy: the common experience of having lived through such periods of stress.

But it was not everyone, that evening in the basement, who
agreed with Melanie. I clearly recall someone sneering at her:
"You're sick. You're very sick, Melanie. Your head is still so full of
that street and gutter garbage that you're actually proud of having
been a screwed-up dope addict."

I remember Melanie quickly swiveling toward her new enemy,
and crashing her obscenities against him. And then the whole group
joining in a battle of hot arguments, a kind of a free-for-all that
could probably be heard by evening strollers up on the top of the
palisades, two hundred yards away.

And meanwhile I said nothing. And in my silence wondered how
sick I might be that I should have envied—even for the space of a
few seconds—that gutter-garbage life of Melanie.

And yet I had. I definitely had.

That's why it was such a wonderful moment for me, some time

later, when in connection with I know not what discussion during the noon seminars of Synanon—I believe that I had brought up the name of Patanjali and spoken of the five obstacles in his book of Yoga aphorisms, namely ignorance, self-esteem, desire, aversion, and the fear of death. And I had stated that the overcoming of these five obstacles in oneself, that is to say insofar as mere human beings could possibly overcome them, constituted an important step in the development of the higher spiritual values—whereupon someone jumped up to argue that I had never been an addict and that strangers ought not to be permitted to come into these noon discussions, bringing with them ideas that were of no use whatsoever to drug addicts who had come to Synanon to save themselves from self-destruction, ideas that were in fact dangerous to people who far from having to overcome their fear of death were hard put to overcome their fear of life and to control their secret death-wish. . . .

At which Arline spoke up in my defense, saying that these noon seminars were free and open discussions, and that anyone who wished to do so was entitled to argue against me, but not to call me a stranger, because as far as she was concerned, Guy had the right to think of himself as an honorary dope fiend.

To my surprise there was a sudden burst of applause for Arline, and I guess some of it must have been meant for me, and I would have said something in gratitude, except that at that particular moment I don't believe I could have pushed any words at all through my emotionally constricted throat.

I have really treasured that title of honorary dope fiend. It was a position that eminently suited me, since it brought me closer to the organization, while at the same time it absolved me from the necessity of having to go through those ordeals that most members had gone through to reach Synanon.

And in this connection I still remember with some irritation a certain moment in San Francisco when Synanon was in the process of opening up their Seawall branch, and I had just come back from Europe and was invited to speak there. During the course of my talk I mentioned how deeply touched I had been, when, by acclamation, I had become Synanon's first honorary dope addict. And someone raised his voice in correction, saying that I was not the first, but the second. The first being Dr. Donald Cressey, the criminologist from U.C.L.A., now dean of the School of Social Sciences at Santa Barbara.

All this is not only strange but also contradictory. For consider this: if I can take pride in being nominated honorary dope addict, and furthermore Arline can feel that she has thereby conferred some distinction upon me, then haven't we really reversed all values, and in particular the values that Synanon is supposed to stand for? And dope addicts are something special after all.

Perhaps there is some sort of solution for this puzzle in a passage that I have several times admired in Dostoevski's *House of the Dead,* that book in which the author recounts his years in a Siberian prison camp, a passage in which he reaches the conviction that criminals are somehow potentially the most gifted and strongest of the Russian people and that it is a great pity that these bubbling energies and fine talents should have been directed into deeds of evil and violence that eventually must land them in the useless occupations of prison life.

Is not this perhaps the beginning of the saga of Synanon? That a man, Chuck, that is to say Charles E. Dederich, was able to see through the external appearances and recognize in dope addicts great reserves of ability and devotion where the surrounding society could see only people fit for prison or asylum? And therefore, on August 30, 1958, he founded an organization that would discover and release these wasted lives.

But when I broached this notion to Reid Kimball recently, he wasn't quite sure.

"That about the dreadful waste, yes, I'll buy that. To take human beings, no matter how crazed with dope, and run them year after year over that endless treadmill of arrest and trial and prison, and then rearrest and retrial and more prison, that is certainly a terrible waste. And it was nothing less than genius—and courage—on

Chuck's part, to have staked his life on the idea that this treadmill routine wasn't necessary. And at the same time to have demonstrated that the old sociologists were right when they said that society prepares the crime, the criminal only executes it—because when Chuck had designed his new society for dope addicts to live in, they stopped being junkies.

"And that's why we have that line from Lao-Tze that we print on all our stationery: '. . . enabling man to go right, disabling him to go wrong.'

"But where I think your illustration from Dostoevski goes overboard is in picturing the sociopath as superior to the ordinary run of the mill human being, as being of some superior fiber. That I find difficult to buy.

"Maybe—just maybe—some of them can be described as having been driven to drugs by a greater sensitivity, a sensitivity that made it impossible for them to conform to our brutal world and by a reverse twist drove them into criminality. But let me disassociate myself at once from that oversensitive type. I can assure you that I, for one, was not made of any better fiber than the average. I never had any particular talent. Unless it was for pimping and robbing. And in fact I wasn't even good at those crimes. Just lucky that I practically never got caught.

"Among the very few paying jobs I ever held in all my years was that of pit boss at a bingo table at Lake Tahoe. Bill Burns, a fellow addict and friend, got me that post at a time when I needed some income in the worst way. Well, Bill Burns is with us now. Here at Synanon. And you can ask him how good I was at my job. I was all thumbs. And that goes for me right down to the present day."

"Oh, come on, Reid," I protested. "You've run this whole plant at various times. And found here people who can cook, who can keep your building in repair, who can superintend your accounts, take care of your supplies—"

"A bunch of fumbling, stumbling bums!" Reid retorted. "Oh, we've plenty of kids here who can fix a TV set provided there's practically nothing wrong with it. They can change a spark plug in your car—in about twice the time it takes an ordinary mechanic. They can put a new washer in a faucet—and with any kind of luck the faucet will stop dripping. And this is so true that we even have a special name for these so-called experts around here. We call them Synanon plumbers, Synanon electricians, Synanon carpenters. But if something goes really wrong with our plumbing or our automobiles, you should see how fast we rush out and grab ourselves some professional help. Our own people can't do it. They have nothing that you could call expertise. Nothing remotely like that.

"And we'd be crazy if we expected it. Because most of the people here—at just the age when they should have been learning their craft and perfecting themselves in it—were too damned busy scratching for dope in order to wipe out their minds. And so they're ten and fifteen years behind their contemporaries. And it will take time—much time—for them to catch up. . . .

"Our real experts, our Shim Teitelbaum, our June Holland, our Tom Hudson, our Ted Dibble and Ron Silva, they're so rare and so valuable that the different branches lay schemes to kidnap them. A good secretary is worth her weight in gold around here. And this branch has had the misfortune never to be able to keep one. No sooner do I find one than she's snatched away from me. Or she marries a member who wants to be in the San Francisco branch or in San Diego."

Reid grabbed up a letter from his desk. "Here! Look at all these mistakes. For years I've been praying for a good secretary. A girl who can spell. But no luck. Oh, they'll work at it. They've got all the good will in the world. But efficiency? They left that behind when they went into the gutter. With a whole bullpen of girls here, I can barely manage to squeeze out a few letters a day. I'm perpetually behind in my correspondence. And God help us if anything unusual should come along. The whole office simply falls apart."

"Now really you're overloading it!" I exclaimed.

"I'm not!" Reid cried. "If anything I'm understating it. But don't get me wrong. We do some remarkable things here. But with people.

Not with jobs. Maybe we don't turn out secretaries who can win prizes at shorthand like Billy Rose, but we do other things."

Reid lowered his voice. "That girl at the desk out there, who looks as if she were busy. I remember her many years ago. On the street. Once, when I was so loaded with heroin that I was in a complete fog, I moved in on her. She took care of me. She went out on the street and turned tricks for me, just so I would have the money to keep up my habit. And then, some time later, still in the same blind fog, I just wandered out of her pad, and never saw her again until one day she came in here for help, herself at the end of her rope.

"We took her in. And now look at her. She's living clean. She's as good at her job as she can possibly be. Only Synanon could have done that with her. Only Synanon. But don't even dream of sending her out into the world to compete against the crackerjack secretaries who can hold down jobs in busy Los Angeles offices. Not for a moment. She'd never make it. Never. You'd just be driving her back to the streets and to dope.

"But she's a wonderful person. You couldn't hope to find a truer friend, a more affectionate sweetheart, a more devoted wife, or a more tender mother. She'll be all those things to some man, someday. Someone who will be forever glad he found her. But for God's sake don't expect her to spell!"

"But to have done just that much," I said, "to have helped to build this place into such an exciting spot that people flock here on Saturday nights and stay so late you have to threaten to turn the lights out on them, doesn't that make Synanon into something that can be safely called a success? Along with you too?"

"Oh, yes," Reid said. "We're a brilliant success. Too brilliant perhaps. And that's why I can't sleep at night, wondering when some ass-hole of an animal, whom we've just dragged out of the gutter and brought into Synanon to turn into a human being, will do something so hair-raising, so scandalous that it will blow our whole club to pieces. I tell you I wake up in the middle of the night shaking. Shaking at the thought of some terrible fracas that would immediately be blamed on Synanon and that Synanon could never live down.

"Think of Synanon disappearing. Think of that. Disappearing in a cloud of lies and accusations and public contempt.

"You talk about our friends. We couldn't live without them. Naturally not. But give a thought to our enemies. The people who don't bother to visit us, ever. The people who don't like us, in front, because we're ex-criminals and ex-addicts. And because at Synanon we refuse to draw any distinction between black and white. Who hate us because we refuse to believe that there is some special therapeutic value in sorting out mankind according to sex and locking them up in separate buildings. The people who want to stop us because we don't care what special brand of politics or religion you may have. . . . People who are just waiting for their chance to smash us. Just waiting . . .

"Oh sure, aside from the question of when I'm ever going to catch up on my correspondence—and on my sleep—I suppose you could call us a roaring success. If you absolutely insist."

Well, at least one man from Synanon can be called a success. Reid notwithstanding. One of the first persons I got to know in Synanon was a tall, thin young man with a long nose, who went by the name of Jake, to which was sometimes added "the Snake," not as an epithet, just a convenient rhyme. I gradually learned some vague facts about him. He had come into Synanon from New York, a common product of our educational system: lots of knowledge and little wisdom. Before becoming hooked on heroin he had been able to hold down a responsible job. In Synanon this badly mixed-up young man eventually began to find himself.

One day, when I had just had a book published and was making the rounds of the bookstores to see how my offspring was doing, I entered a shop in Westwood and found myself warmly greeted by a young man who evidently knew me but whom I couldn't immediately place. Of course it was Jake the Snake.

He explained to me that he was still a resident at Synanon, but working on the outside and commuting back and forth between

Synanon and his job, a condition known as Stage Two of the Synanon program. The owner of the bookstore knew about Jake's past but was pleased with his work, and Jake himself was very happy. In fact so much so that he was considering some aspect of the book business as a lifetime career for himself.

I took to dropping in at that bookstore now and then and doing some of my book buying there. And occasionally Jake would talk to me about his plans. He was now in Stage Three, that is to say he had moved out of Synanon and was living on his own, continuing, however, to maintain contact with the club. His interest in books was greater than ever, and he was beginning to feel that he ought to move back to New York and find his way into the publishing business.

"If and when you decide to go East," I said to him, "I'll give you a letter to my literary agent. He may be able to help you."

It turned out that my agent was able to arrange an interview, and soon Jake was working in the sales department of a major book publisher. But he did not drop his interest in Synanon. He made himself into a kind of one-man New York branch of Synanon, interviewing local dope addicts who wanted to join the organization, and helping many of them get to Santa Monica.

From time to time I had glimpses of Jake's progress, learning that he had moved up from his job in the sales department to other areas of the company. Meanwhile he had found himself a girl friend, a painter, they had married, and once or twice, while in New York, I spent an evening in their studio apartment, talking art, books, politics, but mostly Synanon, a topic we were never able to exhaust.

Several years passed. And then one day I had a call from my lawyer who was renegotiating for me a contract for a book I had somehow been unable to write, a failure that had led to some bitterness on the side of both my publisher and myself.

"You'll be working under a new editor," my lawyer said to me over the phone. "He will be Mr. James Ross."

"Whoever that may be," I said, "I'm sure he'll suit me fine."

And then, suddenly it hit me. Mr. James Ross was of course Jake the Snake.

I had been doing, at that time, a series of short portraits of Synanon personalities for the Synanon magazine, and several people had suggested that I ought to get out some sort of a Synanon book, made up perhaps of a whole series of such sketches. Obviously the constellation was right for some such undertaking. Already the idea was growing in my mind that perhaps the story and development of Synanon would constitute a worthy subject. I immediately got Jake on the phone and tossed my thoughts to him.

Jake was enthusiastic and moved at once to present the plan to his editorial board. And shortly afterwards he reached me by phone at Synanon's Tomales Bay facility to inform me that the project had been approved.

Obviously Reid underestimates the expertise available among Synanon people. At any rate the story of Jake the Snake must not be omitted from the Saga of Synanon. This book would not have come into being without him.

2

This yeasty sense of having hit upon something uniquely precious but still so indefinable that one might wake up in the middle of the night shivering and shaking at the thought of some incident that would compel the police to raid the place and the public to turn its back, and thus eliminate from the world what might well be man's last best hope, this seemingly megalomaniacal conception of Synanon's astronomical importance began to manifest itself in the club before it had even taken on the status of an organization, in fact long before it had been baptized with its present name.

There was obviously something remarkable coming into being here, but just at this crucial beginning something happened that while serving to illuminate the wonder of it, at the same time threatened it with destruction.

What happened was this: into this handful of alcoholics who were still meeting only a few times a week to experiment with a new form of group interaction came a drug addict just released from prison, a man we'll call Rex because that wasn't his name.

Alcoholics Anonymous had at various times tried to extend its self-help methods to dope addiction, but had always failed. The founders of A.A. had taken the position that "We can't be all things to all men," and had let it go at that. But here, in this group of A.A. members something seemed to be working: Rex stayed clean.

Among hypes there is an amazing grapevine communication system. The news of Rex staying clean without being locked up spread, and a slowly increasing trickle of dope addicts began to knock at the door of Chuck's pad. So that even later, when Rex wandered off and fell back into his old ways of crime and dope, there were nevertheless new addicts coming in to more than fill the vacancy he left.

"There came a moment," Chuck's girl friend recalled, "when we had to bed down four addicts on the living room floor of our little apartment!"

Synanon, still nameless, had begun to burgeon. Soon another apartment had to be rented, and then a store, and still another store. And Chuck would go around insisting: "We're stumbling onto something. We're making a great discovery here." It was a tingling thought. . . . Except that there wasn't enough time for tingling. No time for puzzling out just what it was that was happening. Because Synanon was about to be wrecked by its first success.

Because so long as the group consisted only of former alcoholics, the question of boarding and lodging the members scarcely occurred. Alcoholics are commonly able to earn their living at some honest endeavor. In fact they are often very good at moneymaking. And no more likely to fall into criminal ways than the usual run of the population. Thus—with certain exceptions, to be sure—alcoholics, in order to help themselves stay away from drink, require nothing more than a place where they can gather now and then for a few hours of comradely talk and encouragement.

Alcoholics only *over*-indulge in a chemical that is otherwise legally and socially approved, whereas drug addicts are in immediate conflict with the law by the very nature of their habit—no matter how slight their indulgence. And something more: the effects of the drug are such as to make the addict quite generally incapable of earning a living, while the swollen cost of his favorite chemical is such as to break him financially and thus drag him into crime in order to sustain an addiction which is already a crime.

Thus the moment Rex stepped into that early group, he precipitated a revolution in its structure and in its system of conducting its business. Synanon could not ignore the necessity of providing a twenty-four-hour live-in facility for addicts. This meant rustling up cheap places to rent, furnishing them by hook or crook, and scrounging around for cheap sources of food. And from that moment on, down to this present day, Synanon has been involved with an ever-growing problem, not only to provide for an ever-increasing population, but to fight a running battle with neighborhoods who did not relish having great numbers of former dope addicts living in their proximity, and at the same time cope with constant friction from the police and from other legally constituted authorities who feel that no matter what the success of the Synanon program, dope and crime are *their* responsibility and nothing for a private organization to be messing around with.

"So right from the start," Chuck likes to point out, "Synanon put itself in harm's way. Of course we might have told Rex to go shift for himself. We might have done that. But you see, we didn't. The Synanon method is to accept responsibility—and then look, hope, and pray for the means to carry the additional burden."

The result has been that Synanon has grown accustomed to living on the edge of bankruptcy, and close to official suppression, and under the constant necessity of keeping its case before the bar of the public, so that the full meaning of Synanon's importance has often had to be pushed into the background while its total energies were being committed to a battle for the right to exist at all. And that battle—because of the chance intrusion of Rex—had to be fought out in the field of the treatment of drug addiction. At any rate to begin with.

Meanwhile most of the original alcoholic members began to drop away. They didn't fancy the kind of living that hypes were introducing into the club. They felt that the club was being turned into a sideshow for jive-talking bums and for their nut-house behavior and their raucous music. So, willy-nilly, the Synanon idea had to be born among drug addicts, just as a certain religion had to be born in a manger.

Visitors however began to be attracted to this noisy joint with its easy hospitality, its plentiful coffee, and its free peanut-butter snack—and the interesting characters, both male and female, whom one could rub elbows with. Synanon began, in a small way, to be a kind of an ultra-modern fad. All the philosophy, all the heated arguments over Freud, Jung, Reich, Emerson, Thoreau, with which some few tried to plumb this "happening," meant nothing more to some than any other kind of coffee klatsch. Early wild discussions about the basic needs of man and woman—as to whether it was T.L.C., that is to say tender loving care, of whether it was D.V.O., that is to say deep vaginal orgasm, seemed only an extended joke to most residents and visitors who got nothing much out of it except the pleasure of seeing puzzled expressions on strangers who stared at the big meaningless letters painted on the window and passed by along the busy street wondering—but not particularly caring.

Others claimed it was only the dominant figure of Chuck who kept this thing—whatever it was—from falling apart. The way he could hold forth on Emerson was a charm. All kinds of people began to make it a habit to drop in on Sundays when Chuck would give his weekly Emerson talk. Even a couple of cops who had long had their eye on this strange spot where known dope addicts congregated, and who were always on the lookout for a good reason to raid the joint, would come in and listen with interest.

So another theory ran: "Once Chuck gets bored with this place, that'll be the end." It was well known that Chuck had led a checkered life, had drifted about from job to job, and from girl to girl. He was obviously an exhibitionist. At the clubrooms of Alcoholics Anonymous, it had been common to see him make an entry with two beautiful girls on his arms, and obviously enjoy the impression he made. He wasn't the kind to stick with anything very long. Never had.

And yet, once, when one of the early dope addicts decided to leave the place, arguing that he had now been living clean for a month or more, and was tired of going around without a dime in his pocket and figured he'd go out and get himself a job, Chuck begged him to stay on.

"We're solving something here," Chuck said. "We're on to something big, something really big and important. And if you're smart you'll want to have a share of the action. Right now it's ours exclusively. And let me tell you: it's very, very special."

People were arrested by Chuck's powerful seriousness. He had a faculty for vivid expressions that were completely his own. And he had a voice that carried conviction. And yet not everyone was convinced. The facts were against him. How could this thing last? Where was the money to come from? It was known that every rent day presented a problem that usually had to be solved by Chuck's girl friend dipping into her nest egg. How could an affair of this sort go on? This hand-to-mouth existence? It was unreal.

"Things will emerge," was Chuck's confident motto.

But the food situation remained in a state of perpetual crisis. And some of the addicts, tired of the endless coffee and peanut-butter sandwiches, would go out on the sly and do a little shoplifting. TV dinners were notoriously easy to sneak out of a supermarket's freezer.

The morals of the last few alcoholics who had lingered on were offended by this intrusion of petty crime into their discussion club. The whole thing was degenerating since dope addicts began to be admitted. They voted for throwing the dope addicts out and getting back to the original purpose.

But Chuck stuck to his purpose and the alcoholics, outnumbered, continued to drift away. Reid Kimball, with his twenty years of massive drug taking ("It's a wonder my bloodstream isn't pure heroin," he once said after figuring out that he had poured perhaps half a million dollars' worth of the white powder that drug addicts call "shit," down his veins), Reid Kimball, with his wife only recently dead from suicide and he himself only just released from General Hospital after an almost successful attempt of his own, blundered into the store and stayed.

But as to its philosophy, he wasn't buying any of it. He was in a state of despair and absolutely broke, and needed momentary shelter. That was all. He just didn't feel himself capable of going back out into the world. Not yet. Nor strong enough to try to kill himself again.

"When Chuck would come out with some of his clichés, like 'honesty is the best policy,' I'd want to puke," Reid said to me once when we were talking about the old days. "But I'd hide my feelings not too well, saying: 'Yeah, yeah, sure,' or something like that, which would get Chuck sore.

" 'Why you blind idiot bastard!' he'd scream at me. 'Are you really so bloody stupid you can't figure that out for yourself? Do you want to spend your whole life running around like a dog with the rabies? Racking your crazy brains to remember what lie you told this one and what lie you told that one, so as not to get mixed up and have the covers ripped off you? . . . Of course honesty is the best policy. Of course it is!'

"George the Turk and I, we used to talk about this crazy son-of-a-bitch Chuck. We just couldn't make head or tail of him. The Turk was determined that he would eventually put him in the wrong. 'He's got some kind of a scheme up his sleeve. You'll see,' the Turk would say. And we were both just hanging around waiting for this screwball to give himself away, and then we intended to split.

"I remember," Reid went on, "talking to Mitch one day, about Chuck, and both of us trying to figure out what kind of an operation he had in mind that he was gathering all these crooks for. Some new syndicate, obviously. But that didn't fit with the way we were living. And with Chuck constantly scratching for pennies to pay the bills.

"I had a gun hidden under the porch of my mother's home, and I once suggested to Chuck that a little heist, for maybe a hundred bucks, would tide us over until he was ready for his big caper, what-ever that might be.

"Honest to God, Guy, I thought he'd admire me. I was never so amazed as when he turned on me: 'Why you stupid ass-hole, you!' And he went on chewing me out for half an hour.

"'Well just what the hell do you want from me?' I finally challenged him.

"'I don't want a Goddamned thing from you!' he yelled back at me.

"'Well you must want something!' I came back at him. 'Or you wouldn't be letting me hang around here without putting in a dime!'

"'Can't you get it through your thick skull that I just want you to be happy?' Chuck yelled.

"But I wasn't buying any of that crap. Neither was Mitch. And we finally reached what to us—in those days—was a truly brilliant analysis of Chuck that went something like this: 'It takes all kinds of bastards to make up a world. And here's one special bastard happens to get his kicks out of trying to make people happy.'

"In short this Chuck was some kind of a strange pervert. We thought we'd seen everything in the line of perversions, but his was one we'd never run into before."

This was still in those Ocean Park days when the group was occupying nothing but those two crummy adjoining stores, one of which was arranged as the men's dormitory, and the other as the clubhouse, while a neighboring apartment or two was fixed up for the girls. Total membership fluctuated around twenty. And yet such was Chuck's conviction as to the future of his collection of misfits that the moment he had selected the name Synanon for it, he would go around saying:

"You wait and see. Those three syllables Syn-a-non, they're going to be a household word. As familiar to the world as Coca-Cola."

Some smiled. Others, feeling the weight that Chuck can put into his words, as if communicating to his ideas some of his own chunky body, would believe. But on Saturday nights when, after Chuck's speech and just before the bongo drums would begin, a big glass jar with the label "Discover the Joy of Giving" would be passed around among the visitors and afterward would be found to contain no more than a couple of dollars in change, waves of doubt would engulf even the most convinced.

But Chuck never budged: "You wait and see. Those three syllables will someday be as well known as Coca-Cola."

One of the girl residents recently told me that it was the first time she had heard the word "syllable." And she wondered what connection those two strange words "syllable" and "Synanon" might have. She was a girl who had just come out of Lincoln Heights jail. And that hadn't been her first jail experience. Not by far. Although just out of her teens she had been in and out of jail for dope smuggling, for prostitution, for marks, and so forth.

"It was all a fog to me," she said. "I just whirled around in it blindly."

She listened to what the other girls were saying. One of them complained rather openly: "There's nothing specially therapeutic about sleeping with only one sheet," she would say. "And never having the money to have that sheet laundered."

And if one of the girls dared argue back, repeating the words of Chuck, that their problems would be solved, that money would somehow "emerge," then an expression would be heard that was to become more and more current: "Don't give me any of that Synanon-shit."

And Chuck was already being called Fatso. But of course only behind his back. Because dissidents feared his roar. He knew that some of them were managing to turn the club into something of a whorehouse.

Chuck could understand that. Some of these girls had never known any other way of earning a living except by lying on their backs. And Chuck would lace it into them for that. At the same time he knew that many of them were sincerely anxious to adopt another way of life, but when a man has a couple of TV dinners he has stolen, what girl, tired of the club's poor food situation, could resist doing what she had long been doing for bread and butter!

Several years ago I went to see Wanda in her inexpensive upstairs apartment over a garage, where she lives surrounded by her children, who I am sure will some day be as beautiful as she must have been (and still is, in fact, though now beginning to turn matronly), and she told me how upset she used to get seeing Chuck so worried about money, and his club members stealing food on the sly, and putting the whole organization into jeopardy, and she thought she could do something about that.

"All I ever needed for money," she explained to me, "was my little black book and one thin dime."

"What little black book?" I asked, not because I couldn't guess, but because when it came to the kind of life I had never lived, my guesses were sometimes completely off base and I had to keep making sure.

"Well, there was this man I told you about, this bartender. Remember?"

This time I pretended I did, because not to know might seem indelicate, although there were so many men in Wanda's life story that anyone might be excused for getting lost.

"The one with the sharp suits," she explained.

"Oh yes, of course," I said. Although I didn't have the vaguest idea. I had a good enough picture of Wanda's early homelife. That part of it was all terribly vivid. Her father and his stroke and his taking up with another woman, and her mother and her alcoholism which would often end in dt's, and how from the age of twelve Wanda's despair (and beauty) had led her into the arms of many men and into smoking pot and then taking drugs; but Wanda's endless procession of men lost me.

"This bartender worked at a hotel," Wanda went on, "and one day he asked me to drop in there because he had something serious to discuss with me.

"What he said was, 'Kid, you're throwing yourself away. A girl with your looks shouldn't be satisfied with five or ten bucks a trick. With the right clothes and hairdo you'd stop looking like a kid, and you could get yourself the kind of men that are accustomed to treating you like a lady, with dinner, theater, fifty bucks. That sort of thing. You got to step up, kid.'

"He said he could advance me the money for the clothes and for a nice apartment. Maybe even for a car. And I'd pay him back later.

"He explained to me that in his job in this fine hotel where all the men were good spenders, there wasn't a day went by that he wasn't asked if he couldn't fix someone up with a nice girl.

"All he wanted was that I play straight with him. Every fifty I took in, I was to give him half. 'Play fair with me, Wanda,' he said, 'and we'll go far.'

"Of course I promised I would, and that's how I got set up as a call girl.

"Which was fine. Only pretty soon some of the men I got to know didn't bother to reach me through him, but came straight to me, and after a while I couldn't see any reason to keep on splitting that kind of money with someone else. Also these men would introduce me to others. And then some of them would just as soon pay me a hundred as fifty, and I didn't figure that was any bartender's business either.

"After I had paid him off for the money he had advanced me, I just never went near that hotel again. Didn't have to. When I had some free time I would just open this little black book I kept and make a few calls on the phone. Just for a friendly chat, you know, kidding around, having a few laughs, and if a date developed why that was fine, and if not, then not. I had a lot of numbers and no problems at all.

"Except this habit of mine. It had ruined my marriage. It had forced me to leave my children with my mother. It was keeping me broke. I never had enough money left for my clothes, for my rent, for my car, for my children. It seemed like the more I made the worse off I was. Heroin swallowed everything.

"It was a cop who pushed me into Synanon. One night this cop stopped my car for some traffic violation and found me loaded and he was going to arrest me for using, for paraphernalia, for marks, but I cried and I told him about my children, and I took him up to

3

my rooms, and finally he said that he would let me go if I would get down to that club that had just opened up on the beach.

"That's how I got in. And that's how I stayed really clean for the first time.

"But after a while it seemed like at the club it was just the same as before. Never enough money. Never. Everyone always worried about rent and food and other expenses. And there were still my children whom my mother was taking care of. And I knew I couldn't give her too many worries or she'd be back on the bottle.

"Since I went every week to see my kids, there didn't seem to be any reason why I couldn't combine my visit with a date. I still had my little black book, and I thought it was nobody's business but my own.

"I was never bothered with any questions. I was always back before dark, and not only with enough money to keep my mother supplied but with a couple dozen hamburger patties and some big quart cartons of cottage cheese, and some other goodies for the club members.

"I'd tell them it was a gift for the club from my mother, and they were all too busy eating to waste time putting me through the third degree. Besides I was living absolutely clean which was more than some of them were doing. And that was what the club was for, wasn't it? Sometimes the men I dated were users and they wanted to give me a fix, but I told them I was living with a bunch who were all trying to stay clean and I was going to stay clean too.

"I meant that, Guy. Users always try to talk you into just a little joy-pop, but I'd refuse even that, because this time I really meant it.

"Of course, as I say, none of this dating I was doing was overnight stuff. I was always back by late afternoon. But once, when the club needed some real money, like a couple of hundred at least, I figured I could help them by accepting a weekend invitation. One of those group affairs, you know. Four or five men clubbing together to take half a dozen girls up to a hunting lodge to shoot duck and have themselves a real party. The sort of thing that rich married businessmen go in for, because duck hunting isn't anything that wives care to go along with. Men in the wholesale business who would bring gifts for everyone, like a fine leather handbag, or maybe a dozen nylons. And the girls would all get maybe five hundred dollars apiece. That sort of party.

"But being absent for a whole weekend, that wasn't like being gone for an afternoon. This time I was really missed. And there could be only one explanation: I had split, and was back on drugs. Except for one thing: I had taken only one of my suitcases. Most of my clothes were still hanging in the closet.

"Naturally there was a lot of talk about me not showing up Friday night, and then not showing up all day Saturday, and not until late at night on Sunday. But after giving my mother a couple of hundred I had two hundred-dollar bills for Chuck, and I figured that would stop him from making things too difficult for me.

" 'What's this?' he asked me, when I handed him the bills. And I could feel a storm sort of starting up from the basement of his belly.

" 'Some money my mother gave me for the club,' I lied.

" 'Well we don't want it,' he said. 'Here. You take it! It's yours. You earned it, I'm sure. In the only way you know how!'

"When I was slow taking it, his voice rose. 'I said: take it! And pack your stuff and get your fat ass out of this place as quick as you can!'

"But he wasn't yelling. And usually when Chuck would get angry his voice could be heard a block away, and all the girls would be frightened to death. This time his voice was powerful but low.

"Maybe if he had really thundered at me like he sometimes did at us girls, telling us that we were nothing but a gut with arms and legs, food going in one end and coming out the other . . . and no brains. . . . Or maybe the way he shouted at us when we neglected our washing and ironing, telling us that all we were good for was to lie on our backs and get screwed. Maybe if he had given me that kind of a haircut, I would have been able to stand up to him and lie my way out. But this quiet voice of his really shook me.

"I began to cry. And because I was crying I couldn't talk. So I just grabbed Chuck's hand and finally I was able to blubber that I was staying clean and nothing else but the club had ever been able to keep me clean. And I promised I'd never go off again. And that I had only done it for my children. Not for the club. But there was this money left over and I knew that he needed it, and if he took it, I'd never, never, absolutely never go off again. I would swear that on the Bible. But if he kicked me out it wouldn't be twenty-four hours before I'd be hooked again and worse than ever. . . . And it would be his fault. . . .

"And on and on. . . . Until finally he growled 'okay, okay,' as if he wanted to close the incident as fast as possible.

"But afterwards—long afterwards, when I had left the club and was married, I heard from others that he would often tell visitors how, in the early days when the club was so hard up for money, how Reid Kimball was ready to hold up a bank for a couple of grand, and Wanda had been ready to lay the president of the bank for five hundred dollars, to get the money that was needed.

"It seems he was really proud to have members like Reid and me. Very proud. He was against our doing anything of the kind, of course. But still very proud."

Chuck was indeed proud of his little organization of reformed criminals. He felt that there was good there, and these events were proof of it, but he also knew that dope addicts were nothing but little children, nasty little brats arrested in their development. Kids crying for their little white lollypop powder so that they could shoot it up their veins.

They would eventually learn better. It might take years, to be sure. But then weren't criminals sent to the pen for years? Why should he be required to cure them in less time than the state took to punish them? He was sure he could do it in less, but he didn't see why people expected him to do it in weeks.

And meanwhile he assured his flock that no matter what troubles they were having, things were looking up. "Right now," he would often say to the members, "right now is the happiest period of your lives. You'll look back on these times someday, years from now, and you'll remember what I said."

For some of the residents that was just Fatso talking big, and they would often make fun of him behind his back, joking about it among themselves and laughing until someone would warn: "Sh! Here comes Fatso and his trained seals."

Chuck knew about this kid stuff and didn't take it seriously. They'd grow up some day, his prostitutes and his dope addicts. They'd grow up and then they'd regret that they had let this golden opportunity to become one of Chuck's trained seals slip by them.

It wouldn't be true to say that this has happened yet on a large scale, but it is definitely coming to pass that membership in Synanon is considered in certain quarters as such a privilege and an honor that an increasing number of squares who do not have the necessary background of addiction or crime come to live in Synanon, not merely joining one of the various "Synanon game clubs" that are increasingly coming into being as subsidiaries clustered around the various Synanon branches, but actually taking up residence in order to live and work full time for the organization.

"Dope addicts," Chuck said in a recent talk he gave to some forty such "square" residents, "know why they are here. They know that they want to give up their previous kind of life and become ex-dope addicts and ex-criminals and ex-prostitutes. Squares have a more difficult time understanding why they are here. They do not realize that it is because they want to become ex-squares and get away from the kind of life that produces the world we live in, the world of wars and riots and mass-poverty cheek by jowl with vast wealth."

Some squares come to Synanon penniless, bringing only themselves and their willingness to work in the organization in whatever capacity they can. Others come in with money which sometimes is far more than enough to pay for their keep. One young woman, Dorothy Salant, after the tragedy that deprived her of her husband, made a payment of many thousands of dollars and came to live at Synanon with her three little children, and serve as a teacher at Synanon's nursery school.

Milt Cooper, a rich industrialist, joined the Synanon House in San Diego and started Synanon off in a pen and pencil advertising business, which has been profitable to both. Dan Garrett, a lawyer, began to cut down his practice in order eventually to give all of his time to Synanon. He is now the director of the Synanon facility in San Francisco. And very recently Phil Schwabacher of Lancaster, California, has begun to follow the same path at the Santa Monica branch. Ed Siegal, a man in the real estate business, is now about to do the same. Already he is giving one full day a week to Synanon's housing problems. And George Wheelwright, a man of considerable means, talks of perhaps eventually doing something similar, and promises to deed to Synanon a cattle ranch that is all but within the city limits of San Francisco.

How does one explain this infectious Synanon magnetism?

Recently, at the Clay Street House in San Francisco, one of Synanon's growing number of residences and facilities, I was invited to attend an evening's game specially organized for non-addicts who were having marital problems.

In the course of the animated and at times almost violent give-and-take that arose that evening among the fifteen or more people present, there was one young racing-car builder who made this comment about himself: "I just don't know in what direction I want to move. Right now I'm acting as if all I wanted was for one of my cars to win the Indianapolis. But sometimes I think I'll drop all that racing crap and join Synanon. Who can say? Suppose, for example, I went into politics—and even got to be President of the United States—and then found out that the head of Synanon outranked the man in the White House. . . ."

He didn't get to finish his thought because the whole room rocked with laughter.

When there was a moment of quiet he asked in a kind of challenging tone: "What the hell's the matter with everyone? Does everyone here consider me stupid for thinking that Synanon is headed for the top of the political heap?"

Rod Coburn has since joined Synanon and presently runs the club's automotive department, which keeps some hundred or more trucks and automobiles in repair.

Chuck himself refuses to entertain such political ambitions. He has no use at all for the political game. "Me and Henry Thoreau," he will sometimes say, "have one thing in common: neither of us ever voted."

But as to whether Synanon may some day enter the political field, that's another matter. "We're forming a new kind of sub-culture here," Chuck has observed. "Eventually, I suppose, we'll dot the whole United States with branches of our way of life. Naturally such an organization will exert some kind of political pressure. Large blocks of like-minded people do that, you know. That's just the way it is."

But for the moment there's no sign of that. In fact it is sometimes strange to note how amidst some seething electoral campaign in which issues of vast importance are at stake, Chuck's office will remain as calm as some remote medieval cloister. And Chuck himself like some quietly meditating lama, totally oblivious of the world.

At such times, almost unwanted, I find myself remembering Mark Twain's famous line: "Serene as a Christian with four aces."

Which is of course precisely the way it is. Only Chuck usually phrases it differently: "We've built a better mouse trap," he will often say. He is convinced that the answers that the people are looking for are not to be found as a result of elections, and that eventually all the so-called authorities, all the people in the executive branches of the government and on the faculties of the universities, will have to come to Synanon to study its methods.

It is this supreme confidence that gives Chuck the aura of someone divinely appointed. And calls to mind the great saints, the prophets, and the religious leaders of former times. People tend to wonder at the power accumulating around Chuck, and refuse to believe that a man with his undoubted charisma does not cuddle in privacy some great desire, for the moment carefully concealed from his followers whom he will eventually make his dupes.

But this is only representative of the difficulty that people find in coming to terms with someone who has gifts that are beyond them, and whom they must therefore tear down to their own level at least now and then.

Even in Synanon this very human need for equality exists.

Recently while lunching at the Santa Monica facility, Reid Kimball, then still the director of that branch, told me Synanon's latest inside joke. It seems that Chuck, who was for the time being residing in a kind of powerful semi-retirement at the big Tomales Bay property (that was originally built in order to lure Marconi to this spot some fifty or sixty miles north of San Francisco), got to thinking about the possibility of his passing away and took note of the fact that as yet no suitable plot had been selected for his final resting-place.

He thereupon called in one of his best "hustlers," that is to say one of those members trained to work out in the field finding gifts, bargains, sponsors, everything and anything that can give aid to Synanon's many activities, and ordered the fellow to locate a first-class burial site. The hustler soon returned with the information that cemeteries were in no mood to give away their plots, but that he had seen one burial site that he thought was worth the thirty thousand dollars being asked for it, because it looked out on the most magnificent land and seascape. . . .

"Thirty thousand dollars!" Chuck exclaimed. "Ridiculous! Did you explain to them that I want it for only three days?"

This semi-religious ferment in Synanon, whether laughed at or not—and of course there were always some who would—demonstrates something of the aura and the zest that permeates this place. And certainly Chuck, who is well described by one of his admirers as "an earthquake of a man," could not stop this sometimes grudging adoration even if he wanted to.

The organization is already full of those trained seals, men who have adopted Chuck's way of talking, Chuck's vigorous and decisive way of acting, the very gestures he uses. Men charged with his powerful unshatterable optimism, which has kept this club going through its many lean and dangerous moments.

Thus, for example, during a recent Synanon game that I attended, I noticed one of the Synanon directors, in the midst of a violent argument, picking up a piece of Kleenex and as if unconsciously folding it in a certain peculiar way and then rolling it into a spindle.

I watched this man's behavior with such fascination that perhaps I betrayed myself, or perhaps he himself became aware of what he was about to do, for instead of completing the paper spill, he stopped and began to wave the folded tissue as if he had never had any other intention but to emphasize his words with it. And then, as if still further to conceal his original intention, he began to chew at one end of it, while still talking.

Of course both he and I knew that that piece of Kleenex, had it been actually rolled into a spill, would have duplicated a device that is most intimately connected with Chuck. So much so that it might indeed stand as a symbol for him, as much so as the cross. . . . Long before Synanon Chuck had had to undergo a serious major surgery in his right ear, penetrating, some say his brain, a surgery that had resulted in widening the ear canal on that side into a formidable hole. I still haven't quite grown used to seeing Chuck roll up a piece of tissue into just such a heavy spindle and plunge it deep into that side of his head, in order to clean out the passage or perhaps obtain some sort of relief from an irritation there.

And to watch this director, with nothing remotely resembling such a condition in his ear, fashioning just such a spill, was to feel the powerful presence of Chuck materializing itself in this room five hundred miles from his actual abode. As if by this esoteric sign one could summon the power and the spirit of the absent leader.

3

Synanon is of course not a religion.

But it does have certain similarities. It has found passionate adherents and suffered persecution from equally passionate detractors. It began small and endured poverty. It has had its Judases and its heretics.

Arline related to me one of the many stories about Synanon's early money problems: "If ever there was a nut, a total screwball, a dingbat of the worst kind," she said, "that was me when I first went into that beach club that still had no name.

"My mother got me into Synanon. This is how it happened. I was in jail, up on the thirteenth floor of the Hall of Justice, where I was doing ninety days for marks. And I was pregnant. Don't ask me about that right now. Please.

"So one night I felt labor pains. Of course no one would believe that I was in real pain. Prisoners are always putting on one act or another so as to get special privileges. But finally the matron came to our cell and she realized that I was telling the truth and she got me moved over to the County Hospital and had me admitted to the prison ward.

"The next day my baby was born and I hated it right from the start. But that's another story and I don't want to go into that either. Of course my mother was wild about the kid. It was her first grandchild and she couldn't stop feasting her eyes on it. But I wanted it out of my sight as fast as possible and I let it be adopted away while my mother wept.

"What a pest my mother was, and how I hated her! But this much she did for me: she had heard about a club on the beach where addicts were staying clean, and she rented for the two of us a little apartment across the way from the club, and thus got me involved with the organization.

"I was at that time like some animal out of the jungle, my brain as if cobwebbed. I remember Chuck talking to me about something and using the word 'analogy.' That's where he lost me. I didn't know what analogy meant. And then he used the word 'symbol.' And I got lost again.

"But I did understand when he said to me: 'Don't even think of total abstinence from drugs. That's too big for you. Too vast. Take it easy. Think only of staying off drugs for this afternoon. Or even just for the next hour. That's all.'

"You see he tailored his philosophy to my size. And my size was awful small in those days.

"But there was one thing he said that really registered with me. He said: 'Get away from your mother.' No one had ever told me that before. And he did even more. He made room for me at the girl's dorm, which was an apartment down the alley, and I left my mother for good.

"Guy, you'll never understand what it meant to me to be in a place like that beach club. I had been in and out of prisons and hospitals, and nothing ever came of it except records. Just people in white jackets or white smocks, coming around with charts and asking me questions and making little marks in their charts. That's all.

"Now, suddenly, I was in a place where you were encouraged to ask questions and to discuss the answers that were given to you. No charts. No blood tests, no urine tests. And at the head of it a man like no other man I had ever met.

"For example, once I had a terrible toothache. I had to be taken to a dentist and the tooth had to be pulled. And that night, at two o'clock in the morning, I couldn't sleep because of the pain. I felt I had to talk to someone and so finally I went over to Chuck's apartment and knocked at the door.

"I expected to be bawled out for waking people at that hour. I was sure of it, but I really needed someone to talk to. And that was perhaps the nicest thing that had ever happened to me. I wasn't scolded. I was given sympathy. And a couple of aspirins.

"But I was going to tell you about the money problems in those days. Our poverty was there every hour of the day. Sometimes we were absolutely broke. And all we had was Chuck's perpetual phrase: 'It will emerge.'

"Well, you know what? It did. It did emerge one day. And it was one of our big laughs for weeks afterwards. You see, one of the jobs assigned to me was to give a finger wave to any new girl who came in. And on one of those absolutely moneyless days when all we had was Chuck's repeated 'it will emerge' to keep us hoping, a colored girl came in. And I gave her the usual finger wave."

I had to interrupt Arline at this point because I couldn't see the sense of these finger waves for the new girls, and especially not for a colored girl who would be more likely to want her hair straightened than waved. I was really lost.

"A finger wave was just our term for it," Arline explained. "You know addicts are always hiding a bit of dope somewhere in case of a sudden necessity. And the girls have the best place of all: the vagina. They love to keep a condom stuffed with pills up there. Emergency rations. Well this girl said that she was just wearing a Tampax because she was about due for her period, but I always gave good finger waves, and I got out this Tampax and there was this piece of green paper rolled up in it, and when I straightened it out it was a five-dollar bill.

"We had to wash it, of course, and the girls put it in the oven and watched it carefully so it would dry out but not burn, because that was certainly five dollars we needed badly. And the way it had 'emerged' was one of the big jokes about the club, and I wonder if this colored girl, who is still with us, has ever quite forgiven me."

A kind of aura of prophecy began to surround Chuck as a result of events such as this. The residents laughed—and became a little more willing to believe.

Concerning another one of Chuck's prophecies, the following incident deserves to be told:

One day, not long ago, up at the Tomales Bay facility, the mail brought a hefty package which proved to be the new Random House Dictionary of the English Language. On a hunch Chuck decided to look up the word Synanon.

To Chuck's delight and surprise this invented word was now in the dictionary!

"Syn-a-non (sin′ a non′), n., a private organization assisting those who wish to be cured of narcotics addiction."

For a group of people who eight years before had still been without a name to have already broken into the English language, and in a position now to consort with such hallowed personages as Socrates and Shakespeare, and to rub shoulders with such common nouns as "ice cream" and "grasshopper," was certainly a monster step toward that goal that Chuck had once envisioned: "to make Synanon a word as well known as Coca-Cola." Considering the millions spent by the bottling company compared to the extreme lack of funds in which the club had been spawned, this was quite an achievement. And Tom Patton, the scholar of Tomales Bay, undertook to celebrate the occasion in suitable prose:

"We're all pleased to see Synanon welcomed into the mainstream of the English tongue," a communiqué from Tomales Bay proudly announced to all its branches, "but what we are really after and hope to see in the next edition of the dictionary is the word Synanon defined without limiting it to the small field of narcotic addiction, but extended to the vast numbers of encapsulated peoples everywhere and anywhere.

"To accomplish this new goal it may be necessary to bring lexicographers into our square games," the communiqué went on, concluding confidently with Chuck's still favorite phrase: "It will emerge."

It was not just the fulfillment of still another of Chuck's prophecies that aroused all this gloating and back-slapping, but the fact that for Synanon the dictionary, the words of our language, has a very special significance. One of the most important aspects of Synanon is its language therapy, a laying on not of hands, but of words. A theory of mankind as essentially a species of intercommunicating animal, to whom a perpetual buzz of words is as important to life and well-being as air, and just as the lungs must forever expel foul air and breathe in fresh, so the human psyche must perpetually renew itself by exhaling and inhaling words.

"How can one hope to help people who commit crimes and insanities," Chuck has asked, "by the present practice of locking them up in jails and asylums which can only result in their becoming even more encapsulated than they were."

According to this interpretation, that elusive essence of Synanon which I have been trying to pin down is merely intercommunication between human beings raised to the nth degree. A kind of gift of tongues. And whatever the club has been able to accomplish must be largely ascribed to their never-ending verbal therapy. As to what such a therapy might effect, if expanded to the world, that is something that some members of Synanon occasionally speculate about, and one often hears it said about this or that figure who happens to be in the news, whether about the war or the riots or what not: "Boy, would I like to get him in a game! Just once!"

Early disputes over dogma, disputes that seemed to threaten the very existence of the movement, are yet another aspect of Synanon that links it to the religious. But this was only the natural result of the sense of importance that the first members attached to their ideas and activities.

But from such disputes came Synanon's first heretics and first martyrs—or pretended martyrs.

One of these figures—a person who has vigorously denied me the right to use his name—when I visited him for material about the early days of the club became so aroused as to drum the table with his fists: "No, no, no! You're missing the whole point! You're missing it completely."

"Well, what is the point?"

"The point is very simple. Why must something true and beautiful become so distorted that instead of serving the good of all mankind, it becomes nothing more than the vehicle whereby one man elevates himself over others? Why? That's the point! That's it, and nothing else."

"How do you mean that?"

"Well, isn't it clear enough? That no matter how wonderful something is, there are always ways of spoiling it."

"You're accusing Chuck, aren't you?" I asked, because my martyr-friend's constant allusions, without ever bringing up Chuck's name, were beginning to irritate me. "You're saying that Chuck has ruined Synanon as a social movement and turned it into fraud for his own psychological and financial enhancement."

"No, no, no! Why do you keep refusing to understand me? There's this you've got to know about Chuck: he's a powerful personality. Powerful. And association with him is bound to be a genuine experience. But as to whether it turns out to be a gratifying or devastating one, that's another matter. Personally, I left Synanon just in the nick of time."

"Explain yourself," I said.

"Chuck would have destroyed me if I had continued to oppose his methods."

"How so?" I persisted.

"How he would have done it? How do I know? Except that he would. But fortunately I didn't stay to find out."

"So how can you be sure that he would have destroyed you?" I prodded. "Perhaps he would have saved you?"

"How do I know? Isn't it clear enough? Have you ever seen the papers of Synanon's incorporation?"

"What papers of incorporation?"

"I should think that you, as a student of Synanon's history, would know the papers I'm referring to. The papers that gave Synanon its name and established it as a California non-profit organization."

"Oh, I know about that," I said. "But what about those papers?"

"Well haven't you ever seen the names of the five signers?"

"Of course," I said, and I ticked off the names, ending with Chuck's.

"That's right. And of that group of five names, how many are left? Well, are you going to answer me or not?"

"One," I said.

"That's right. Charles Dederich. Chuck. Chuck and no one else. Doesn't that tell you anything? Aren't you reminded of Stalin? How he got rid of all the original founders of Communist Russia until he had made himself the one-man ruler? Is it possible you can't see that?"

"I can see that he's the only one left, that much is undeniable, but—"

"But what?" he challenged.

"But I don't know that he ever threw any one of the others out. They resigned. They quit. They left."

My martyr-friend smiled and shook his head unbelievingly. "Is it possible that you're so completely snared by him that you will believe that?"

"I won't deny that I admire Chuck," I fenced.

"It goes far beyond admiration," he declared. "Far beyond. I pick up in you a person who has already been hopelessly hoodwinked by the master hoodwinker himself. Which is no surprise to me. He has that power. He most certainly has. But why do I talk to you at all. It's so damned useless. None of this will get into your book. Chuck won't let you put it in."

"That would certainly be the negation of everything that Synanon stands for," I said, "if he won't let me write the truth as nearly as I can discover it."

"You mean the negation of everything that Synanon formerly stood for," he retorted. And then amended himself: "Oh, I suppose that Synanon is still doing more good than harm. I'll allow them that much." Then he burst out passionately: "Oh God! If only

I could put across to you the excitement of those early days. I felt as if I were burning up. All day long my nerves vibrated. Those early discoveries of ours! Before we realized what Chuck was up to. Before he became a victim of his own powers. God, how I wish I could make you see that!"

He stopped as if overcome. As if these memories were more than he could bear. "Because that's the terrible part of it; this great advance into the unknown, this loophole for humanity to escape from all its ancient chains, and then, right in our own midst we discover betrayal—and not just by any old somebody. But betrayal by the very person who was most responsible for our discovery. But that's what happens when the spirit of aggrandizement seizes a person: his first victim must be himself. That you understand, don't you? That Chuck had to destroy himself first. He's to be pitied more than any of us, Guy. He really is. The wonderful Chuck his early friends knew and loved—he was the first to go. . . ."

I waited for him to continue. But he remained silent. And after a moment I urged: "Go on."

"What's the use. You know how our first little group of A.A. members got together in order to probe deeper into ourselves for the source of our urge to obliterate our rational minds with alcohol. And you know how Chuck, with his grasp of Emersonian philosophy, gave us our two basic axioms: that only the truth, the unadulterated truth, could set us free, and that anything that was good for us must be good for all. That's all we had to start with: just those two ideas.

"And now picture us in the grip of this all-consuming faith that caused us all to shed every vestige of selfishness, with everyone's purse open to everyone else, freely stripping ourselves down to our most hidden moments, the most intimate and secret details of our lives, and pitching into each other with verbal weapons that loving friends had never before used against each other, in order to compel ourselves to this state. Who needed alcohol: I tell you, Guy, we were drunk with ideas. Drunk with the possibilities that this method was opening up on every side.

"The whole sexual question reexamined. Prohibition, inhibition, total permissiveness. We argued it out endlessly, cutting it up in all directions. . . .

"And then this test case, just walking right into our hands, straight out of jail. And with that first one, I mean Rex, this thing revealing to us unimagined vistas. All those difficult areas of life where mankind had been struggling for answers for millennia. It was all there!

"Right away we were off to the races! In business, up to our ears. We had to expand. We rented stores and apartments. There was nothing to stop us from spreading right across the whole United States. The whole world! Except that already Chuck was beginning to dream his dreams of personal grandeur.

"I can't explain it. It's beyond me. Except that he got scared that this fantastic thing would escape him. Would run away from him. Would get too big for one man alone. The ego in him demanded that he remain more important than the idea he had given birth to. Who was it? The ancient Greek god Cronus who devoured his children: Or was that Saturn: Well, it was Chuck doing the same thing. Holding on, smothering, choking this thing that wanted to explode too fast."

Overcome again he stopped. Then he shrugged as if it were all useless: "I can see you don't believe me."

"But you see that I'm taking notes as fast as I can," I pointed out.

"Well, then take this down. You're close to Chuck. You watch him. That man is a born intriguer. He's operating full-time, and all the time. His every word is calculated. I don't know how he does it, but he never stops figuring things out. He never stops plotting and scheming. And at that sort of thing he's a genius.

"But he's a sick genius. I can give you ten or a hundred illustrations. As many as you like. But listen to just this one. Listen to the words that came out of his mouth when we moved from that little storefront in Ocean Park to the big armory building in Santa Monica. Here's what he said, and I'll never forget it. He said:

"'I now have a bigger house—beside a bigger body of water—than my stepfather has.'

66

"Think of that! That pronoun 'I,' as if he was Synanon. As if he owned it. And as if Synanon was only his compulsive need to outdo his stepfather!

"That's when I realized how Chuck's tie to his mother and his hatred for his stepfather were incidents of his life that were still boiling around in his insides, and that it was this jealousy, this envy, more than the problems of the poor addicts, that constituted the basic motivating factors in his creation of Synanon. It was this still unresolved Oedipal complex directed against the stranger who had come into his home and taken the little boy's mother away, away to his own bed, that was still raging in Chuck's gut. I was horrified. I understood all sorts of traits in Chuck that had hitherto puzzled me. And I saw at once that this desire of his to outperform his stepfather spelled danger for our club. I saw that Chuck was already moving to use our once honest and vital club of dedicated truth-seekers as a means of self-glorification. To raise himself above the man he hated. And that the situation had in fact gone too far for the club to be saved."

"Why was it too late?" I wanted to know.

"Because he had already rigged the place for himself. He had all those poor addicts already looking up to him as the Great White Father. He had turned the place into a political machine of which he was the sole boss. It was impossible to breathe a word of criticism against Chuck in the new atmosphere of one-man rule that he had established. What could I do? What could any of us who saw what was happening do to stop it? Nothing. We saw Synanon being ruined and all we could do was stand by and weep.

"Let me give you another illustration. Really, Guy, believe me, there was nothing to stop us from sweeping across the nation. Everybody was on our side. I know that Synanon now has enemies everywhere. For example in the police. But that wasn't so in the beginning. If they had been, couldn't they have raided the place at once? Couldn't they? Answer me that! But no, they helped us. They shut their eyes to the fact that our club was breaking the law. You know about the non-association rule of the parole department that says it is a violation of parole for one parolee to associate with another one, and in particular for one drug addict out on parole to associate with another former addict. You know that don't you?

"But one particular parole officer kept right on sending people down to us. And cops kept directing addicts toward us. Everybody wanted us to succeed in curing these poor victims. But Chuck's nature required him to have enemies. The more the better. He wanted to take on the whole world. So that he—and he alone—might stand out as the one man capable of handling the addict situation. See how this great man is being crucified! See how this saintly man is being martyred. Chuck the hero! Chuck the persecuted one! Chuck the heaven-sent messiah!

"And it is that utterly false image that Chuck has been able to put across. In spite of the fact that when the chief of the Santa Monica police came down to visit our place, and saw us housing dope addicts everywhere, even in our own apartments, he was overwhelmed: 'You're doing the Lord's work,' he said. Yes, that's exactly what he said.

"But all these officials had that non-association rule to contend with, and when they were pressured by their superiors and had to obey by pulling out some of the parolees as violators, Chuck turned on them, calling them 'pea-brained civil servants' and 'Mickey Mouse bureaucrats.' . . . That was cruel and unfair towards people who had been so helpful, people who had extended themselves to the limit for us!

"You understand it took me a little time to catch on to what was happening. I was confused. Chuck as the enemy of Synanon? I couldn't grasp that right away. It was too much. Of course I knew Chuck had had something close to brain surgery. And I knew he had had LSD. But Chuck and I had been seeing eye to eye for so long I couldn't believe he was changing his goal so completely.

"And when I began to stand up against him, why he had all those poor drug addicts on his side. You can't blame them. They're just children. Frightened children. And Chuck had made himself into their savior who was protecting them from the world. When actually the world was only too anxious to help them get well. And the proof was how many merchants, how many professional people gave us money, food, free medical advice, legal assistance.

"And that is where the honesty of Synanon went out the window—never to return.

"Instead of explaining to the public the problem we had with dope addicts . . . I mean with respect to sex, girls who had been prostitutes and men who had generally been impotent and were afflicted with all kinds of sexual fears. Instead of explaining how we were trying gradually to bring them to a healthy sex life, we turned it into a dark secret. We lied about it.

"Do you see the paradox, Guy? Do you understand?"

"Of course I see it," I said. "But wasn't the community aroused? Wasn't there a danger of this truth about sex being used to kill the organization?"

"We're the world," was his reply. "We're part of the world. And if we're going to help this planet, if we're ever going to have the world of truth that we want, we've got to begin with ourselves. With ourselves first! We can't compromise with ourselves and then turn around and demand strict compliance from others. Can we?"

"So that's why you left," I asked.

"Yes. And because I couldn't stand this sense of persecution that they were building up about themselves. Chuck constantly afraid that everyone was trying to steal Synanon from him. Why I would be insane to think that I could run any kind of organization, whereas Chuck is a fantastic executive.

"Let me put it to you in its simplest form, Guy. I was ready to do anything, give all my money, give all my time, my life if necessary—but only to an idea, a great idea—and never to an ego—no matter how great that ego. And that's the point, you see. When Chuck identified himself with Synanon, when he himself became Mister Synanon, then I had to go.

"The great goal of Synanon had changed from dedication to an ideal to dedication to a man—and at that point I had to leave."

"Why didn't you form your own club if you felt that Chuck was ruining Synanon."

"Many former members wanted me to. They begged me to do just that. But, Guy, I'm not a business person. I'm not much of a speaker. I'm just not the kind of man who could build an organization. Not me. No. I thought of it. Yes, I thought of it many times. But I couldn't."

The spectacle of this tiny club of fifteen or twenty recent alcoholics and a sprinkling of recent drug addicts cleft by Grand Canyon arguments, the spectacle of these people who were often individually and collectively so broke that they couldn't be sure of their next meal, and yet were ready to choke with apoplectic fury over their proper philosophic stance, all this would be laughable if it were not indicative of the sense of history in their midst, a sense so powerful that it acted like a magnifying glass, ballooning their least arguments out of all proportion. Because the leaders of this little group saw all mankind eavesdropping in the wings, prepared to invade the stage of Synanon by the millions the moment they heard the proper cue.

"This thing is bound to explode some day," is the phrase I used to hear time and again. And when Synanon didn't explode but just kept growing, there was talk of the "critical mass" not having been reached yet. The explosion was not abandoned, just postponed.

And in the meantime those who left were of two kinds; those who thought of themselves as somehow graduates of an educational institute, a place where they had been taught how to live without chemicals, and like alumni all over the world they continued to maintain some relationship, however infrequent, to their alma mater, while others were splittees, that is they left in anger, carrying with them ashes of ancient grudges and disputes, ashes always ready to burst into flames again on the question of Synanon.

Synanon is often attacked for the way it holds on to its members, but the truth is that the Synanon umbilical cord is tough to cut, so that both those who leave in a rage and those who leave with blessings continue to find Synanon holding much of their thoughts and emotions. And the disgruntled ex-Synanon members are of course constantly on the lookout for the kind of news that will confirm them in the vindictive position they have taken.

Recently, for example, one of these former members wrote a magazine article about his dropping in at the newly opened San Francisco branch of Synanon, a big house in a stylish neighborhood, and told how a butler met him at the door and commanded him to wait while he got permission from the master to admit the visitor.

This picture of Chuck turned into some sort of a Mussolini of the addicts delighted these ancient mourners, as I found out from talking to several of them. The truth is that the writer had actually toned the picture down. This particular Synanon House did not have just one butler, but possibly four or five. And probably as many as six cooks, plus seven or eight upstairs and downstairs maids, and God only knows how many janitors, chauffeurs, and social secretaries.

The explanation for the princely existence in which Chuck was indulging himself at what has since become known as the Clay Street House is that it is Synanon's policy not to locate itself in slum neighborhoods. However, in fine neighborhoods there arises the powerful opposition of those who do not wish their children to live near former crooks and prostitutes, no matter how "former" they may be at the moment. And in this case the opposition had the familiar weapon of the zoning ordinance to stop Synanon from putting up one of their houses in an area restricted to single family dwellings.

To save Synanon from eviction proceedings, Chuck resorted to a legal trick. He and his wife became the single family inhabiting the Clay Street mansion. And since the zoning provisions had nothing to say about the number of servants a family might have, all the drug addicts of the place were turned into butlers and maids and kitchen scullions.

So much for that.

But of course heretics are not necessarily looking for the truth. They are more likely to be looking for any excuse that will permit them to cry out: "You see! What did I tell you? Remember what I predicted?" The perpetually hopeful cry of old-timers trapped in pleistocene conflicts that would be scarcely worth a footnote if these issues did not keep cropping up again and again.

Involved in one of these footnote disputes of long ago was a person deeply devoted to the early Synanon, a woman whose gentleness and generosity are still vividly recalled by many of the early members—a person of culture whose collection of books formed Synanon's first little library.

And then suddenly, this person was gone.

For a time all sorts of opinions and rumors circulated as to why she had left, since the official communiqué "for reasons of health," did not wash. But there is such a constant churn of events in Synanon that her case was quickly knocked into a corner and forgotten. What with the population turnover and growth, it may be safely said that today ninety-five—maybe as much as ninety-eight—percent of Synanon doesn't so much as know she ever existed.

A graduate who remembers her well had this to say about the case: "She was all tea and sympathy, Guy. And her message had quickly spread throughout our little club: if Chuck ever gives you a vicious dressing down for some infraction, don't let it affect you too deeply. Just hop, skip, and jump over to your good friend, the club-mother, with her wide-open hotel bosom where there's room for everyone, and she'll soon have your hurt soothed.

"Chuck was gradually getting sore as a boil. All his tough shock therapy was being frustrated by an all-loving mother-figure. And this just when he was realizing more and more that you can't run Synanon on mother love.

"Who would struggle to improve himself? Who would battle to change his character? Who would fight his inclinations? Mother's love just doesn't do those things. Mother's love is something that never fails. Deserve it or not, Mama is always there with her kisses and her bandages. No. It's the father-figure that puts spine into you, instills a superego into your make-up. Because Papa's love is something that has got to be earned. And that's what we addicts needed.

Not the everlasting loving bosom of Mama. But Papa and the wood-shed.

"We were all sorry to see her leave, I'll say that much. We knew that she had opened her heart and her purse to Synanon. Generously. But she had to go. She just wasn't good medicine for drug addicts. Period!"

I discussed this matter once with Chuck. "You had originally intended to call your club 'T.L.C.,' meaning *Tender Loving Care*, hadn't you? Those were the letters painted on the window of your storefront?"

"Yes," he said. "But we learned that there was already a T.L.C. club."

"But suppose," I said, "that this name hadn't been pre-empted. With T.L.C. nailed to your masthead, would not the doctrines of your organization have moved in the direction of mother love instead of stern paternal affection?"

"I can't imagine what would have been the fate of our foundation if we had been burdened with that name," Chuck replied after a moment. "We were very fortunate, I suppose, that some other organization had prior rights to it.

"I remember very clearly our day of baptism. Our phone was near the coffee counter, and I was leaning on it with my elbow and listening to our lawyer, who at that time was Jim Kemper, and he was kind of getting impatient for me to pick some other name. But the words *Tender Loving Care* had got themselves so chiseled into my brain that I just couldn't think of anything else.

"Then this word that everyone was using around the club occurred to me. It was one of our early alcoholic members, Graham Thompson, who had coined it. For our seminars. One of his many malapropisms. We had always thought of that word as an in-joke, good for a laugh among ourselves and nothing more. But wasn't that precisely what made it our very own? And therefore just right for us? So I said to Jim: 'We'll use the name Synanon.'

"Jim Kemper said: 'How do you spell it?' And I had no answer.

I just didn't know. It was a word that had never yet been written. Only spoken.

"So I began figuring it out on a piece of paper that was there. I wrote it one way and then another. And then still another. I remember trying it out first with a 'c.' Cynanon. But that looked tough and hard, probably because the sound suggested the word 'cynical.' And then I tried beginning it with an 's,' but I didn't follow it with a 'y.' I wrote it with an 'i,' and I ran into the word 'sin' and that obviously wouldn't do either. And then I wrote it with a capital 'S' and a 'y' after that, and suddenly I felt that I had it. With that 'S' reaching up above the line, and then the 'y' going down below, the word seemed anchored right from the start. It looked solid and strong. Structured. And already I could see it in print, on letterheads, and on our literature."

"What name had you been using on your literature so far?" I asked.

"We didn't have any literature," Chuck explained. "Not of our own. We had been distributing A.A. literature. The same stuff that you can find in any A.A. clubhouse. I guess you could say that the word 'Synanon' was our first piece of literature. And perhaps our best."

Happenstance? Possibly. And then again not. Perhaps the word "Synanon" was like that five-dollar bill. Something that "emerged." A bit of a miracle.

4

At the origin of Synanon there looms a strange figure: a man who came first and then left, making way for one who was greater.

This John the Baptist was Gray Thompson.

Arline, when she first came to the club, and was still wrapped in that fog in which she had lived for so long like some jungle animal, as she herself described it, couldn't help but admire this handsome god-like figure who towered over everyone in the Ocean Park store. She often stared at him, unable to understand how anyone could be so big and so beautiful. And she would watch him wonder-eyed, as he went roaring off to the beach, to race up and down along the sand like a madman, then dash into the sea to cavort like a seal or a walrus. Then back to the club where he had rigged up a punching bag which he would beat with the fury of a maniac until the sweat poured from him in streams.

And then, while Arline tried in vain to comprehend this manifestation of masculine ardor, he would utter in a deep voice a line that she didn't as yet recognize as a quote from Thoreau: "The masses of men live lives of quiet desperation."

He seemed then to Arline like some soothsaying spirit out of the Bible or out of mythology, pronouncing doom upon all mankind. It made her shudder.

When Rex, the dope addict whom Gray Thompson introduced to the club, stayed clean, Chuck tried to puzzle the matter out. A drug addict who simply gave up his desire for dope, voluntarily, with no coercion, with no medical assistance, with no walls to shut him in, was practically unheard of.

"I puzzled over this," Chuck told me. "I didn't realize we were developing anything so remarkable in our evenings of prying out truth, until the results became manifest in Rex. This fascinated me. Somehow we had developed a peculiar piece of machinery. Throw a drug addict into it and it cleaned him up! Dope fiends who weren't forever chasing that white powder just didn't exist—so far as anyone knew. Rex himself was unable to throw any light on his new condition. Just that he had stopped looking for dope. Didn't crave it. Didn't go mad looking for it.

"Of course junkies often kick their habit when they find themselves needing too large a dose to produce the desired narcotic glow, but this is usually only in order to start all over again as soon as they can. This is just part and parcel of the race that every addict runs with his habit. But Rex staying clean was something else again. I knew we had something here. A new discovery, a new mechanism, a new method of working with human beings."

Gray Thompson, elated over the Rex success, went around spreading the news of this discovery. One who heard of the still nameless club through Gray was Vivian G. Recently, during moments she could spare from the needs of her little boy, she recalled for me the painful road she had traveled until she reached the club. Vivian was a woman whose whole being cried out for physical perfection, and she was not physically perfect. Her soul cried out for beauty and she was obsessed with the dread that men might find none in her.

Alcohol first gave her the courage to be promiscuous, and in the arms of men she found some precious moments of relief from her dread of not being liked. But the sense of guilt that followed these sexual bouts only added to her fears and her anguish. And thus her need for the escape that alcohol offered grew right alongside the relief she got from it.

She became an alcoholic.

Promiscuity furthermore brought in its train the probability of disease and pregnancy, and soon a cheap abortion had given her a case of extensive peritonitis. Her doctor gave her morphine to ease the almost intolerable torture of her inflammation. And now she knew of another road to a state of blissful forgetfulness.

Her body became well again. Her doctor stopped the morphine. And once again life lost all joy. She began to associate with boys and girls who shot dope and she stepped into this new experience with trepidation and eagerness. She didn't want to go too far. She knew all its dangers. She even knew that the road she was choosing was false. But what other way out was there? Except the bottle or the needle?

She started by sniffing the heroin, hoping to go no further. But this made her feel so good, with all sense of guilt, all anxiety, all dread vanishing in the wonderful glow that the drug induced, that her fear of the needle gradually diminished. She began with the little injections known as skin-popping, until finally she became a hardened trooper who could mainline it right into her bloodstream with no compunction whatsoever.

But a narcotized pain is still there, even though you don't feel it for a while. Afterward it comes back with twice the power it had before. Promiscuity soon turns into prostitution when it becomes a question of how to afford the expensive drug. Endless vows are made to break out of this evil circle. But dope erodes one's will-power. And the circle becomes ever tighter.

Then suicide begins to beckon. Isn't that another way out? Perhaps the easiest and the best? What did she have to live for? A father who was a sewing-machine repairman, who, at best, was stuck in some poorly paid job, at worst had no job at all. And a mother who was a scold and a slattern who filled the house with endlessly repeated variations of her many complaints. Home was hell.

Vivian's suicides failed. Her marriages failed. She could only cure her drug habit by turning to alcohol, and could only cure her alcoholism by going back to drugs. And again and again she went to jail. For using, or for prostitution. She went to a hospital when a dirty needle gave her an attack of hepatitis from which she barely escaped with her life. Her woes never stopped. It was either one chemical or another.

"I tried A.A. but it didn't seem to work for me," Vivian related. "I needed something stronger. I was then in an alcoholic phase and at A.A. no one knew of my addiction. But one evening when it came my turn to get up and make my testimonial, I surprised myself and everyone by suddenly admitting that my real problem was more than alcohol. I remember weeping and confessing. . . . And a woman came up to me afterwards and urged me to go to a branch of the organization, a branch called Hy-Al, developed for those who had both problems.

"I was going around with a boyfriend at the time, Abe, whose problems were similar to mine, and we both attended the Hy-Al meetings together. And one evening there was this tall handsome man all steamed up about a queer cat at the beach, a guy named Chuck. With this Chuck, he told us, it wasn't testimonials. It was something totally different. So different that it couldn't be explained. It was something that had to be experienced. Powerful!"

"What did you think of Gray Thompson?" I asked Vivian.

"The closest thing to God," she said. "The size of him. That bubbling enthusiasm that never stopped. The drive and the energy he could put into whatever he said or did. I can't really describe him to you, Guy. He was just overwhelming.

"And he was so right. The difference between A.A. and Chuck's method was something that couldn't be described. One had to live it. And drug addicts were already beginning to flock to the place. There were no dormitory arrangements yet. Everybody was doubling up. A couple of cheap apartments had been rented so that as many as possible could squeeze in. Both Abe and I joined up immediately.

"I loved the closeness in which we all lived. The comradeship. I felt warm and protected. And that was necessary because in the therapy sessions you were not called upon to offer up your own testimonial. No. You were like an oyster whose shell was being cracked open. It was painful and terrifying. You were exposed and you struggled to cover up. You hated it. But at the same time it was exactly what you wanted. And it was so good afterwards to have the crowd around you—still warm and friendly. In fact even friendlier.

"I felt as if reborn."

But about the subsequent estrangement between Chuck and Gray Thompson, Vivian was not too clear. "I was pretty mixed up myself, Guy. But I sided with Gray. I felt that Chuck was power-hungry, and all my sympathies went the other way.

"And when Gray left, it was as if I had lost my brother. I felt totally miserable. It took me a long time to realize that I owed my life to Chuck. Not to Gray, who hadn't done anything except make the introduction."

"Have you ever seen him since?" I asked her.

"Yes. Several times. Just bumping into him by chance. The last time was maybe two and a half years ago. On the street in Santa Monica. He was the same old Gray. As bubbly as ever. 'I've just bought a bar,' he told me. Which surprised me, coming from a former A.A. 'So?' I said. 'Whereabouts?' He told me: 'In Venice. Wish you'd drop in.'

"The same old Gray. Just as attractive as ever. And just as anxious to make every girl he saw. I had to tell him quickly that I was married. 'Well, bring your husband along,' he said.

"I never saw Gray after that but I heard that he had sold this bar and gone off with some of his crazy friends on a trip to the South Pacific. Or somewhere. Kind of sad, isn't it? For such a wonderful man to go wrong. Especially when I think what I owe to him."

Gray apparently fascinated everyone. Almost all the early members sided with him when the big quarrel broke out between Chuck and Gray. It was only later that most of them realized in which man lay the real strength and the real warmth of Synanon.

Jesse Pratt, an imposing Negro, with the features and the stance of one of those Mongolian warriors who conquered the world from Central Europe to the Pacific Ocean, but who is now shipping and wrapping clerk in the basement of a local bookstore, recently recalled for me his first encounter with the two men.

Jesse first heard of the club on the beach from his parole officer. "Jesse," the officer said to him one day, "you're still young but already you've done eleven years of your short life in road camps, in honor farms, in jails, and in penitentiaries. Where are you heading now? Have you given it any thought?"

Jesse's only thought was: "Once a hype, always a hype," an expression that was common among the people of his world. He lived in a state of chronic despair, punctuated by periods when he was loaded with money gained by theft or gambling and could indulge in his appetite for drugs and for women, for both of which he had an enormous capacity when he happened to be out of jail.

He had been bitter about himself and the society he lived in since his childhood, ever since, at the age of nine, he had watched his mother go off to work day after day and come back ten or twelve hours later, having earned a total of ninety cents.

"That was when I made up my mind, Guy, that I'd be a Negro, since that was the way I was born, but I was damned if I was ever going to be a nigger. No white man was ever going to stretch out his leg in front of me and have me kneel before him with a brush and a tin of shoe paste. No, sir. Not ever. And no white employer was going to stick a mop in my hand and give me orders to clean out his shitters. I'd break the mop over his head, if he did."

It was that sort of fierce pride and the inevitable series of humiliations that life forced him to swallow that took Jesse into the world of drugs, graduating him from weed to heroin, and turning him into a gambler and a burglar, but never erasing the picture of his mother, who wanted him to be a man of education and who had scrounged pennies to buy him a book for his birthday or for Christmas. Always a book. Never a toy. That's the kind of mother he had had.

And now, here he was, sitting beside the desk of his parole officer and listening to the mathematics of a life that had attempted to escape the economic domination of the white man only to discover the white man's prisons.

"What do you propose to do about it, Jesse?" his parole officer asked.

Jesse shrugged. "What is there to do?" he asked. "When you're hooked, you're hooked."

The officer said: "There's something happening at the beach in Ocean Park. I don't know exactly what it is. I haven't had time yet to go down and see for myself. But I've heard a lot about it. It seems that it's the one place where dope addicts can really clean themselves up. Why don't you give it a try?"

Jesse smiled. He had been through all the big narcotic hospitals and had never found anything that could stop his need for a fix. Nevertheless he was willing to promise his parole officer that he would look into it.

And so one day he went down to Ocean Park and looked for the address that his parole officer had given him. He was rather startled to see that it was not in the least the sort of place he had expected. No imposing entrance. No guard in a booth. Not even a reception clerk. Just a store. And inside some white people sitting on chairs that didn't match, around a table that was ready to fall apart.

"I guess the total membership at that time," Jesse said to me, "must have been no more than fourteen, probably less. And most of them were still A.A. people, but with the dope addicts just about to win the majority. I thought I'd be invited to sit down with them and talk this thing over, and cut it up with them as to whether their method would be worth a damn for a real boss hype like me.

"But we never got to a discussion. It seemed like the moment I opened my mouth these white people shouted at me: 'Shut up! Move in, and when you get some of that street garbage out of your head, then we'll listen to what you have to say.'

"That kind of reception, inviting me in, while kicking me in the face at the same time, was so unexpected that I didn't know what to say.

" 'Okay!' I was told. 'You're in. We'll show you where you bunk.'

"This was going too fast for me. My mind was confused. I had wanted to debate and had found myself ordered around instead. But I had promised my parole officer to give these guys a chance, so I explained that I'd be back in the morning. . . .

" 'We're offering you a pad right now,' they told me. 'If you're serious about wanting to clean up, now's your chance. Move in at once.'

" 'But I haven't brought my things with me,' " I pointed out.

" 'What things?' they yelled at me. 'You mean your needle? Your stash of drugs?'

"Their laughter was insulting. But I checked my temper. 'My clothes,' I explained. 'My bathrobe, my pajamas, my toothbrush, my toilet articles . . . I'm a man who likes to be clean. I guess I make a fetish of it.'

"Well that really set them off. Apparently it was the best joke they had heard in years, a dope addict who made a fetish of being clean. Because you know, Guy, addicts call the stuff they shoot into their veins 'shit,' and here I was, saying I made a fetish of being clean and at the same time was shooting 'shit' into my body.

"So they told me again that I was sick, insane, stupid, with nothing but gutter-garbage in my head, and either to move in at once or get lost.

"All I could see in this, Guy, was the same white guys who had always yelled at niggers. I didn't realize then how cleverly all this was stage-managed to keep the issue off the intellectual level and bring it down to the gut, so that I was moved to get out of that Goddamned place, get back to my room, pack my things, and come back, just to prove to those Goddamned white bastards that they weren't going to keep me out of their place because of the color of my skin.

"But that's when they flabbergasted me again. Because they were pleased when I really showed up again. And they turned me over to one of the handsomest men I had ever seen in my life. A Greek statue turned into six feet four of flesh.

" 'I'm Gray Thompson,' he said to me and shook my hand. 'Come along, pardner.' And he took me around, led me over to his apartment, and showed me where I'd be sleeping.

"Then he opened up a dresser drawer and pointed to a little pile of small bills and change.

" 'This is where we keep the kitty,' he said. 'Empty your pockets, my friend. Here we share and share alike.'

"I explained to him that I had just got out of jail and didn't have a dime to my name.

" 'That's okay,' he said. 'We happen to be ahead at the moment. We've got a couple hundred here. So if there's anything you need —here it is. Just come and get it. Only you must remember one thing.'

" 'What's that?' I asked.

" 'Well, it's the arithmetic of it,' Gray said. 'This money belongs to the whole club—so every cent you spend on yourself is a cent that the rest of us can't have for what we need.'

Jesse paused in his story. "I wonder, Guy," he said to me, "if you can realize what a beautiful moment that was. *The* most beautiful thing that had ever happened to me in all my life. If it hadn't been for Gray Thompson I think I would have moved out of that club ten minutes later. Because it was right afterwards that I collided with Chuck.

"I had developed such immediate warmth and love for Gray that although I reacted violently against Chuck, I nevertheless didn't run off. I stuck it out. But that Chuck! Right away I felt this is the white man I've hated all my life. The white man who sticks a mop in your hand and says: 'Clean out the shitters, boy!' Which is exactly what Chuck did.

"I backed off and I said to Chuck: 'Look here. Now you listen to me. Because I want you to get this straight. No white man hands me a mop and tells me to clean out his fucking shit-house!'

"Chuck said to me: 'Now you—*you!*—YOU!—pay attention to what I'm saying. Because I'm not crazy. And you are! Don't tell me that a person who commits a crime in order to get the money to buy a little bit of white powder to shoot into his veins, so that pretty soon he has to go out and commit another crime in order to buy some more of that same white powder, don't tell me that that person hasn't got garbage in his head instead of brains.

" 'So you listen to me! And listen carefully. Everybody in this organization has a job. How the hell do you think this place is run? We don't hire help! We do it ourselves. And of course the last man in has the lowest job. Or are you so Goddamn insane as to imagine that you're going to step in at the top? You want to be president here? Are you totally out of your mind?

" 'So your job is mopping up! And do a good job. Because this toilet is not just mine. It's yours too. And if you want a clean crapper, keep it clean.

" 'And one more thing. The next person coming into this place— white or black!—is going to take that mop from you! And you're going to move up! That's the way it is! Like it or lump it. You don't expect to start work at General Motors as the president of the plant, do you? Well, do you? Well, what about it? I'm asking you: what about it?'

"I didn't believe him, Guy. I didn't believe a word of what he said. I just didn't like that guy Chuck. It was instinctual. But I yanked the mop out of his hand and I went ahead. I mopped, and I swept, and I emptied ashtrays, all the things I had sworn I'd never do in my life. And I hated every minute of it, but I gritted my teeth and I did it.

"And the more I saw how the whiteys in the place were sitting around on their asses, chewing the fat, pretending they were having very serious discussions about things too deep for me to understand, the more I hated them. And particularly Chuck. All of them except Gray Thompson. That fellow I loved.

"Really my hatred for Chuck was eating me up. But I did my job. I watched those guys drinking coffee, leaving their dirty cups around for me to pick up and wash, and my hate just kept on growing.

"I think I wouldn't have been able to stand it, except for Gray and one or two of the other members. It seemed to me at first that the more Chuck made himself hated, the more Gray and a couple of others would go around after him, and sweeten things up.

"It was one of them who gave me my first book to read in Synanon. And when I had read that, gave me another. In a couple of weeks I had read maybe eight or ten books. And then I noticed that Chuck would now and then talk to me as if I were a person of some knowledge and intelligence. Talk to me about the books I had read.

"And then one day there was a new face in the club, and they took my mop away from me. And I was put on the coffee counter.

"Mind you, Guy, I still couldn't like Chuck, although dimly I had the feeling that he had engineered everything. That his rejecting me, his insulting me, his forcing me to mop floors, those were prods that he had used to compel me to churn over in my gut all my feelings, stir things up in me, so that while other guys would be shooting the breeze over cups of coffee, I'd be compelled to face myself, deep down inside of myself.

"And pretty soon I was looking forward to the discussions that I would have with Chuck. But he was still no Gray to me. I was catching on to his methods, however. And when the club got so large that we couldn't all of us meet in one group, it was me, not Gray, whom Chuck picked out to head up one of the groups, with himself leading the other, but with the members of these groups changing places all the time.

"I guess the reason for my being selected was my hostility. I could get roused. I could get sore. Awful sore. And then I could really unload. I could pour it out. Hot and heavy. Almost as good as Chuck.

"But Chuck. I could never quite get over my reservations about him. And sometimes I would let my old hatred come gushing out against him. Like for example once when I wanted a couple of dollars out of the kitty for a trip to the barber.

"'Two bucks for a haircut?' he roared at me. 'Are you out of your mind? There's a pair of scissors around somewhere. Ask one of the girls. They'll know where to lay hands on some shears for your golden locks.'

"Guy, I tell you, he'd irritate me to the point where I'd yell at him: 'You dumb bastard! Don't you know the difference between any old haircut and the real thing that only a good barber can give you?'

"He'd give me the two bucks, maybe, but along with it some remark about 'suedes' which would make me boil even though he had often explained that words were just noises that come out of peoples' throats, and the real meaning lies in the feelings that go with them. But he couldn't understand that for me a 'suede,' an immaculate appearance, was my one way of outranking the whites.

"Toothpaste was another matter we kept quarreling about.

" 'Brush your teeth with salt,' he would say. 'That is what I do.'

" 'And that's why you got the lousy teeth you have,' I'd tell him. I've always been proud of my good teeth, Guy. Chuck's teeth are miserable. You know that."

"Yes, I know," I said.

Jesse continued: "He'd make some dumb remark about everybody ending up with store teeth anyhow. But in the end I'd argue him out of a few cents for toothpaste.

"Another time it was a question of food. I wanted twenty-four cents for a box of Wheaties. It was during a period when all the food we seemed to be able to get around the place was day-old bread and ready to curdle cartons of milk that hadn't been sold and were due to be sent back to the dairy.

" 'Wheaties?' he shouted. 'What the hell is Wheaties?'

"And when I tried to tell him that it was a breakfast food he interrupted me, exploding: 'Well it's wheat, isn't it? And isn't that what bread is? So what Goddamned difference is it to your stomach whether your teeth grab hold of it in flakes or in a slice? Your gut doesn't care whether it's sold in a box or in a wrapper.'

"How could you argue with a man like that? How could I explain to him if I had to eat one more slice of bread and milk I would puke it up in his face!

"Guy, it was a real bitter tug-of-war to get that twenty-four cents out of Chuck. And even when he finally gave it to me, he had some insult to go along with it. 'You're a baby, Jesse. Not a man. Do you know the difference between a baby and a man? Babies are unreasoning animals to whom you have to give things to make them stop squawking and squawling. And that's how I have to treat you. Here! Here, take it, infant! Take it!'

"I took it. Yes. But feeling all the while that I'd like to shove it up his ass.

"How different it was with Gray. He'd give you his last dime without a word. Of course, Chuck never spent a cent on himself. Never. Maybe he does now when I understand that things are going easier at Synanon. But not when I was there. Not one penny."

"You admire Chuck in spite of everything, don't you?" I once asked Jesse when we were having a bite together during his lunch hour.

"With reservations," he said. And then added: "Of course you understand that he saved my life. You understand that, don't you? I wouldn't be alive today if it wasn't for Chuck."

"Nevertheless you split with Chuck. Or at any rate you split with Synanon."

It was a question that I had asked him several times before, and had gotten various answers, so that I had decided that perhaps there was something here that Jesse didn't want to discuss. And the differing explanations he had given me were thus only the changing rationalizations of a mind that didn't want to come out with the truth.

In a Synanon game I would have said to him: "Jesse! You're taking me on another trip." "Trip" being the word that has come to be used at Synanon for elaborate attempts to evade an honest answer.

"When Chuck began to split with Gray," I asked Jesse, "how did you line up?"

"You mean on the question of incorporation?"

"Yes. And on the move to Santa Monica."

"At first, Guy, I was all for Gray. The club was doing fine. We were having a wonderful time at the beach. Things were bubbling all the time. I couldn't see anything illegal in what we were doing. Why shouldn't we just keep on going the way we were?

"But I could understand Chuck's side of it too. We were getting bigger and bigger all the time. We needed real dough. We couldn't go on begging stale sandwiches from catering trucks, and spoiled vegetables from supermarkets. We had to organize, put in an accounting system, keep records. I could see that. But still I was drawn to Gray's argument that we shouldn't do anything that would destroy the tree-house feeling of having a gay old romp. Gray felt that Chuck was going to ruin things.

"Gray was impetuous. He was whimsical. He was a delight. While Chuck was authoritarian. He had a sense of humor, yes. But only as a veneer to his seriousness. I loved and respected both men but for Gray I had more love than respect. And for Chuck more respect than love. And when the big blowup came and I saw the whole club splitting wide open, coming undone like the pages of a newspaper in a rainstorm, I realized suddenly that the glue that held this thing together was not in Gray, but in Chuck. And so I sided with Chuck.

"Most of the others sided with Gray. At first it was only Vivian and myself who were for Chuck. And then, after a few hours, Crawley joined us. . . . I guess most of those who sided with Gray got lost and many eventually went back to drugs. . . ."

"But you too quit," I said, trying to get him back to the original question.

"Yes I did."

"Well why?"

"Chuck has his faults," Jesse said. "I know Chuck. He and I averaged nineteen hours a day on our feet trying to keep the club going during those times when there was practically no outside interest. During my first six months in Synanon not a single newspaper, not a single magazine, not a single radio or TV program so much as mentioned us.

"I used to ask myself: 'Why. What is he doing it for?' I knew my own motives. I wanted to live clean. But his? What were they? Then I began to notice something. His love for shocking people. Knocking them off their feet. What did he get out of that? Why obviously a sense of power. A sense of having control over people's lives.

"And in Synanon he had that. Plenty of it. He could take people into his foundation and save them from suicide or prison. He could release them from the chains of their addiction. But once he had these people in Synanon he could also throw them out. And it was almost one hundred percent certain that anyone he threw out would shortly land in jail—or be dead from an overdose. That's an absolute fact, Guy.

"Don't you see that this power of life and death made him a kind of god? Don't you see that? And don't you see that the more people he got into Synanon the more he could become the great father-figure? That's why he never wanted anyone to leave—unless they dared to stand out against his ideas. Then from being the man who never wanted anyone to leave, he would become the angry god who expelled you from paradise! Plunged you back into hell.

"So you see I had to escape from Synanon. I had been there a little over two years. I felt I was ready to go back into the world. But Chuck didn't think so. What counted, however, was that I did. And I got out. And I was right. I stand on my own two feet now. I'm married. I like working in a bookstore. I have peace of mind. This is where my mother would want me to be. Here among all these books."

"Did it ever occur to you," I asked Jesse, "that Chuck might feel that with his organization growing so fast, he had first call on the people whose lives he had saved, that he needed them to help him and work with him, rather than go out and back into that world that had never done anything for them but drive them to shooting dope? Did that ever occur to you?"

"Yes, of course that occurred to me," Jesse said. And he continued with deep seriousness: "I did think of dedicating my life to Synanon. It would not have been difficult at all. . . . Only . . ."

"Only what?" I prodded.

"Well, I didn't want to be a fanatic. I just haven't got that dogmatic makeup. But I'm still following the philosophy of Synanon, am I not? Right here in this basement. Doesn't it say that a man must accept himself as he is, for better or for worse? Doesn't the Synanon philosophy say that a man should bestow his toil on that plot of ground which is given to him to till? Well, what else am I doing down here in this bookstore? Books are what my mother used to save her pennies for. And I like it here, surrounded by books."

5

"That's a lot of lies!" Arline cried out one day when I had been speaking to her about Jesse. "Jesse didn't quit because Chuck was power-mad. Jesse got thrown out!"

"Thrown out?" I exclaimed. "Why I understand that Chuck admired Jesse."

"He did. We all did," Arline declared. "Jesse was one of the smartest men I've ever met. Such insight into the feminine mind! Donna used to say that Jesse could guess what was on her mind even before she began thinking of it. None of the girls could hide anything from Jesse. It was uncanny. And Jesse could lecture the girls—give them a haircut—as we say, better than anyone else. Maybe even better than Chuck. The girls got exactly what was coming to them from Jesse. They knew it too. There were three men to every girl in those early days, and it was no problem at all to get some fellow to do your work for you. Chuck was absolutely right when he said most of the girls were still peddling their asses inside Synanon, as if they were still out on the streets, hustling."

Arline wanted to show me exactly where the old club was. And the alley going off it, where Chuck had had his pad. And Gray Thompson's place. But an urban rehabilitation project had taken over the area. She took me around, trying to locate the exact spot of the club's beginnings, but found it impossible. Great blocks of land had been cleared of all houses. Two immense skyscraper apartment buildings already thrust high overhead. Bulldozers and piles of crated plumbing fixtures and other mounds of construction material dotted vast stretches of plowed-up sand.

Arline couldn't get over it. "They've torn it down. They've torn everything down," she kept repeating, as if it were unbelievable that a spot that had been so important in her life should have left no vestige of itself. I had the feeling that she looked upon all this devastation as something of a sacrilege. Holy ground had been defiled. A shrine had disappeared. It smelled of blasphemy.

But then she shrugged. "I guess all this should have been destroyed long ago. It was nothing but junk. I remember when we rented the store across the alley to make the men's dorm. It had been some kind of auto-repair place. . . . You can't imagine how filthy it was. Floors, walls, even the ceiling, were caked with oil and with dirt. Such grime. We scrubbed and scrubbed. And the place had no water—or something. Anyhow I remember we ran a hose out of the club window, and across the alley and into the dorm, so the men could shower. . . . The shower was right in the living room."

Arline was filled with memories and I hesitated swinging her mind back to Jesse.

"Nothing but junk," she repeated. "Yes, you could rent a place around here for peanuts. In those days. I bet it's going to cost a fortune to live in one of those skyscraper apartments. Overlooking the ocean. What a view! But what kind of a club for junkies could you start here now? You couldn't."

As we walked away I brought her back to the question of why Jesse was thrown out.

"Didn't he tell you about his epilepsy?" Arline asked.

"Epilepsy? Jesse?"

"Oh he can control it," Arline said. "But he has to take his medication. And he got careless. One time he felt it coming on while he was taking a shower, and wearing nothing but a couple of soap bubbles, he ran through the house. Chuck caught him. Forced a spoon into his mouth, and took care of him during his fit. And not long after that Jesse packed up and left."

But later I talked to Lena. She didn't agree. "Arline doesn't have all the facts," she said. "I think I ought to know best why Jesse left. I was Jesse's girl."

I could see that. She would have been Jesse's girl. And what a handsome couple they must have made! Lena, very dark, beautifully built. Both of them with fine free figures and intelligent wide-awake features.

"How did you and Jesse get along?" I asked.

"I was very fond of Jesse," Lena said. "Perhaps because he was Chuck's right-hand man at the time. And I was just a nobody. A nothing of an addict. From the earliest I can remember I was always reaching out for the immediate pleasure. And with little or no sense of guilt. For example smoking marijuana right in front of my mother. And she saying: 'Well, if you got to smoke pot, I'd rather you did it with me knowing about it, than behind my back.'

"Maybe it has something to do with the kind of family I was born in. So that I can remember any number of times when my mother would say to me: 'Guess your father must be lying around somewhere, drunk as a dog. Go find him.' And I'd go. I was always the strong one of the family on whom the others leaned. My mother had a weak heart. My sister was always ditching school. My father gambled away his earnings. And I was determined to hold our family together. And get through school too.

"I was Mama Lena, the head of the house. But I didn't make good at it. Because I too wanted to live it up. I wanted some of the fun of life for myself. So I began to run around with older kids. At fourteen I was already shooting dope. Soon I was stealing. And then turning tricks, getting arrested and thinking: 'Well, fuck it.'

"Then I had one of my two illegitimate children. My boy. I said to the nurse: 'You don't have to give *me* any sedation. I'm loaded.'

"So I had my boy by 'natural' birth. And I felt fine. And proud. But not my baby. He couldn't sleep. He whined. His nose ran. He kept throwing up. And his little body shook with spasms.

"The doctor said to me: 'Your baby was born a drug addict. You've been fixing him for nine months through your bloodstream. And now he has to kick *your* habit. Has to kick it "cold turkey."'

"I was so conscience-stricken that I cried for my poor baby and said to myself: 'Never again!' But who ever heard of a dope addict keeping a promise? I didn't keep mine. Not even when I got a six-month conviction for marks and Judge Younger said to me: 'It's so close to Christmas. I guess you would like to spend the holidays at home with your children, wouldn't you? I'll excuse you until New Year's. You can start your term then.'

"I wept once again. But it wasn't until I came home and my little boy was so wildly happy to see me that I began to have real conscience pangs and promised myself: 'Absolutely never again!'

"But once again, in typical hype fashion, I didn't keep my resolution. I was no sooner out of jail than I was back with the needle. But one day, on an Art Linkletter show, I saw a report about Synanon and my mother said to me: 'I'll take care of the kids. You try Synanon.'

"And even then I delayed. Then, when I finally did go, it was only with the secret thought of just cleaning myself up for a while. Say ninety days. And then back to my old ways. But I met Jesse at Synanon, and became his girl, and I stayed. I guess that saved my life. Synanon and Jesse.

"Chuck loved Jesse. And he needed Jesse. But Jesse had a sex thing—especially for white girls. And I was given my first job in Synanon: to straighten Jesse out.

"But how could I? He was so anxious to lay his hands on white girls that he'd even have eyes for a newcomer while she was still puking it out on the couch. I'd keep trying. Trying everything. Trying to talk him out of it. Telling him I was through with him. And pitching into him in all the games, telling him he was stinking up the club.

"But Jesse was kind of irresistible. So attractive. Such a gift for language. He could always talk me back into going together again.

"Maybe if the woman who was kind of our club-mother hadn't been herself so fond of Jesse, maybe something could have been accomplished. But whenever Jesse had done something terrible, there she was immediately trying to patch it up. Not that she condoned what he did. But she lectured him so gently that it was almost as if she did."

"You were rather fond of her, in spite of that, weren't you?" I asked Lena.

"Who wasn't?" she replied. "Certainly all the girls were. Maybe some of the men weren't. She was the mother-figure of the place. Always sweet and kind and willing to give you another chance to make good. In her opinion women were the flower of civilization. And every woman, as a potential mother, shamed man out of his brutality. Men were the doers and the artists, but it was women who were the inspirers of beauty and the guardians of the arts. She was always lending us books, and calling our attention to some beautiful passage in Emerson or in Kahlil Gibran. It was difficult for someone like me not to worship her. But later I realized that with all of her sweetness wrapping itself around me she was only making it harder for me to come to grips with the hard facts of my life. . . ."

"How do you mean that?" I asked.

"Well, she let me believe that as a woman I had everything coming to me, just purely from the fact that I was born with one set of sex organs rather than another. That feeling of superiority delayed my cure for a long time. And her methods were no good for Jesse either. If not for her maybe Jesse could have been saved for Synanon. She didn't help him any—with all that easy forgiveness of hers—she didn't help him to get over his terrible sex mania."

Rita, to whom I talked next, didn't go along with Lena on this sex-mania business. "Lena exaggerates. Jesse didn't have any more of a sex thing than all the rest of us. You have to remember how short of everything we were in those days. Synanon didn't have a cent to spare. Meanwhile addicts by the dozen were clamoring to come in and get cleaned up. And there was no space to hold them. We got double bunks and shoved them so close together that our house looked like one of those Nazi concentration camps. Some of the guys were saying that they had had more room to move around in when they were in jail. A lot of people—potentially good Synanon candidates—split just because of the crowding. Went back to the gutters. In fact it's a wonder any of them stuck it out.

"And then our slopping around all day in half-undress, that didn't help to give us Puritan morals. But you've got to remember our clothing and our laundry problem. It just kept getting worse and worse and we didn't seem to know how to lick it."

I tried, in my mind's eye, to see Rita slopping around. But I couldn't. I felt sure that she, at any rate, had always been as neat, as trim, as precise and as dainty as she was now. Even though I knew a lot about her life as a drug addict, engaged in activities that anyone can imagine and that were anything but dainty. . . .

"At the same time," Rita continued, "we were all of us coming out of a narcotic state. You know of course that hypes are pretty generally impotent. The girls often stop menstruating. They're generally frigid. In bed they just pretend that their customers are taking them to cloud nine, so that they can get themselves an extra five dollars. As for most of the men, they stop having an erection. Hell, you're so loaded that you're on the nod. Half-asleep most of the time. And the rest of the time you're running around like mad to get some more heroin to feed your habit. The men go out to steal cars or hang paper—you know, pass out phony checks—or break into drugstores at night. And the women go out and do the thing they know best.

"And of course everyone pretends that he is having one hell of a time, beyond anything that squares could possibly understand. I used to be crazy enough to think that myself. And even now I'm still crazy enough to wonder about it now and then.

"Now pack all these insane people into Synanon. Pack them in there with no drugs, and with all their genuine appetites rushing back. All their healthy and normal drives. But still without brains. Because if they had ever had any brains in the first place they wouldn't have become drug addicts. And the functions of the body bounce back long before the mind wakes up.

"Can you imagine now the kind of mess these dimwits must make of their lives when they first start getting back their health and living normally? Don't forget that even in the world of sanity, sex is still the most difficult and dangerous area of all. How much more so then inside Synanon!

"Of course we had the Synanon game working for us. But too slowly. Health would come back to us in a matter of weeks, and along with it a rekindled desire. But education was not so fast. That needed years. Chuck would sometimes refer to the club as 'my animal farm' or 'our playpen.' We just looked grown-up. Actually we were still babies. Or animals—which is what babies are. Except that babies and animals couldn't possibly have gotten into all the mischief we got ourselves into.

"So it's not fair to speak of Jesse's sex mania. As if that were something special in our club. He wasn't any worse than the rest of us. And I want to say this for him: he never touched *me*. Except to massage me when I was kicking. He had powerful hands, but a delicate touch. And that's about as sexy as he ever got with me. Never gave me the eye. Never said to me: 'Look baby how about us two making it.' None of that. And for all I know I might have been very willing. I was still nothing but a dingbat. And there was this Jesse. Already a director. And a fine strong figure of a man. Absolutely unlike Chuck, who went around looking like the worst slob of all of us—walking around like an unmade bed, as someone once described him—while Jesse was always so neat. His pants sharply pressed. His shirt immaculate and with razor creases. And always a book under his arm. Perspiring freely, but always freshly showered and smelling of eau de cologne—not the very best, but still a cut or two above the five-and-dime stuff.

"No. Jesse didn't have any special sex thing. He got most of the blame for the famous incident in the library, because he was a director. But he hadn't been in the club so much longer than the others. I know that when the mayonnaise hit the fan and people were buzzing about it all over the club, a lot of members thought they had a right to put on white wings and think of themselves as angels, just because they hadn't been involved in the famous 'incident in the library.'

"I was disgusted with this hypocritical attitude. I hadn't been part of the orgy either. But I didn't go riding around high and mighty about it. All I said was if those schmucks wanted a sex party why didn't they go down in the basement, instead of locking themselves up in the library where everybody had to know that something crazy was going on.

"I suppose there must be a million or more sex orgies taking place in the United States every year, in country clubs and in hotel rooms, at sales meetings and Shriners' conventions. But that doesn't mean that all these people are sex maniacs. Everybody lets go once in a while.

"Of course someone had to take the blame, and it was Jesse. . . ."

"Rita hasn't got her facts straight," Bill Crawford told me later. "She seems to think that Jesse got bounced because of the incident in the library. That's not so. Rita wasn't involved. I was. I remember everything very clearly."

Bill is a gentle, scholarly looking man, who has risen in Synanon to the kind of positon that Jesse once had. And this after years of addiction to cough medicine, which he would drink by the gallon if he could get hold of the stuff.

"There were ten of us," Bill told me. "Including Jesse. About six guys and four girls. And Jesse was lecturing to us on Emerson. He really was. He was very strong on Emerson. I don't know how one thing led to another, but the talk got to be very sexy, and the question arose as to who had the courage to face the world stark naked. Hiding nothing.

"Maybe this nakedness idea had some connection with the time that Jesse had felt the aura of an epileptic attack just as he was in the shower and had run through the club dressed in a soap bubble, as people afterwards described it, or maybe it was something else that triggered it. Anyhow Oscar got to urging Jeanne to undress, and Jimmy began to badger Frances. And pretty soon everyone was taking off his clothes. . . .

"And there was such shouting and laughter and screams that we could be heard all over the building until finally someone had the bright idea of locking the door. That was just when the coordinator, who had the supervision of the house, came to the door, and finding it already locked, rapped on the panel. But Jesse yelled that he was in charge, and that everything was okay, and for the coordinator to get lost.

"Of course it all had to come out. I don't know who blabbed, but it makes no difference. With our Synanon games the truth has to come out eventually. And Chuck's attitude was simple and direct. Not that he spared us each a good haircut liberally sprinkled with references to us as 'punks' and 'ass-holes.' But he wanted none of our apologies.

" 'You don't owe *me* any explanation or apologies,' he said. 'You haven't done anything to me. I'm not Synanon. Synanon is the whole organization. And you've endangered the existence of that organization. You've endangered the existence of the one hope for the cure of dope addiction that there is on the face of this earth. So you go out and make it right with the membership. They are the ones that may have to suffer from your stupidities if this should break up the club. So you go out there and clean it up with the people in the house.'

"The result was a general meeting before the fireplace, where the whole population pitched into us, calling us every kind of dirty name in the English language, and demanding explanations for our infantile behavior.

"The girls wept. And I felt like sinking through the floor. I know that Jesse, and all of us, never spent a more embarrassing hour in our lives.

"But this incident didn't get Jesse bounced. If it had he would have left immediately. As a matter of fact he behaved himself afterwards. His continued role as director depended on his toeing the line. He had more to lose than the rest of us. What Jesse neglected was his medication. When he had his next fit, Chuck decided that that was enough.

"I know this is true because I can remember the meeting that Chuck called and what he told us. Namely that Jesse had a medical problem and that he was leaving the club in good standing, and that we were all sorry to lose such a fine director. But that it couldn't be helped. There was always the possibility that Jesse would recover his health at some time in the future, and that the club would always be ready to welcome him back."

"That's not the real story at all," Ted told me some days later. "Either Bill doesn't know the truth, or else he really believes the story that Chuck used just to cover up Jesse. Naturally Chuck wasn't going to tell the whole membership exactly why Jesse left."

Ted is a wiry young man, soft-spoken, gentle-featured, and almost painfully serious.

When I asked him what had brought him into Synanon he said quietly: "Despair." And he told a story of having just served two years in San Quentin and having two more years to go on parole, and meanwhile with such a huge habit that he couldn't possibly go to see his parole officer loaded as he was. . . . And then being stopped on the street by narco bulls and propositioned to turn in his connection and be let off. Somehow he managed to talk them into taking him to his parole officer, and somehow he talked the parole department into letting him come into Synanon.

When I interviewed him he was part of the San Diego facility, in charge of the living requirements of over two hundred people, who had to be supplied out of gifts in kind and out of cash disbursements with homes, clothing, furniture, spending money. In short everything.

"Seems like all I do, Guy, is give. Eighteen hours a day," Ted complained. "This one wants a new TV set, that one wants a lamp. So and so needs a larger apartment since the birth of another child in his family, and someone else has to have a car to carry out his work. It's give, give, give, all day long, until deep into the night.

"Advice on personal problems—hell, just to cope with all the jealousies is a full-time job. Why did this one get new carpeting? Why did that one get a better apartment? I have twenty-six pieces of real estate to manage: mortgage payments, taxes, insurance. I'm going crazy. And when I come home late at night from my office, my wife says to me: 'Seems to me you have time for everyone's needs except those of your own family.' And you know what? She's right."

"What are you going to do about it?" I asked.

He shrugged. "I wish I knew. I can't quit Synanon. I owe my life to Synanon. And my future, whatever it may be, is with the club. But sometimes I figure maybe I'll be lucky and have a nervous break-down and just go to pieces and then there will have to be some kind of a reshuffling of jobs."

"Do you want to talk about Jesse?" I asked him. "Or would you just like to rest. Have a cup of coffee or something?"

"I know everything you want to know, Guy," he said. But then, seeing me pick up my pad and my pen, he added: "I'm not sure that this is something you ought to put down."

"No matter what you may tell me," I said, "I couldn't publish it without Jesse's permission. And yours too. I have to have releases, you know. I may have to change names, and slightly alter circum-stances, but in any case I must do the best I can to satisfy both the truth and the people involved."

Still Ted hesitated.

"Is this something that is difficult for you to talk about?" I asked.

"It's on account of Frances that Jesse had to go," Ted said. "And Frances was my girl. At Synanon. And later, outside of Synanon."

"Can you tell me when you got to Synanon?"

"September '59," he said. "Just a month or so before the club moved from the store building in Ocean Park to the armory building in Santa Monica. I think our total population was about forty-five. Now we're eight hundred or more you know—and with a real popu-lation explosion just around the corner. I can feel it coming. I know it's coming."

"Do you want to tell me something about your life?"

"Seems to me like all my life up to my joining Synanon was just running scared, and somehow managing to have a ball at the same time. Fun and trouble came together. Home was a place where my drunken father would kick my mother—but there was always the street corner where I could hang around with a bunch of kids like myself, and we'd steal cars and go joyriding, siphoning gas to feed the tank, cause it was wartime.

"But the cops were always on my heels," Ted added. "I'd wake up in the morning, maybe in San Bernardino, but already the cops were at the door. The stolen car was on the hot sheet, and the next thing you know I was in Juvenile Detention, or I was in a road camp. . . .

"I can't tell you the number of times I was arrested. For smoking weed. For stealing cars. For breaking in. For dope-dealing. For putting out phony payroll checks with a stolen check protector.

"I married a beautiful girl who didn't mind my being addicted until she got pregnant, and then she put her foot down and told me she didn't want her baby to have a dope addict for a father. I told her to take a powder. I was in jail when she had the baby—my baby —but she was already married to another man and all she wanted from me was my consent to have the new father adopt it. I hated to give up my child. It was mine. . . . It was really mine. It really was, you know.

"But I had to resign myself. I knew I was an incurable addict. I never knew an addict that was forty years old. They were all dead by then, or else in the pen for life. I knew that a short life was going to be my fate too, but I didn't care. I told myself that once a hype, always a hype, and that I was having a great life, and that I loved it.

"And all the while I was really running scared. Scared to death. And the proof of it is that in a dozen years I moved at least a hundred times. Maybe more."

He paused. After a moment I asked him: "Do you want to tell me about Jesse and Frances?"

"Jesse was crazy about girls. No matter how many he had, he wanted more. He couldn't keep his hands off them. Why once he went after a girl who was kicking her habit on the couch. It was late at night, and Jesse switched off the lights for the action.

"When the nightman came by he turned the lights on again and told Jesse to knock it off. But just as soon as the nightman left, Jesse switched them off again. And was back at this girl. . . .

"She was terrified. She had come to Synanon as a last resort, and didn't know what might happen to her if she dared resist. Maybe this was something she had to do here. She nearly went out of her mind.

"Chuck lectured Jesse again and again. He needed Jesse. The club lacked responsible people. Reid Kimball, who was to turn out to be a genius of a director, was still in a fog from I don't know how many years of addiction. So Chuck kept hoping that Jesse would straighten out. And Jesse in fact always would straighten out—for a while—and then go right back to being the same old Jesse.

"It was in the summer of 1960 that Jesse happened to see Frances on the beach. She was in her bathing suit. He was in shorts.

"And he suggested a walk. Nobody turned down a walk with Jesse. He was a fascinating talker. He said he had a friend living near Muscle Beach. Perhaps they might drop in on him.

"His friend wasn't home. But Jesse walked right in. And there he grabbed Frances, tore at her suit, ripping it loose. She tried to fight him off, but he choked her, until she figured that the only way to save her life was to get through with whatever he wanted as fast as possible.

"She came running back to the club, clutching her torn bathing suit against her body. She wouldn't even look at me. She ran right to Chuck. And Chuck was waiting for Jesse when he came back, and told him to pack his bag. Told him that his lack of control was endangering the existence of the club.

"Jesse argued that he had had an epileptic fit, and had grabbed Frances to keep from falling. Maybe so. Who can really say. At any rate Chuck was willing to let the club think that Jesse was leaving for medical reasons. And that's how it was given out to the membership.

"I remember how we all stood in the dining room and watched Jesse leave. We watched him go across the Pacific Coast Highway and up the concrete steps there, and on up the hill until he disappeared from sight. . . ."

"You still liked Jesse."

"I hated him—and yet I liked him. Chuck himself looked like he was holding back tears when he saw Jesse with his bag packed and ready to leave. But perhaps getting booted out of Synanon was just what Jesse needed. I know he's straightened out since. He doesn't use. He's married. He works at a job he likes. . . . He's doing fine, I guess. But he should be in Synanon. That's where he belongs."

"What happened to Frances?" I asked.

"Remember the seven parolees who had to leave Synanon?" Ted replied.

"Yes I do," I said. "That was just shortly before I first came to know Synanon. The club was still talking a lot about it."

"The parole officers didn't mind us being in Synanon—not at first. They figured they knew where we were and that consequently we weren't involved in dope or crime. But then the higher-ups decided that this was in violation of the rule that said that parolees are not allowed to associate with people who have crime records. And how can you be in Synanon and not associate with former criminals? So they ordered us all out of Synanon."

"I remember now," I said. "Frances was one of the seven."

"No," Ted said. "She wasn't. But she left Synanon too. To be with me. Because we were in love. But we weren't ready yet to be out on our own. We were still far too immature. Almost immediately we started using again. And then it was the same old life. Getting picked up for this and for that. The inevitable routine. Running scared. Changing our address. And convincing ourselves that we were having a whale of a time.

"Then Frances got pregnant and I wanted to get her an abortion. But like the dope fiends we were we decided that we could do it ourselves. With a catheter. So first we took a really big fix, and then when we were loaded up, we performed the operation. But not successfully. Frances got very sick. Some infection. I rushed her to the County Hospital in Torrance.

"Over the New Year's holiday they let me take her home, but I was warned that she was very anemic and must not do anything strenuous. She knew she oughtn't to have a hot bath, but she took one anyhow. I had gone out to score—you know, find some place where I could buy dope—and when I came back with some friends she was in the tub.

"The fellows and I went into the kitchen, to fix, and then I prepared some for Frances, and went into the bathroom and fixed her too. And then I went back to my friends in the kitchen. Then later, when I went into the bathroom I saw that she was lying under the water.

"I picked her out quick and carried her to her bed and yelled to my friends to blow. Then I tried artificial respiration. I was so scared that though I had just fixed, it all left me. Of course I knew she was dead even before I yanked her out of the tub, but I ran across the street and called the emergency, and they got there so fast that I scarcely had time to get back across the street and put her bathrobe on her. And all the emergency could do was certify that she was dead on arrival and order her body taken to the county morgue for autopsy. There her death was eventually described as 'accidental.'

"I was very much in love with Frances, Guy. Very much. And she with me. And if we had stayed in Synanon, I would not have this on my conscience. . . . But that's water over the dam. I guess. After her death I began using more heavily than ever. And in and out of jail all the time.

"But one day my brother drove up to the County Fire Camp. I was being released. And for the first time in many years I was neither on parole nor on probation. I was really free. And my brother drove me straight to Synanon. . . .

"You know I'm married now, Guy. You remember Carol Scofield?"

"Yes, of course."

"We have two kids. You couldn't pry either of us loose from Synanon. Not with a crowbar . . ."

6

"Why does everyone insist on missing the point?" Chuck exclaimed when I consulted him on all these various Jesse theories. "Of course I wept when Jesse left. Jesse was just too good to lose. And of course I was sorry to see Gray Thompson go. We needed him. Psychologically they were both wonderful people. Gray, Jesse. Several others. Everybody liked them. I liked them. They had real quality.

"And if the club had remained small—say twenty people—or twenty-five at the most—everything would have been fine. But when we grew to forty, fifty, then it became a matter not of psychology but of sociology. There's a borderline in there—I can't pinpoint it— where they could no longer function.

"My girl friend of that time opened her pocketbook to us—but it wasn't bottomless. And we couldn't keep depending on her pocketbook and a glass jar labeled 'discover the joy of giving.' She couldn't see that. She couldn't move up into sociology. She just couldn't.

"And letting her relationship to me get in the way of her relationship to the club, that was part of it. And totally unrealistic. Which was more important? The personal emotions of the two of us, or the welfare of fifty addicts who would live or die depending on whether the club continued or not?

"You see she was stuck in time. She couldn't grow. And the club was determined to grow, whether anyone liked it or not. So we outgrew her. Which was unfortunate because she was a hell of a fine person. If she had been able to ride along she could only have gained in dignity. And in personal recognition too. She could have sailed into a graceful old age as the mother-figure of a thriving community that is perhaps the most unusual and promising community that ever existed in this world. But she evidently couldn't see that far. And that must be the reason why she never quit her job during the two years she was with us. Never really committed herself, you see? Never made the decision to sink or swim with Synanon. Never threw herself in, come what may.

"And it's the same with Jesse. He had this terrible sex drive. Well —so long as we were nothing but a kind of crazy beach club, something out of the South Sea Islands, what difference if you were totally uninhibited? What difference if you walked around naked with your pecker in your hand? What difference how much your behavior might stink, since your heart was pure.

"You're having your sexual fling. Great! Crazy! But only up to a point. When a beach club grows up and becomes a movement, then you've got to take another look at the world in which you live. Then you've got to think for example of the question of what to do about broads who get knocked up. You can't solve that by slopping around the beach, strumming a guitar and singing songs. Not in Santa Monica, you can't.

"It seemed for a while as if I was the only person who could see this sociological thing coming in on top of the psychological one. It seemed as if I was the only one who could see this organization growing constantly in size and importance and requiring all the executive talent we could find.

"My girl friend, for example, was so far from thinking in this big way that when we had any guests to the club you could see that she identified with the guests rather than with us. Whether it was the parole department, or the probation department, or the police, or the authorities of Santa Monica, or the judge who was trying our zoning case, she was always seeing it *their* way, and not ours.

"And maybe this is understandable. Here we were, a bunch of prostitutes and dope peddlers, and there she was, a woman of culture and refinement, with an excellent library of books that she read and understood. . . . But she never really saw herself as a member. She saw herself as lady bountiful passing out the goodies to the afflicted. Genuinely concerned about them, yes, of course. But not herself one of them. Whereas I thought of myself as a former drug addict, even though I had never been one.

"Then, when she realized that things were moving out of her sphere, instead of trying to catch up with the club, she chose to feel hurt, to feel neglected, discarded. Which was nothing less than a hallucination. And a greaty pity, because she had made a very important contribution to the founding of the club. And she might, in the future, have made even greater contributions."

"Wouldn't you say that Gray made the biggest contribution of all?" I asked.

Chuck nodded. He leaned back in his chair and stared at the ceiling. He spoke soberly: "Gray was extremely important to the birth of Synanon. I would say in fact that he was essential. He had qualities that you don't find around easily. Really I never met anyone to equal him. First of all the sheer physical perfection of the man. Six feet four. Two hundred and ten pounds. Could wear out a dozen girls jitterbugging all night. A strapping bumptious hunk of virility that no woman could resist. And absolutely shameless.

"There was never anyone to top him in sheer gall. He'd make no bones about calling up one of his married girl friends and inviting himself in to dinner. But first he would find out what she was cooking. And if it wasn't what his appetite was after, he'd tell her so flatly, and call up some other girl friend. He had a string of them, so there was no reason for him to limit his menu.

"Gray was all feeling. The nearest thing I've seen to a natural man. A great big animal. Handsome, powerful, fearless. During the war he ran amok, behaved like a savage, collected I don't know how many citations. A magnificent soldier.

"And yet he was full of love. Ready to hug the whole world.

"I remember the first time I met him. In 1957. That was before Synanon. At a time when I was talking at all the A.A. clubs in Southern California. I drove up to Malibu to speak to a group of swanky drunks at the sheriff's station, and I went out of my way to be brutal to those socialite lushes. And after my talk this tall massive man came rushing at me as if he wanted to kill me. But of course all he wanted to do was kiss me. He was like a huge dog. A Great Dane wanting to slobber all over me.

"I looked up into his nostrils and said coldly: 'Look here, Buster, I never have anything to do with nuts like you until they've been dry for at least six months.'

"But you couldn't insult Gray. Not if he liked you.

"Then, some months later, I saw him at another A.A. meeting, and we got to hanging around together. He had a pad at the beach and he would invite me down. We were suited to each other. Gray was the first person I'd ever met who could match my energy.

"No matter what party we went to, Gray and I would still be going strong when everyone else would have dropped away. We used to speak of stacking up the fallen guests like cordwood. We outlasted everyone. We were twin Falstaffs.

"Gray was good for my ego. He was the first person ever to hero-worship me, and there was nothing I needed more. I was just getting over a bad case of shattered image. After all what was I but a common drunk who had failed in business, failed as a husband, failed as a father, failed in every department of my life. And now came this wonderful figure of a man to give a blood transfusion to my wounded psyche.

"Gray worshiped me to the point of imbecility. And I loved every moment of it.

"When, for example, we'd go out for a swim, he'd run ahead of me on the beach, screaming: 'Make way for Monsignor! Make way! Everybody out of the ocean! Monsignor is going to swim! Clear the Pacific! All out! All out!

"It was an insane performance. And he was so noisy, so big, so flamboyant. Calling me Monsignor. And patting the sand where I wanted to lie down, so that all the girls would have to stare. It was as if he were drunk. And yet he never drank at that time.

"To match his flamboyance I would have had to get looped. A

few drinks and I could out-Orson Orson Welles. But Gray could do it cold sober. I would have to grab the cocktail shaker to work myself up to that pitch. But somehow, when Gray was there to trigger me, I didn't need any liquor. His admiration for me, and his example, were enough.

"We'd go to A.A. meetings together. Pick up a couple of broads. And then eat and argue all night long, while the girls would yawn, or go off to a corner and fall asleep.

"Gray never had any money problems. Any firm in the world would have been glad to hire him. But working or not working, Gray's pocket was open to all his friends.

"But more than his money, more than his worship, was the role he played in bringing certain important elements into the Synanon game. Gray was with our first group when it began reaching out for something more effective, more penetrating than the A.A. testimonial method. It was Gray who roused me to the point of finally using the game not for polite conversations, but for emptying out the vials of my hostilities. He could needle me like no one else.

"Under the influence of Gray we blew out the moderator and conducted our meetings without this hangover from the past. And it was Gray too who first cast aside all the rules about polite speech. Our language got rough and gut-level. And the Synanon game with all its fire and fury, all its fun and laughter, all its tears and heartaches, finally came into existence.

"But even then no one would have known how powerful a therapeutic instrument we had concocted if again Gray hadn't brought something new to it, namely his friend Rex, a dope addict just released from jail. Gray lodged him in his own apartment and made him part of our circle.

"Thus it was that we ran our first test case. Not that we knew it in front. We had no idea how important this was going to be. What a landmark in our development. And even while it was happening before our eyes we still didn't immediately realize that we had constructed a machine that could clean up one of the most difficult problems of modern psychiatry: drug addiction.

"But Gray did even more than that. With his mania for changing words (for example he would say 'solicitate' instead of 'solicit,' and he would call the coffee urn the 'coffee urinal') he invented the word 'Synanon,' which was exactly what our totally new method needed, namely a totally new word.

"For all this Gray has a permanent place in the heart of Synanon.

"But Gray himself was unable to adapt himself to what was taking place. In particular he didn't like the way Synanon was coming between him and his best friend, the Monsignor who no longer had time to go out and sun and swim on the beach. He could no longer call upon the world to clear the Pacific Ocean because his Monsignor was going to bathe.

"I was too busy cleaning up dope addicts, too busy trying to pay bills, trying to pay rent, making sure of food, trying to find people in the club who could help me with some of this load. The time when all the savages danced around the campfire without caring whether there was another coconut around was over. It was a time for hard work. I had to keep insisting that everybody in the club must have a job. And there must be no shirking. And Gray didn't like that one bit. Not one bit.

"I saw what was coming and I tried to pull him my way. I put him on the board of directors. But he didn't last two weeks. He particularly hated the idea of leaving Ocean Park and moving to Santa Monica. He'd grouse to the members, telling them that this was really his club and that I was stealing it away from him and worse than that: ruining it in the process. He was the first of all those people who didn't want to run the club and left me to do all the running, who would later accuse me of stealing it from them.

"Of course I wasn't stealing his club at all. It was the addicts who were stealing it. And that was something he himself had initiated. But he refused to see this.

"I guess he felt that I had turned rat. He had been so nice to me —for example—insisting on taking me down to a store and buying me an outfit from the ground up, shoes, socks, underwear, suit, shirt, tie, hat, everything. And then I didn't wear any of it. Dressed myself up twice. And then gave it all away to some hype, someone who didn't even stay in the club, but split, going off with all those expensive clothes.

"Gray still kept hanging around, walking about the place, grumbling, grousing. But his heart was no longer with us. And then it became obvious that he was drinking again. And once, filled with his frustration, he went up to Jesse, who was sitting calmly in a chair, and slugged him hard. That was totally unlike Gray, who, at bottom, for all his strength, was really a very sweet and gentle soul.

"In fact his action frightened him more than it did Jesse, and he didn't pursue his advantage, even though he had the whole club scared. He quickly turned away and went over to his pad.

"It was I who had the job of calling up the cops and having Gray arrested.

"That was the worst blow of all. I, his best friend, had blown the whistle on him. I had called the bulls. I had had him locked up like a common drunk.

"Well that's what he was. So what else could I have done? It was a question of protecting the club. He didn't stay in jail long. He called up someone, I forget the name, who could spring him. And he came straight back to the club. Burst in through the back door, pushed his way through the crowd there, and was obviously so ready to explode that he had the whole place cowed. Absolutely cowed.

"I guess there's no one more frightened of physical violence than myself, but I walked right up to him and said: 'You come with me, Buster!' And I turned my back on him and walked out the front door expecting obedience. And in fact he did follow me. Meekly. Completely subdued.

"I took him over to my pad and shouted at him: 'Now what the hell are you trying to do?' He just sobbed, not saying anything, as if his heart were too full for talk, and just slowly simmered down.

"And then he left.

"His connection with Synanon didn't end abruptly. It sort of trailed off. He moved away, but would visit us now and then in Santa Monica, and would behave eccentrically, throwing his weight around, talking far too loudly. As if taunting us to start something with him. Daring us.

"It was obvious that he had a full-blown drinking problem again. And I heard later that he was going to the Hacker Clinic and was taking an LSD treatment. And then he disappeared. Dr. Casriel, who wrote the first book-length study of Synanon, claims he ran into him while on a tour of some West Indies island, running some kind of combination nightclub and whorehouse, living it up there on the beach, brown as an Indian with a red-check bandanna around his hair and big gold ring in one ear. And drinking a lot more than he should.

"That would be just like Gray. Just the sort of thing he'd do. Flamboyant to the end."

Chuck paused in his reminiscences. Swiveled his chair to look out over the great bay of Tomales and the wooded peninsula beyond.

In the silence I could hear a bulldozer at work on one of the slopes of property. A foundation was being prepared for a big structure that was being proposed for a center for art and culture.

I had to think of Gray, Synanon's John the Baptist, and the Synanon game he helped to invent, and the movement that has grown out of it. How fantastically this seed had developed. And Gray left behind.

7

Gray Thompson was only the beginning of what was to become a flood of worshipers at the shrine of Chuck Dederich. Sometimes this adoration can go to rather embarrassing lengths.

Only recently, for example, I heard Zev Putterman proclaim loudly at a Synanon game: "Chuck is my god, and Synanon is my religion!" He flung it out like a banner. A crusader's challenge. *"In hoc signo vinces!"*

To hear this sort of thing from an intelligent, even a brilliant man, such as Zev undoubtedly is, a man who was once a fine student, who enlisted to fight in the Arab-Israeli war, and who is now making himself a reputation as a talented TV producer, is shocking—and deeply disturbing to someone like myself who generally tries to maintain a cooler and more detached position—though not always with success.

The point is that I can readily find excuses for Zev's ardor. But not so readily for mine. I have never had a dope problem. I never balked the efforts of seven or eight of our best institutions and hospitals to cure me. I did not puzzle eight or nine of America's most noted psychiatrists and psychoanalysts who were all unable to halt a nine- or ten-year run of addiction and crime. Zev did all that.

Only four years ago Zev might have read in the New York *Herald Tribune* the opinion of Dr. Casriel, who had just finished many years of study on dope addiction. Dr. Casriel's opinion was precisely that of the dope addicts themselves, only more professionally phrased.

Instead of saying: "Once a hype, always a hype," Dr. Casriel said: "Either put him away for the rest of his life in hospitals or jails—or give him all the heroin he wants." (This, of course, was written before Dr. Casriel encountered what he was later to call the "miracle of Synanon," thus himself coming close to joining the throng at the shrine.)

Zev's conversion into a militant Synanist, with Chuck as his god, is therefore understandable. Or at any rate pardonable. In view of the fact that today he is married, has two children, earns a good living, and is free from both crime and dope. Naturally he tends toward hyperbole when he considers the cause of his cure.

But what excuse can I find for myself? Except that history shows such religious fervor to be contagious.

I think it was Jeanne Camaño, who, five or six years ago, first suggested to me that something resembling a deification of Chuck existed in the minds and hearts of a number of the Synanon residents. It seems to me as if I can still hear the passion with which she said to me: "I adore him, Guy. I'm crazy about him. Really, Guy, I just can't tell you . . . but I worship him!"

And I recall vividly the expression on her face—something that El Greco might have painted—because Jeanne's emotions were always too big for her to cope with, and at such moments her words would come tumbling out of her mouth, tripping each other up as they passed her lips, while her breath would go whistling audibly past her teeth.

There was an intensity there, difficult to describe. . . . But for Jeanne too I can find excuses. I still have the notes I took of Jeanne's history, and the pages are spread before me now as I write. Pages that read like a shriek from a torture chamber, a cry for help from a child whose only crime was that she wanted more love. More love and more understanding. And neither was available.

Of course dope could never give Jeanne precisely what she craved. But at least it could make her feel temporarily comfortable. It could help her smudge out for a short while the ugly record of the past. It could make her forget for a short period of time her mother saying to her: "Jeanne. Jeanne, I warn you! You're driving me to an early grave!"

And dope could help her to forget the nun-teacher at the parochial school ordering her to stand in the corner, facing the walls, and then saying to the class: "Jeanne's been bad. Nobody play with Jeanne. Jeanne's been very bad."

Jeanne was so profoundly aware of the disapproving adult world surrounding her that she would sometimes be too terrified to voice her desire to be excused from class. And then she would have to die and die again, because of the shameful wetness of her panties that no amount of leg contortion could erase or conceal.

Even in college when she experienced the miracle of being loved by a boy whom she loved too and her whole life seemed about to be magically transmuted, it was only to face her mother's inflexible opposition: "Frankly, Jeanne, I would sooner you were dead than married to a Jew."

And thus, in time, she found her way to Synanon. With her wrists still bandaged from her latest suicide attempt. What more natural then that she should apotheosize that bulky man who with his kindness and his harshness, finally, after months of trial and error, slowly began to straighten her out. Slowly and painfully. One little bent part after another. (So slowly and so painfully that sometimes Jeanne was compelled to wonder if continued dope addiction and crime and early death were not after all preferable.)

And now she too is married, and about to have a baby. . . . A baby that I am afraid will be suffocated with affection. . . .

But of course what bothered me most about Jeanne's expression of adoration for Chuck was the feeling that there was a danger of myself succumbing to some such hysterical passion. There had indeed been times when I felt something of the sort surreptitiously invading me. Communicating itself to me perhaps through his mere physical presence: his heftiness, his big belly, his gravelly voice, which could thunder like Jehovah and then switch abruptly to love and laughter.

Chuck is such an obvious father-figure, and the dope addicts are so evidently his children, his pets, whom he alternately chastises and caresses, that he is without a doubt a casting director's dream for precisely the role he occupies: namely that of lord and master. The shepherd of his flock, who will not let one lamb go astray. The Moses come down from Mount Synanon with the tablets of the holy Emersonian writ in his fat arms.

Those of us who like to live in the light of reason are always made uneasy by religious passion which so easily plunges into that horror of horrors: religious fanaticism. The Inquisition, the witch-burning, the Nazi concentration camps and gas ovens.

I remember Jack Hurst telling me about his early days in Synanon and saying: "Chuck seemed to me like the Second Coming." Then, as if afraid that I might be taking him seriously he added: "Or at any rate the greatest thing since Lydia Pinkham." Obviously he felt something of the same sort of fear and embarrassment that I have experienced in this connection.

Frank was, I believe, the first person who didn't merely express an opinion of this sort to me, but backed it up with strong arguments. Frank was one of the last of the Alcoholics Anonymous group to linger on in a Synanon that was becoming almost completely dedicated to addicts. And when Frank himself left, there remained only Chuck of the old A.A. bunch.

"For me," Frank said, "Chuck is just about the nearest thing to Christ."

I made no note of whatever I may have said, but I must have expressed some sort of shocked disbelief, for my next note has Frank arguing: "Well, look at it this way, Guy. Didn't Christ say: 'Give up all your worldly goods and follow me?' Didn't Christ say that? Now you tell me how many Christians you know who have actually done that? Chuck's the only one I ever bumped into. The only one.

"And this thing about loving your neighbors. Christ didn't say: 'Love some of them, and hate others, and be indifferent to the rest.' Did he? He didn't say: 'Don't bother about dope addicts and criminals.' What Christ said is simply: 'Love your neighbor!' And love him with no ifs, ands, or buts! And damn few Christians do that.

Just look around you, Guy. Look at the Negroes, the Mexicans, the Jews, the convicts, the dimwits, and the misfits that are here. . . .

"It says in the Bible," Frank continued, "that you should cast your bread upon the water. And again the only one I know who has done that consistently is Chuck. And looking at those guys who call themselves 'Reverend' this, and 'Reverend' that, and whom you then see joining up with the Citizens Committee to throw Chuck and Synanon out of Santa Monica, I really wonder, Guy. I really wonder how they can have the nerve to think of themselves as Christians. But of course the best people in Jerusalem, they didn't want Christ around either, did they?"

And Frank went on justifying his feeling that Chuck was the closest thing to Christ. Frank is a tool and die man who still works somewhere in Santa Monica, although no longer living in Synanon, and in fact very rarely seen there nowadays. He had first come into contact with Chuck at an A.A. meeting, at a time when Frank was having one hell of a struggle with the bottle. Those were the days when Chuck would come barging into an A.A. assemblage, surrounded by his admirers, and shoot off a blistering lecture against John Barleycorn that held everyone fascinated and everyone ready to swear on the Bible never to touch another drop in their lives.

"But it wasn't doing me any noticeable good," Frank admitted. "I'd swear off again and again, but then—just as soon as Chuck had left—that old feeling of needing only one drop more would start to come over me. In fact the spell that Chuck could exert on me wouldn't last any longer than his voice in my ears.

"I remember asking myself if what Chuck had that I didn't have might be the LSD treatment that he had undergone at U.C.L.A. I thought that perhaps it might, and so I tried it too. But it didn't help me one bit, although I must say it was one of the most memorable experiences of my life. I'll never forget it.

"I suppose it was only natural for me to have a sort of machinery vision under LSD, but what was so startling was that I didn't just see this machinery, I was myself the motor, I mean not just inside of it, but also outside of it, and feeling the whole thing as if I were all the working parts and functioning at a great rate. In fact I was more than all the parts. I was also the oil moving between all the contacts, slipping and sliding between all the moving pieces. In fact it was like I was in every drop of that oil, inside the molecules, and even inside each atom, and even inside every electron whirling furiously around each nucleus—and then suddenly the most astonishing transformation: all these whirling atomic systems suddenly blew out into the universe, with each atom of oil becoming a planetary system, in which I felt myself to be the moon, the sun, the earth. . . .

"It was really a tremendous vision, Guy," Frank said. "But it didn't separate me from the bottle for one moment. I began to feel that nothing but a long stay at Camarillo would ever get this terrible craving out of me. But Camarillo was simply impossible. I had a divorced wife that I had to send alimony to, because she took care of my children. How this could be managed if I went to Camarillo, I didn't know.

"But at the same time, to go on working was also becoming almost impossible, because I couldn't function except in a half-drunken haze. And it was getting worse every week. It seemed like one way or another I was headed for self-destruction. I was rapidly reaching a point where earning a paycheck would kill me while at the same time I couldn't live without it.

"But once every week I did manage to keep sober. But that was because I was determined to stay off booze and go down to the beach and listen to Chuck read from Emerson, as he did every Sunday morning. But during the rest of the week I just went to hell.

"One Sunday, after the lecture, I went up to Chuck and explained my problem to him: how I needed Camarillo and yet couldn't afford to go there because of my wife and children.

"'Why not move in with us,' Chuck said immediately. 'That way you can stay off the bottle and keep your job at the same time.'

"By 'move in with us,'" Hank explained, "Chuck meant for me to move into that little group of six or seven alcoholics who had just begun to take in dope addicts. I would say the entire membership, at that time, wasn't more than eleven or twelve.

"I accepted Chuck's offer, but the moment I moved in, I regretted it. I was certain that this madhouse couldn't possibly keep me from drink. In fact I was sure it would drive me to it. You have no idea the dingbats we had here at that time. I remember Arline down on all fours, crawling around like a wild animal except for the big cigar in her mouth. And I remember someone else doing one painting after another. And always the same insane painting: just nothing but a great big red ball. And the whole club split into crazy disputes as to whether tender loving care or deep vaginal orgasm was the basic cure for addiction.

"That this crazy place was somehow keeping me off liquor was something I couldn't believe. I mean it amazed me. Because it certainly wasn't doing it for everyone. I guess I was a real square, Guy. Because I just couldn't get used to the nasty language. I was constantly shocked by it. And the fact that some of the addicts cheated. Smoked pot, or even shot some dope, while laughing behind Chuck's back at how far they could go to make a fool of him.

"The alcoholics felt the club was theirs and that the addicts were ruining it, and when Chuck wouldn't side with them, they began to drop out, one by one. Which only made the place worse because new addicts took their place and the madhouse just got more and more wild.

"The girls too were getting away with far too much promiscuity. A promiscuity that seemed to me only a step or two removed from prostitution. And those who wouldn't play along with them couldn't get a shirt ironed or a meal cooked. And as if that wasn't enough trouble the whole place felt the growing differences between the mama-figure and the papa-figure of the house. It was a civil war that was getting ready to burst, but taking its time. Perhaps because no one knew how the club could survive. If the mama-figure left, who would pay the rent? And if the father-figure left, who would hold the group together?

"This sense of insecurity—the feeling that Synanon would fold this week or next—was such that although new addicts were drifting in all the time, others were leaving almost as fast, so that by

Christmas the membership was no more than fifteen. There was lots of sex of course, and lots of sex talk, but scarcely enough food. We had no electric lights, just candles. And nothing to do on evenings when there were no games, except lie around on the couches with the hi-fi going. So that an impression got spread around the neighborhood—an impression that was peculiar to put it mildly. And one evening a couple of fellows came in and asked how much the girls were charging for a trick.

"We threw those bums out, quick, Guy. But they weren't totally off base. And I do believe that anybody coming into that place at that time and doing any kind of real investigation might very well have come to the conclusion that the club ought to be padlocked.

"And what a terrible mistake that would have been! Because something was going on there. Something new and not yet quite formulated was coming into existence there. Sometimes I thought it was just the presence of Chuck, and at other times I thought it was in the games. But whatever it may—or may not—have been doing for others, it was keeping me off alcohol. That was a fact from which I couldn't get away. Maybe my trouble was that I was seeing too many of the little things that were wrong, and thus failing to note the big thing that was right.

"Now and then I'd speak to Chuck," Frank went on, "about the things I saw happening around me and of which I felt he was being kept in ignorance. He'd listen and nod and shrug. He wasn't worried. Never flew off the handle. 'We're still in the experimental stage,' he'd say. 'And we'll just have to go along, pursuing our policy of no policy, and see what develops.'

" 'But you've got to draw the line somewhere,' I insisted.

" 'Of course there have to be rules of proper conduct, here as well as anywhere else,' he said. 'But you can't stuff morality down the throats of people who have been breaking all the rules for ten or twenty years. It won't work. The group will have to develop its own rules.' And then he would generally add: 'Don't worry. It will emerge.'

"But I couldn't see anything emerging. Every sort of crazy sex theory would run hog-wild through the club and then be discarded for some other crazy idea. For a while everyone was acting as if he were convinced that there was nothing in the world that couldn't be cured by removing all fetters from sex. Inhibition, that was the enemy! But it didn't take long before some of the residents began to see that absolute freedom made for all kinds of additional problems, and didn't so much cure neuroses as cause them.

"A couple of dope addicts would fall in love and become absolutely elegiac about their passion, convinced that they had found the solution to all their troubles. They dreamed of walking off into the sunset down the lane from honeymoon cottage . . . hand in hand into a glorious future. And the next thing you knew they were both out of Synanon and lying in some gutter somewhere, strung out on dope and at each other's throats for the mess they were in.

"Chuck coined the comparison of the love of two dope addicts to a couple of lengths of cooked spaghetti getting tangled up in each other and imagining that they were both deriving strength from their infatuation. What a delusion!

"Then from people being encouraged to have sexual relations, as if sex were some kind of medical prescription, the needle swung sharply to the reverse: people were kept apart, until the club had good evidence that the two lovers had developed enough strength of character. But this didn't solve anything either. Synanon has never had a locked door. Two people who were being kept apart by the club had only to walk out of the place in order to be together. Often ending up in the same gutter with the lovers who had been encouraged.

"It seemed that we just couldn't do things right. In spite of which Chuck always remained confident. He was always saying, whether it was a question of money or food or a code of behavior: 'It will emerge.' And another thing he'd often say was 'It seems that at Synanon we first have to do all the wrong things and get them out of the way, before we finally do it right.'"

"And still you say that he was the nearest thing to Jesus?" I asked Frank.

My question didn't embarrass Frank in the least. "Yes, that's my opinion. He was a Jesus who just didn't think he had all the right answers ready-made. Not immediately. That's all."

What surprised me was that Reid Kimball should take such a completely opposed position in this matter of Chuck's resemblance to God. Because of all the people in Synanon it seemed to me that he owed more to his association with Chuck than anyone else.

"There's no great mystique about Chuck," he said sharply. "He was just a guy who liked to beach-bum around, huddle with other fellows like himself, and bullshit till dawn about religion and psychology. It seems to me that if you're trying to make some great religious leader out of Chuck, you have to have some evidence of an inner spark, some sacred fire. . . . You know: the finger of heaven. But Chuck would be the first to deny anything of that kind. And if *he* didn't, I would.

"Now listen to this: I've often heard Chuck say something of this sort: 'Now I'm going to talk to you about something I know nothing about, and for that reason I'm going to pontificate.' No religious leader I've ever heard about was ever that candid. Chuck never tried to pass himself off as anything more than he is. A guy with a great idea. He doesn't even pretend that he is the sole inventor of that great idea. He freely gives credit where credit is due.

"But what is really wonderful about Chuck is that when the thing was there—I mean the Synanon idea—Chuck snapped to it as no one else did. And while Chuck was saying: 'Hey! This is something big! We've solved something here that all the doctors in the world have failed at!' these others hesitated, or joined only halfheartedly. In other words Chuck committed his life to this. And isn't that how things really get done in this world? By absolute dedication? Dedication to the limit of one's being? Well that's Chuck!

"What's important about Chuck is not whether he had—or did not have—wisdom from on high, but that he did have the brains to keep developing whatever wisdom he had as he went along with this project. Growing with it. And if he did not have any great charisma given to him from birth, at least he made sure of acquiring it as this thing went along.

"Chuck sometimes claims that the great turning point of his life was his LSD experience. I wonder about that. Maybe it did help him to crystallize all sorts of vague notions stirring around in him. Maybe. But I had an LSD experience too. It was terrific. I'll never forget it. But it didn't change my life one iota. Not in the least. And I don't think it did anything special for Chuck either. In my opinion Chuck would have been Chuck without LSD.

"People talk a lot about Chuck's prophetic powers. But I doubt that too. Because Chuck never predicts anything he doesn't lend a hand to bringing about. I don't call that prophecy. That's just plain old determination. If Chuck prophesies now that the Synanon game will spread to all the colleges in the United States, it's because Chuck is making every effort to bring about that very thing. And will let nothing stop him until he has made his vision come true.

"At that rate a lot more of us could be true prophets if we would just put our balls on the line for what we really believe. But how many of us will do that? How many of us have the guts to risk everything?

"In short I see Chuck as a great man—maybe even one of the world's greatest—but not because of any special superhuman equipment given to him by the angels—but because he is that man whom Thoreau speaks of: that rare man who steps out confidently in the direction of his dreams. Furthermore I'm convinced that such confidence was nothing native to Chuck. He drove himself to it.

"You know as well as I do that Chuck made a failure of his college career, made a failure of his business career, made a failure of his marriages, made a failure of himself with his addiction to alcohol and Benzedrine. You know the story of how he decided to go to California and for no good reason bought himself a pickup truck and a trailer, and then had to stay overnight in motels because he didn't know how to get into his trailer. You know how he was so wishy-washy, so undecided, that when he got as far as Las Vegas he turned right around and drove like mad to his house back in Toledo, but never reached Toledo because when he got to Kansas City he whirled around again and headed West once more.

"I defy anyone to deduce from this kind of behavior a man stepping out confidently in the direction of his dreams—unless his dreams were some kind of a nightmare.

"So what I see in Chuck is first of all an opportunist who just didn't happen to discover the opportunity he was looking for until he was past forty years of age. Not until he saw this Synanon thing develop right before his eyes did he realize that he had found what he had all along been looking for.

"That's when he locked his bulldog grip onto this thing.

"Of course I have to admit that I never knew that early wishy-washy Chuck. And any lawyer who had me on the stand would very quickly force me to admit that all this is just hearsay and gossip. The Chuck I first met up with was already the Chuck all of us know today: strong in his purpose, full of insight, sometimes too patient and too loving, sometimes too irrascible, but always stepping out confidently in the direction of his dream. Yes, always. And the Synanon I entered, while still in its formative stages, was already basically a working machine. Crude, but functional.

"Not that I was able to appreciate that fact when I stumbled into the place. I was such an absolute smashup when I got there. I was really something for the crows to peck at. And spit out if they had any sense. I had been that way ever since Yla's death. . . . You remember Yla, don't you?"

Yes, I remembered Yla. Not that I had ever seen her. But Reid had so often spoken to me about her, telling me how when he first came in to Synanon he dreaded the necessity of sleep—tried in every possible way to stay awake—because the moment he fell asleep there was his dead Yla in that recurrent dream he had. Yla alive again, and more beautiful than ever, dancing and singing across a flowery meadow in a picture of unforgettable loveliness, thus stirring up in Reid all the pain of her death again, so that in the midst of his sleep he had to scream out loud.

I recall Reid telling me about this recurrent dream and wondering what there could be in this pretty dream that would cause him to emit blood-curdling-yells. "I could understand it," he said to me, "if it were some horrible dream of death. But everything's so beautiful . . ."

"That's how you are punishing yourself," I remember explaining to Reid. "By seeing her at her loveliest, and being forced to realize all over again that she is dead. And that you were largely to blame. That's what makes you scream."

Yla was a ravishingly beautiful girl who sang at a nightclub in Hollywood and with whom Reid fell madly in love. And Yla with him. Reid was then a handsome young man, bold as brass, with a cocky stance and a sense of humor so remarkable that he could keep you in stitches for hours on end.

Naturally Reid didn't tell Yla right off how he earned his living. He pretended sometimes that he was a successful Hollywood writer, and at other times that he had inherited money. Eventually, of course, he did have to tell her the truth, but by that time she was so much in love with Reid that nothing could make any difference.

The truth was that Reid had grown up in Santa Monica, and had earned his first money watching out for cops at the foot of the amusement pier, in order to warn the carny men who were often carrying on some forbidden gambling instead of their legitimate prize-games.

Reid learned to drink, he learned to smoke pot, he watched and admired the carnies and especially the pimps whom he considered big shots because they carried around hundred-dollar bills. He soon got involved with girls, learned how to run a floating crap game, became partners with a girl who was running a whorehouse, and took a liking for the profession of pimp. He felt that he was set for life. Not much work. Lots of money. Lots of girls. Lots of fun.

This idle and totally useless life suited Reid just fine. He loved every part of it. The liquor, the pot, the girls, and the money. And when, one night, Mitch, a friend of his, invited him to an opium party, he loved that too. "I really dug opium," Reid said. "From then on I smoked opium every day." Great!

Of course he had heard that it was habit-forming, but what was wrong with that? Provided one satisfied one's habit? He had never yet experienced the misery of being hooked, and so threw himself gaily into the rocky abyss. It wasn't until one day, when for one reason or another, he had skipped the nightly opium party, that he realized something was dreadfully amiss. He woke up the next morning feeling horribly nauseous, he started to sweat profusely, and was seized with uncontrollable fits of yawning. He felt so miserable and weak that he could scarcely drag himself out of bed.

It was then that a bartender introduced him to the habit of carrying around some protection in the form of edible opium pills, so that at any time he felt this sickness coming on, all he had to do was reach into his pocket, grab a few pills, and swallow them. And at once all symptoms would disappear.

Great! All problems solved! Just become an opium eater, that's all, then party or no party, one was prepared against sickness.

But now another aspect of the opium habit began to manifest itself: the expense! But that too was easily solved.

"At that time," Reid told me, "a can of hop was to be had for seven hundred and fifty dollars. And I could dispose of about one a week. A lot of money yes, but Virginia and I were working this call house, and she and I could count on a couple of hundred a day each. So the money problem didn't worry me one bit. Or at least not until I began to feel that I had to have something quicker and surer than opium, and took to sniffing heroin. That's when the costs really began to mount."

It was at this point that Reid met Yla.

Reid has never forgiven himself for what he did to Yla. Even though at the time when he did it, he was absolutely unconscious of any wrong. "Yla wasn't making more than a hundred and a quarter a week at the nightclub," Reid argued, "and she was superbly beautiful, so why not capitalize on it? I was already running one call house with Virginia, so why not another with Yla and some other girls? That's how I saw it.

"Why the very first week I set her up she took in over a thousand dollars as her share. We limited our business to the rich movie people, running our house from only noon to seven o'clock, and it was all dates, all the girls going outside for their appointments, and every date a minimum of one hundred dollars.

"So what's wrong with that? Yla loved clothes, loved spending money, and now she had all those things."

But in addition to making a prostitute out of Yla, Reid also turned her on. First to heroin sniffing. But again nothing wrong with that. Wasn't he doing it himself? Just that same old money question popping up again, because heroin was so expensive. But that too was solved by changing over from sniffing to shooting, because that way you got more mileage out of a given amount of heroin.

But sometimes such a habit, which seemed momentarily bearable, with all the necessary financing assured, would turn out to be unbearable. The police would suddenly mount a big drive. A smuggler would get picked up with a suitcase containing millions of dollars' worth of H. With every port being watched no new supplies could come in and the price of the drug would not only shoot way up, but whatever was available would turn out to have been cut and cut again. Formerly stable sources of supply would disappear, and panic would sweep through the ranks of the dope addicts.

Under such conditions a two-hundred dollar a day habit can mount up quickly to five hundred dollars a day, and life is made almost impossible. The hounding of the police, the rise in the price of the drug, caused Yla and Reid to flee Los Angeles and seek refuge in San Francisco. And then move on to Las Vegas, and then to Watsonville. Always on the go. Always trying to make out and never quite succeeding.

"There's nothing special to tell about those days," Reid would say. "You'd think there would be lots of experiences, lots of exciting adventures for people who were always racing on, one step ahead of the police. But actually one day would be precisely like another. We were always loaded, or else sick from lack of dope, or else out scratching after something that was getting more and more difficult to find."

That's when Reid started to pull some occasional holdups so as to add to what Yla could make. And thus they managed to get by— at least some of the time.

"Of course that meant that our whole lives were dedicated to only one purpose: getting all the dope we could, And therefore one day had to be exactly like any other. Yla would be out working at some call joint, and I'd be laying up in some hotel or other, or maybe going out to pull some kind of swindle, or else myself dealing in dope, and pushing it so as to make some other sucker pay for the cost of my habit."

But the price of the drug wouldn't stop going up, and the dealers kept cutting the pure heroin with more and more milk sugar, and the race with their habit kept getting more and more impossible.

Reid tried cures. Tried holing up somewhere and kicking cold turkey. Tried Camarillo. Tried everything. He separated himself from Yla, took up with another girl whom he also turned into a heroin addict and sent out as a prostitute to help pay for their habit, until her relatives came down on her and put her away in a clinic and Reid had to run from their fury.

The easy life with no problems, lots of girls, lots of money, lots of fun, and lots of dope had changed into a phantasmagoria. That's how Reid summed it up. "Only not so exciting as a phantasmagoria. More like a nightmare. I missed Yla dreadfully, but was so stoned that I didn't know what it was that made me so miserable. I thought all I needed was more dope."

Then, in 1957, when he was working in a bingo parlor in Las Vegas, Yla walked in, and Reid suddenly snapped to what was eating him. She too had missed him, and told him so, but somehow Reid couldn't respond. He couldn't tell her that he loved her too. He couldn't resist some deep impulse that compelled him to be rude and cold to her no matter how warm she was to him. For some obscure and perverse reason he had to conceal from her his joy and pretend that she meant nothing to him. And all the while he was dying with happiness, went out and bought a beautiful wedding ring for her, and was just waiting for an opportune moment to reveal to her his plans for a completely new and different life for the two of them.

Yla was so badly strung out that Reid offered her his apartment to kick in, but he did it in a manner to imply that it was something he would do to anyone who was so obviously in the grip of a bad heroin habit. And a couple of days later when Yla had recovered somewhat, and said she had left all her clothes in Los Angeles and was going to fly down to get them, Reid only said "okay," coldly, just like that, as if what she did or what she did not do was a matter of complete indifference to him. But privately he decided that her return would be the right time to expose his plans to her. She said she'd be back on Tuesday, and if Reid didn't want her around, she planned to go on to Chicago. "Okay, okay," Reid said as if impatient to have her out of the way.

So Yla left for Los Angeles, and on Tuesday Reid waited anxiously for her return. By nighttime she had still not showed up. Instead a friend came to Reid's apartment and said: "I've got bad news for you, Reid. Yla's dead."

That's when Reid's life finally went to pieces. He scarcely listened to the story of how Yla had gone to Los Angeles only to rent a room for the purpose of killing herself. The days and months that followed were totally without meaning to Reid. Whether he stole or borrowed or drank or shot dope, or went to Camarillo to clean up, it was all just a jumble of boring incidents in a life he no longer had any intention of living. The only thing he was waiting for was the courage to do away with himself. And the only plan he had meanwhile was the vague one that the more he messed himself up the less he would mind finishing himself off.

It didn't take long to reach that bottom. When he had cheated all his friends, when he had borrowed and stolen from everyone he knew, when he had used up all the good will of his relations by the promises he never kept, when he had sunk to dribs and drabs of heroin and lots of cheap wine, and was staggering and stumbling around sick with vomiting and dysentery, until people would cross the street to avoid this stinking beggar, then he knew he had reached the end.

He was finally ashamed to be alive, and in this condition went to see a doctor from whom he had used to buy dope, a doctor who had had his opiate license lifted because of too many infractions, and Reid whined a lot of crazy stories to him about not being able to sleep, until the doctor was moved to give him some thirty sleeping pills.

Reid had just enough money left to go to a cheap hotel nearby and rent himself a room, telling the clerk some cock-and-bull story about having driven all night and not wanting anyone to disturb him. Then he locked himself up and sat on the edge of the bed and began to throw pills down his throat, some five or six at a time.

Until he passed out.

8

A couple of days later Reid woke up in the General Hospital and became aware that he had tubes sticking out of every orifice of his body. He was immediately overcome with the sick realization that he had failed! And that now the whole terrible business would have to be gone through again. In addition he was evidently kicking, and his body, aching for its heroin, was so weak and dizzy that he couldn't move his head without the whole room revolving.

He learned later that the cleaning women at the hotel had become worried about his failure to respond to their knocking, that the door had to be broken down, and that the manager finding this body there, coal-black and without any sign of breath, had hurriedly summoned the police. But on the way to the morgue an orderly had observed some faint evidence of life. They had rushed the body to the Georgia Street Receiving Hospital, where it was pumped out and flushed out and then sent to the General.

As soon as Reid could manage somehow to stand up on his wobbly legs, he begged a doctor for a release, and then managed somehow to put on his clothes and stagger out—and make his way back to Santa Monica, there to bum a few bucks from whatever friends he could find, whining to them about his suicide attempt, and so totally without pride as to seek to extract some gain from his miserable story. But what did he care what people thought of him now? He was intent on only one goal, namely to screw up his courage again to the point of taking his life, and meanwhile in one way or another to get himself some heroin and some cheap wine, and keep himself so drunk, so sick, and so crazed that people would hurriedly hand him a dollar just to get rid of this unshaven, untidy mess that shambled along, grabbing now and then for support at some wall or lamppost, throwing up, and then having to find a bench where he could park his shaking body and catch his breath.

One day he had conned a friend into a last loan of a few dollars and was on his way to Olympic Boulevard, where he knew he could find a dealer. But he could barely stagger along, and kept having to rest at every bench.

From one bench where he sat for a time, he could see across the street an old storefront, its windows painted over. Above the corner door he could read T.L.C. And while he was watching he saw that door open up and a colored man and a young girl, with their arms about each other's waists, walk out and take a bit of a stroll, up and down. From the open door came the sound of music, hi-fi accompanied by bongo drums. The two strollers took only a minute or two and then returned to the inside, closing the door behind them.

The music, the friendly relations between black and white, all this suggested to Reid that perhaps this might be a place where he could score, and thus save himself the difficulty of a walk to Olympic Boulevard. He rose from his bench and crossed over to the door and opened it slightly to get a better idea of the place. His first thought was that it might be a beer joint, because he saw a counter in the rear. But the rest of the place was all couches where some twenty or more people were sitting around, and a small space where some four or five couples were dancing.

And then—opening the door wider—he recognized one of the many faces. It was that of a fellow I will call Harry, a man who made a specialty of burglarizing drugstores, to rob them of opiates, sleeping pills, and so forth. Reid had often bought dope from him. So he had been right in guessing that he might score here! He was in a "shooting gallery."

Just then Harry turned and cried out: "Hey, Reid! Come on in!"

And as Reid tottered in and Harry saw him better, he exclaimed: "Holy hell! You look like you're dead!"

"I am dead," Reid said. "Who's place is this?"

"It's for addicts," Harry explained. "We clean up here."

"Then I was right," Reid said. "I thought I would have to crawl all the way to Olympic to score. And I wasn't sure I could make it. Okay. Who's got the shit?"

"I guess I'm not getting across to you," Harry said. "Nobody's got any dope in this place."

They argued at cross-purposes for a while. Reid remained convinced that Harry was dummying up on him. He didn't believe a word about addicts cleaning up here. "You're telling me all these people are clean? Why for Christ's sake, they're leaping and dancing. They're high on something. That's for sure."

"We're all clean here, Reid," Harry insisted. "And this is the place for you to come to, if you really want to kick your habit. Not Camarillo. Not Fort Worth."

Reid was too tired and to disgusted to argue the matter. For some reason he was being cut out of a share in whatever was available at this place, so all he said was: "Oh, yeah?" and stumbled out to face the ordeal of getting up to Olympic Boulevard in Santa Monica. There he eventually managed to buy a couple of caps of pretty poor heroin and a bottle of wine. And then, feeling a little better, even though drunk, he began to puzzle over that episode with Harry. And when passing the place on his way back, he decided to stop in again, just to let them know he was on to them.

This time he was given short shrift. The colored fellow whom he had first seen coming out of the place with a white girl confronted him: "You're drunk. And loaded. So why don't you get lost, before we have to throw you out."

Reid tried to deny it. He wasn't drunk at all. Nor loaded. Just sick from his recent suicide attempt. That's why he looked drunk. And could hardly stand.

But one of the residents snapped: "We don't take in bums like you. If you're serious about wanting to clean yourself up, then go home! Sober up! Come back tomorrow looking like a human being."

But the next day Reid was even further away from any sort of human appearance. He was first of all totally broke, and secondly suffering all the pangs of withdrawal. He knew he ought to be dead. But even with his body shaking with chills he somehow couldn't find the courage to face death. He passed in review all the methods he could think of to do away with himself and each method only scared him worse than the one before. But what was he to do, with his legs like soft rubber, so that he could scarcely stand up on them, and not a dime for dope or wine in his pockets?

It was then that the storefront marked T.L.C. loomed up in his mind as a last possible refuge until he could somehow gather himself together. He got there one way or another and looked so pitiful that instead of being thrown out on the spot, he was taken down the alley to Chuck's apartment so that the boss might decide.

This was the first time he looked upon this bulky man in open shirt and old slacks who might have been a beach bum but certainly didn't look like the superintendent of an institution for the care and cure of addicts. Reid was not at all impressed. But there was one thing for which he was grateful. Namely that Chuck didn't take long to decide. One glance at Reid and he said: "What is it? Oh, well no matter what it is, give it a blanket and some eggnog, and put it on a couch. There's a bare possibility there may be something human inside all this garbage."

Thinking back, Reid is unable to discover any other sentiment in himself than gratitude that Chuck didn't kid around any more than he did. "Because my legs couldn't have held out if he had." But as for staying in Synanon, he never even thought of it. For despite the violence of his kicking, despite the spasms and the shivers that traversed his body so that one moment it felt as if it were freezing and the next moment as if it would boil over with heat, Reid was still Reid.

"I was convinced that I was at death's door, Guy, but it was still in my carny nature to size up this place and see what advantage I might get out of it. I was soon convinced that only part of the people here were on the up and up. The rest were just hypes temporarily holed up in a storm cellar. Like myself. So I played it both ways. For those who looked as if they might be on the level I played the shit for all it was worth. While at the same time dropping coarse lugs for the benefit of the cynical ones, so as to make sure that if any stuff was around the joint I would be getting my share eventually.

"And while drowning in sweat and diarrhea I was still letting the broads know that I had eyes for them. And for two guys in particular, namely Charlie Hamer and Mitch, both of whom I had long known on the outside, and who—it was obvious to me—were both cheating on the sly, I had winks and hints to let them know that we were three of a kind.

"In short, Guy, even while my mind was still contemplating suicide, I was working like mad—same as I always did—to make a real ass-hole out of myself. And all the while thinking I was being the smartest con man in the world. Just think of it: here I was, with people who were trying to save my life, and all I was thinking of was how I could fuck over them.

"And then, maybe on the third day I was there, when I was just about as low as anyone can get, when I was exhausted from days of kicking, plus suffering from all my years of addiction and the accumulated sins of malnutrition, so that I must have looked really God-awful, considering the sweat and the running nose and the dysentery, suddenly there is this big fat flabby fellow in a beach bum's outfit again, and he comes over and sits down beside me.

"A god? Guy, I swear to you, not for one second did I take this fellow to be the Second Coming or the nearest thing to Jesus Christ. Not for one second. To me he didn't look like anything else but the kind of slugs I had cheated by the hundreds in my floating crap game.

"And this is what Chuck says to me: 'I hear that out on the streets you really rate. That you had one of the biggest habits any man ever had. Is that a fact?'

"I have to admit, Guy, that I fell for his line of crap. And started to boast of the five hundred or more dollars a day that I used to spend for the shit.

"Chuck pretended to be impressed and drew me on, saying things like 'Great!' and 'Crazy!' so that I kept on building it up. Until he pointed to my body lying there in a cold and stinking sweat, and said: 'So you poured hundreds of thousands of dollars into that body of yours, and you and all that money put together don't add up to more than this fucking mess I see before me now?'

"I remember thinking: 'This is not going to be an easy man to con. I better be careful of this sucker.'

"And then Chuck went on: 'Everybody agrees that you had a reputation for being a very funny man. Why don't you give us some of your wit. How about it?'

"Naturally I couldn't think of anything funny to say. Not in my condition. While Chuck continued to urge me: 'Come on, say something funny. Give us a laugh.'

"I mumbled something about what could you expect from a guy who was flat on his back, and Chuck immediately picked up on that: 'Don't worry. You'll be up and about soon enough. But I'm sure you'll never be any funnier than you are right now.'

"I got the message. Chuck was telling me that he was hep. He was letting me know that he was on to all my curves—and that I'd better knock them off. But of course years of behaving like a total idiot were not to be wiped out by one conversation.

"I still couldn't see Synanon as anything more than a stopgap. And neither could some of the others. Mitch, for example, who was one of my oldest friends. I had known him for maybe eighteen years or twenty years. He was a con artist, with a hell of a line of patter. Could stick anyone with a watch worth maybe five dollars and make him grateful to get it for twenty. Mitch was never at a loss. A good con man never is.

"He had come to Synanon ahead of me and turned me on almost the very first day, cutting me in on what we call 'chippying,' that is to say, very light doses that keep you feeling good without getting you visibly loaded. It was with his help, and the help of some of the others that I was able to provide myself with a Benzedrine inhaler, some wine or some 'turps,' and even join others in occasional blowing of some pot.

"I can't explain it, Guy, except that I was still going by the code of the streets. And also that I was overcome with such a sense of helplessness at the mere thought of being without my usual chemical crutches, I was so terrified, that I had to start out my stay at Synanon with lies, deceit, treachery, all manner of furtive behavior.

"This didn't prevent me from being genuinely grateful to the club for taking care of my needs in this particular emergency. But not for one minute did I buy the philosophy of the place. In fact I couldn't help being derisive and cynical about this crazy attempt to cure addicts of their yen for dope. I just didn't believe it was possible. I had experienced too many attempts of one kind or another.

"And I recall that very early, perhaps about the time of my third experience with the game, I began to drop criticisms such as this: 'What's all this shit about an Oedipus complex?' And I'd laugh and think I was demonstrating a truly brilliant insight. And I remember that the board of directors had a staff meeting every morning with Chuck. And one of them, hearing me one morning dropping one of those lugs, said:

" 'We better let Chuck know about this newcomer who keeps knocking the game. I'm sure he'll be interested.'

"And with that he went off with the others to Chuck's apartment.

"Guy, I could have bitten my tongue out. Not because I had any sense of remorse about behaving so ungenerously and so crudely towards a man who had reached out a helping hand to me when I needed it so badly. No, nothing of that kind. But for being such an idiot as to throw out one of my nasty remarks when there were people around who would report it to Chuck, who would naturally throw me out immediately from this comfortable refuge I had blundered into by pure chance. I could just hear Chuck yelling: 'Tell that fool to get his ass out of here. But fast!'

"I waited in misery for the directors to come back from Chuck's, and when they did I expected the ax to fall. Finally I asked Charlie Hamer: 'Did that bastard say anything to Chuck about my knocking the game?'

" 'He sure did,' Charlie said.

"Again I waited, sure that he had something more to say, and when he didn't I urged him: 'Well? What did Chuck say?'

" 'Chuck said: "Thank God we have someone here who thinks for himself even if he hasn't got the brains to do it with." '

"I felt deeply relieved. I recognized this as another one of Chuck's slams at me, but I didn't mind. I knew now how completely transparent I was to this cat. And it was a learning situation for me too. Because I began to understand the word 'projection,' which I had heard used again and again in the games. The reason I was so worried about what Chuck might do was because I was not really thinking of what the actual Chuck might do, but what I might do in Chuck's place. I knew damn well that if I had been Chuck I would have yelled: 'Get that dirty ass-hole out of here!'

"But I wasn't Chuck. And Chuck wasn't me. And he couldn't have cared less what some dingbat, just out of the gutter, happened to say about a method that he had already spent a year or more trying to perfect. Chuck had long ago come to the opinion that addicted people were never to be blamed. Never. They were only children. You can praise or punish children, but you can never hold them responsible for their acts, and you can therefore never control them with hostility.

" 'The square world,' so I have since heard Chuck say many times, 'the square world handles these children with cops and guns and jails. With the result that instead of getting rid of crime the square world only perpetuates and increases it. It's all done out of frustration. Parents who feel frustrated, parents who are tired and overworked, or simply ignorant, handle their children in the same way. But children aren't born with a sense of moral responsibility.

They're little animals. They have no conscience. Therefore to saddle them with a sense of guilt before you have given them understanding is to wreck them, just as much as if you tore out one of their arms for stealing from the cooky jar. Addicts are no different. They're children who haven't grown up. You've first got to inspire them with love and with loyalty. Then you can gradually make them aware of their crime against themselves, against society, and against their Creator. Not before!'

"Chuck knew that there was a considerable proportion of the residents who weren't obeying the rules. But he also knew that there were some who were staying clean. Jack Hurst, for example, and Jesse Pratt, and Frank, and so forth. And he also knew that the clean guys whom we derisively termed 'the vice squad,' were not yet the decisive group, they were not yet strong enough to give the club its tone and its leadership. They were not yet the power core which they would eventually become, and from which others who might want to stay clean could draw strength.

"In other words, Guy, it was still considered hip in Synanon to fool the 'vice squad' even by some of us who were beginning to look up to Chuck, beginning to respect and even admire him. And of course not one of us would have ever 'copped out' on any of his friends. Never. No criminal ever snitches on his comrades. That's the lowest of all sins in the ethics of the street.

"Then, in June of 1959, when I had been with the club for about five or six weeks, something happened that precipitated the issue and faced everyone with the decision either to get the hell out of Synanon or stick with it and live up to it."

The incident that Reid was referring to is the so-called "night of the big cop-out," recognized at once by all who took part in it as a landmark in Synanon's history. It started late one night when the "vice squad" was returning from a session in Chuck's apartment, to the dorm down the alley. It was then that Oscar Camaño saw Mitch behaving in a very suspicious manner. Oscar was certain that what Mitch had been doing up the alley was stashing away some dope. And he confronted him with that accusation.

Mitch indignantly denied it, but the "vice squad" marched him off to the club and proceeded to question him sharply. Some of the other members began to gather around, and though it was obvious to most of them that Mitch was at least half-loaded, they sat on the sidelines, as if this concerned Mitch and the "vice squad" and no one else.

Reid was there too and had mixed feelings about the matter, his mind swaying from one side to the other. Since he himself had been using as well as drinking in a small way, he wanted Mitch to get away with it, so that both of them could continue to break the rules of the house without penalty.

And yet something was stirring in Reid that kept pulling him over to the other side. He had been doing considerable thinking about this, and had to admit that at times he felt rather lousy about the double-cross he was pulling.

"There were times when I thought of myself as a real shit," he told me recently. "I really did. It bugged me to be screwing up in Synanon. Not that I was actually conscience-stricken. I wasn't. It just seemed such a shoddy and petty thing to do. To go on acting like we were out on the street, when we were actually in this club. I used to say to myself: 'Chuck isn't a narco bull looking for a reason to bust us. He's a guy giving us a break.'

"I think this feeling was gradually getting to all the people in the place. I remember this, for example. Just a few days before the cop-out, Charlie Hamer, who still kept on blowing pot, said to me that he was thinking of giving it up. 'It's a lot of chicken-shit anyhow,' he said to me. 'And I'm not going to pull any more of this crap in here.'

"It was just talk, of course," Reid said. "Because both of us went right on doing just exactly what we had been doing all along. Still . . . there it was."

But for Reid especially, this interrogation of Mitch was a moment of real sweat. He and Mitch had worked together over many years. In fact Mitch and Reid had turned each other on. To opium smoking. And together they had started to sniff heroin. He and Mitch had been associated in many ventures having to do with drugs, with the smuggling and pushing of dope. And once, while carrying out a mission for Reid, Mitch had been busted and had taken a five-year rap for it. And of course it had never occurred to Mitch for one second that he might cop out on Reid and thus get him busted too, and thereby earn himself a shorter sentence. The cops were always trying to get hypes to do that, but no self-respecting hype would ever stoop so low as to squeal.

But this situation—it was different, wasn't it? Squealing on the outside was one thing, and squealing on the inside another, wasn't that so? Reid felt somehow that it was, but he couldn't quite formulate the difference. So he listened in silence to the arguments of the vice squad, who were trying to make Mitch see that Synanon was not a court. Synanon was not the law.

"Don't you see that we can't lock you up?" the vice squad pointed out to Mitch. "Not even if we wanted to, which we don't. We don't have any jails here. And we're not a bunch of deputies. We just want to clean this place up. That's all. And it's high time we knew who was with us and who was against us."

Mitch refused to accept that. No one was getting him to cop to having stashed away some dope. Stashing dope was possession. And wasn't possession a felony? Why all it would take was one telephone call to the police and the bulls would be down here before one could say paraphernalia.

"Don't you see that this is precisely what puts Synanon in danger?" the vice squad contended. "What happens if this place is raided? And the bulls find dope on the premises? Then it's the whole club that is in violation of the law. And everyone here—not just those who are staying clean, but everyone, even those who aren't, could land in jail. And Synanon might never recover from such a raid. Is that what you want? Well we aren't going to let it happen. With us the club comes first. And those who refuse to live up to our rules can get lost!"

Reid saw that his best friend might be expelled, and he felt the threat of loneliness. Impulsively he added his voice to that of the vice squad: "Look, Mitch. Look at it this way. All you've got to do is say, 'Yes, okay, I did use.' So what's wrong with that? Then all you get is a bawling out."

Mitch stared at Reid. What? His best friend was urging him to cop out? Mitch couldn't believe it. Reid working for the bulls. Impossible.

Reid saw that look of amazement and knew what memories of many years lay behind it. But Reid knew too that this meant that Mitch wasn't grasping the difference between the Synanon code and the street code, and desperately he tried to make Mitch see what he himself was just beginning to see.

"For God's sake, Mitch," he cried out. "This is no federal beef! This is something you can cop to." It wasn't that Reid was questioning the validity of the code of street, but that he was already beginning to see that Synanon was somehow an exception to that code. That at least while living in Synanon one owed something to the club, and that it was only right that one should throw them a bone now and then.

But Mitch refused to budge. "I didn't have anything," he kept repeating. "I wasn't stashing anything." And with sudden truculence he rushed to his cot, yanked his old suitcase out from underneath, and began chucking in his few belongings.

It was a sight that shook Reid. With a voice almost choking with tears he yelled: "For Christ's sake, Mitch, why don't you tell them the truth!"

Mitch exploded: "You son-of-a-bitch! *You* know damn well why! And what the hell are you trying to pin on me?" Madder than hell Mitch cursed Reid for being a stoolie, and tearing off his flip-flops, he began to put on socks and shoes, which was a sure sign that he was leaving.

Reid grabbed him by the arm: "Don't be mad at me!" he pleaded. "If you go, I've got to go too!"

"Not with me, you don't!" Mitch shouted, trying to tear himself loose. "Not with me! Not ever again!" He was determined to put on his shoes and Reid was determined to prevent it.

It looked for a moment as if it must come to a fight, here in Synanon where all physical violence was strictly forbidden. "Jesus Christ, Mitch," Reid cried out, "you mean to say you never used anything in this club?"

"That's exactly what I'm saying!"

Hearing this lie drove Reid over the dividing line. "But God damn it, Mitch, I know I've used. And you know I have!"

"I don't give a fuck what you've done!"

"Mitch," Reid begged. "I could stop using here. And so could you."

"You cock-sucker," Mitch yelled. "It's with you that I used!"

Reid relaxed and let go Mitch's arm. "There. It's out, fellows, it's out, Mitch. And nothing's going to happen to either of us."

But one member of the vice squad wasn't satisfied. He directed himself to Mitch. "Let's hear more about this. Like for instance, just exactly what did you two use together. And when?"

"Tell them, Mitch," Reid urged. And as Mitch remained stubbornly silent, Reid went on: "For Christ's sake, tell them, can't you? Tell them that you and I fixed today. Tell them we blew a little pot together. Tell them everything we've done. Come on, Mitch, let's get it all out. It's all a bunch of bullshit anyway. Hell, if we absolutely must keep on using, we can go someplace else and do it. So let's give up this crap while we're here."

Mitch finally muttered: "Okay. We used. I used with you, Reid." It was a grudging confession.

But Reid now turned to all the others around, saying: "Anybody else? Anybody else want to cop out using with me?"

The first to respond was George the Turk, a guy with a romantic background of gun-running and other illegal operations, but who also kept one foot in legitimate undertakings such as haberdashery shops or the representation of women's wear manufacturers, in short a very capable many-sided character. George admitted to having had a cap with Reid now and then.

That was the signal for Charlie Hamer to admit that he had blown pot with Reid and shared an occasional bottle of turp.

Meanwhile someone had sent for Chuck, who came barging in

144

right on top of these confessions, and shouted: "Come on! Let's roust the whole membership. Get 'em all out of bed and over here. Broads and all. Let's ask everyone."

A slow drift of members began to fill the rooms with half-dressed men and women who gradually crowded into the double bunks, making the place look something like those pictures of German concentration camps. They came from the girls' dormitory across the street. And they came from the neighboring cheap hotel where rooms had been rented by the club. . . .

And every sleepy-eyed newcomer was confronted with the question: "Have you ever taken anything since joining the club? With whom did you use? And what kinds of drugs? Morphine? Heroin? Turps? Amphetamines? Exactly what?"

And the immediate response was always the same: "Who? Me? Of course not! Never." Answers that came forth so automatically and so repetitiously, that it was as if people had studied their roles. And the whole room would burst into gales of raucous laughter.

At first there would be indignation and reassertions uttered with even greater force. Until one person would say: "Well you needn't deny it, because I've already told about us two using together. . . ."

Then there would be such imprecations as: "Why you lying mother-fucker!"

But the newcomer's resistance would have to melt before a whole barrage of voices reciting their cop-out stories. Not only had Reid and Charlie and George copped out, but everybody, and thus the newcomer would be compelled or cajoled into copping out too. And then they would have the right to share in the laughter when the next newcomer came in and produced the same line of outraged denial.

It was a weird experience. All this laughter and these confessions as the day began to dawn, and eventually with even the Princess copping. She was an actual princess, being married to a real European prince, and with her money she had been the most prolific source of dope being used in the club. But when she began to tell how many caps she had given to this one and how many to that one, and it turned out that she had favored some of the members over others, hot arguments developed out of a jealousy that no longer had any right to exist, but flared up nevertheless, starting with those who had gotten less and figured they should have gotten more. A retroactive and ridiculous fury that finally wound up in torrents of laughter and confused arguments.

Some few held out to the bitter end. Mitch, for example, still hadn't taken off his shoes, remaining sullen and refusing to join in the general game. Another member, a notorious addict, renowned for his linguistic gifts (it was he who first called Chuck a 'herd of one elephant'), continued to deny everything out of hand.

Last to come in was tiny Tina, a diminutive girl who worked in a doughnut shop. Suddenly introduced to this shouting, laughing mob, and faced with the question as to whether she had ever used since joining, she also played the role of indignant innocence, declaring stoutly: "Well, I should say not!" Whereupon the whole gathering went silent, and Tina looked around herself with wonder until she began to realize that she had just made a perfect ass of herself.

And now Chuck spoke. No one quite remembers what Chuck said. Reid can only recall Chuck facing the group in his usual undress, and rocking back and forth on his bare toes. Perhaps Chuck doesn't come across so much in words as he does in the communication of elemental forces. Listening to him is like feeling the sun shine and then thunder growling and the lightning flash, and then the sun shining again. His speeches are emotional experiences that catch you up, whirl and kick you around, and then deposit you softly back in your place again.

But as near as I can come to reproducing it, his talk went something like this:

"Well, we've all had a lot of good laughs," he began quietly, "but now let's see if that's all we've got out of it—just some laughs. You've had a great time fucking over me, you see. But that's because I'm such an easy mark. It's no great trick to outsmart *me*. I know that one addict can somehow always spot another, and can somehow tell if he's loaded or not. But I can't. I'm dumb—*that* way. That way I'm dumb, and you'll outsmart me every time. Every time. You see?"

And now his voice rose: "But did anyone ever really imagine for one moment that he had *me* fooled? Did anyone here really think that he had *me* outsmarted? Why you ass-holes! Didn't you realize that by fooling me you were only outsmarting yourselves? Didn't you realize that? That no junkie can outsmart me?

"Never! Never! He can only outsmart himself! Don't you see that?

"Because when you take a crap here—on the living room floor—your living room floor—who's nest are you fouling? Why your own! Your own. Of course. It's your Synanon you're shitting on. Don't you see that? And when you're caught with your pants down and you swear like a bastard that you haven't been crapping up the place, that you just let down your pants for a moment so you could scratch your ass—is it me you're fooling? Or is it *yourself?* Think about it. Think about it for a moment.

"Don't you see that this is your club? Your Synanon. Don't you see that? Look at it this way: when you're in a hospital and there's a vacancy in the medical ranks, does the chief surgeon or the head doctor—does he go around among the patients to pick out one of them to make a doctor out of him? Did you ever hear of such a thing? Well did you?

"And when you're in Lexington or Fort Worth or Camarillo and the place needs another superintendent or administrator, do the authorities go around among the nuts looking for one whom they can put in charge? Who ever heard of such a thing? You know that's impossible. And in jail, when a new warden is wanted, do they look among the prisoners to find a candidate for the job? Are you crazy? Of course they don't.

"Then what in hell ever gave some of you the idea that Synanon was a hospital? Or a jail? Or a nuthouse? Synanon is Synanon. And don't go looking for another one, because there's nothing like it in the whole world. Nothing! Here, when I need a new director to help me run this organization, do I go outside to find someone among the college graduates in business administration? Do I go around trying to lure away one of the directors of General Motors? Do I advertise for him? Do I go looking for him among my relatives? Or do I go begging some rich man to come in here with his money?

"No! I find him here among you nuts! I find him among you people who have come to Synanon with your wrists bandaged, who have come here fresh out of jail, who have come here out of flophouses, or on parole, begging for a place where you can kick your habit. That's where I find him. Right here!

"Now can't you see that if you must have your laugh, if you must prove to yourself that you can fool me again and again, why here's your living room—go ahead!—piss all over the place. It's not up to me to stop you. It's your room. It's your club. And if that's the kind of place you like to live in—if that's what makes you feel comfortable —why go ahead—stink it up!

"Because I don't give a damn. You see? I don't give a damn if you idiots want to foul up this place. Synanon will survive. You can be sure of that. It's *you* who won't survive. And if you absolutely insist that you want to spend the rest of your lives in jails, it's no skin off my ass. Well, is it? Of course not! Of course not! If you are determined to die in the gutter, why God bless you! That's every man's privilege. Go right on doing to your last day what every dope addict is always doing: hunting for that little bit of white powder that he wants to shoot in his arm. If that's your conception of man's highest ambition, who am I to say no?

"Because it's not me who needs you sons-of-bitches! I couldn't care less. Is there anyone here who still can't get that simple idea through his fucking skull? That it's you who need Synanon, not Synanon who needs you. That there is only one Synanon—but drug addicts, they come by the thousands. They're all over this country. They're all over this world. Synanon doesn't have to find them right here on our doorstep. We can find them in Chicago. In San Francisco. Addicts are dirt-cheap! In Harlem they say every third man is a user. So why should I care if this batch we have here is hell-bent for the morgue. We can find plenty of others. Synanon, you know,

148

doesn't care if an addict's skin is green or orange. Race doesn't matter here. People are people. In Synanon!

"So don't imagine even for one moment that Synanon must go out of existence if it turns you ass-holes out of here and starts fresh! Starts fresh with people who aren't so blind that they can't still tell a turd from a frankfurter. Why should we break our necks here working with people who are shit-headed? Why?

"If nothing that I can say to you will ever make you understand that in Synanon it's your duty to cop out—and by copping out I don't mean just copping out on yourself—NO!—I mean copping out on your best friend. Of course on your best friend! Your best friend above all. Not because you hate him. No! But because you love him! Not because you want to send him to jail—but because you want to save his life!

"And incidentally your own too. Because this is your living room too. You see that? You see that? Of course you see it. We have just had the proof that some of you see it, and others are beginning to see it, we have had that proof here tonight. And those who can't see it—well they have to go out and die. Because that's the way it is. That's the way it is."

9

Chuck wasn't really sore. And if he left his audience gasping after the pounding of his "haircut" speech, it wasn't because he was sore at them in the least. In fact he was proud of his dope fiends. They had begun to find themselves. Not just as individuals. Quite a number of individuals had already emerged as human beings in the club. Others would soon emerge. But something else had happened here this night: that group pride that he had so often predicted must eventually emerge had finally done just that. There was an esprit de corps now in Synanon. It had just begun to show itself, but there could be no doubt that it was already in existence. And that it would grow. And as it grew it would develop a code of ethics that would be mandatory on the whole group.

Synanon had grown in size and understanding to the point where, like a body of water, when it grows big enough, it eventually becomes a self-cleansing entity. "Synanon had become a family," was the way Chuck put it. "We had found cohesion."

Some of those present that night would leave, unable, or else unwilling, to draw upon this newly found group strength to keep away from their habit. Mitch, for example. But the great bulk would remain. Some of them, such as George the Turk, would become real powerhouses in the move to Santa Monica, furnishing not only the muscular strength but the skill as well, and in fact the money too. And it would be only the dire need for money that would force George out, along with a number of other members, such as Pete and Mort and Herman, who were prematurely advanced to Second Stage, so that they might work on the outside and bring back to the club what they could earn.

They've all done well. Financially. In fact phenomenally well. But the outside world gradually severed them from Synanon, and one sees them only occasionally nowadays. All of them, however, have remained clean.

It might have been better for Synanon had the club been able to hold on to them, because Synanon is forever short of executive talent.

"It wasn't because I knew what I was doing that I stayed on," Reid told me. "Cop-out night didn't really make a new man out of me. Or only to the slightest degree. I still remained cynical. I was still full of wisecracks at the expense of Chuck and Synanon. I stayed because I was too scared to leave. I had no place to go. No friends left on the outside. And besides, I had my nightmares. Christ, if I had wandered out I would have died. My loyalty to Synanon was purely selfish—if anything so completely self-centered as what I felt can be described as loyalty at all.

"You see I had no way to make money. No easy way, such as we call a 'stick.' I mean I couldn't boost. In other words, shoplift. There were guys who could always count on some easy money by their skill at pilfering. Not me. I was no good at it. I had always made my dough out of broads who hustled for me. Or by getting guys to go out and smuggle in dope for me to push out to the dealers. Or with my floating crap game. Or maybe an occasional heist.

"I was really just about helpless at this stage, Guy, so I didn't budge. What I did was wash dishes. Take care of the garbage. Sweep up. That sort of thing. Menial work, but I didn't feel too bad about it. I said to myself: 'Hell, I can make it here. I have a place to sleep. My food. Cigarettes. A dollar a week WAM (that is to say Walk Around Money, which starts at one dollar a week at six months and after several years rises to the princely salary of five dollars a week, which until recently was tops)—whenever the club could spare it, which wasn't often. And I can get laid once in a while. So what the hell more do I want?'

"And then slowly I got interested in the place. Very slowly. You can readily see why. Christ, no one had ever counted for beans in my life except me. I had to make a full hundred-and-eighty-degree switch. A complete about-face. After eight months I was no longer on the service crew. I was in charge of it. And then, after nearly a year, when Pete had left, I got his job as head of maintenance. But I couldn't cope with it. So Chuck relieved me of it and found me a job writing thank-you notes to people who had sent us clothes or furniture or even checks. And Arline was my secretary.

"And that's when I first began to feel in myself a certain sense of dedication. Perhaps the realization of how many kindhearted people it took to make our Synanon. . . .

"But I never thought of Chuck as God. Or anything remotely like that. . . ."

"That isn't quite what I would gather from your fifth birthday speech," I argued.

"What fifth birthday speech?" Reid asked.

"The speech you made to the club on the fifth birthday of your coming in. You know, the speech where you began by expressing how pleased you were that Chuck wasn't present because what you were going to say was something you would find very difficult to say with him around. Don't you remember?"

Apparently he couldn't remember, and was even inclined to deny having ever made such a speech . . . until I offered to play the tape to him.

"You mean it was taped?" he exclaimed in surprise. "Yes, play it. I want to hear that."

"Maybe this is something you would prefer to forget," I suggested, as I prepared the machine for playing.

"Isn't it funny," he said. "That entirely slipped my memory." And he listened with excitement to his own voice coming out of the tape recorder.

"This portion of our Saturday get-together," the tape said, "will

be devoted to our usual ritual: the observance of what we call 'Synanon clean birthdays.' That means a year of accumulated time spent at
Synanon free of the use of any drugs and all their concomitants,
such as going to the bughouse, hitting citizens over the head and
taking all their money, and one thing and another.

"Several years ago, when I was in San Francisco, I ran into an old
crime partner of mine, whom I hadn't seen for a few years, and I
asked him: 'Say, what's happening?' And he said: 'Reid, I'm staying
clean.' And I said: 'I'm certainly glad to hear that.'

"Of course I wasn't glad at all because I suspected he might be
telling the truth. So I had to find out how he was accomplishing
this remarkable feat.

" 'What do you do, to stay off junk?' I asked.

" 'I just keep active,' he said. 'Like for instance I get lushed two or
three times a week. Couple of days I'll take sleeping pills. And over
the weekend I'll blow a little pot. And two or three times a month
I'll go out and pull a couple of capers. And in that way I manage to
stay straight.'

"I was really impressed. I looked up to him as a tower of strength.
If only I could regulate my life so intelligently. But I never could.

"Recently, here, we've been able to observe many clean birthdays.
Some of the people had been here one year, others two years, or
even three, four, and five years. And now it's my turn to speak my
piece on my fifth birthday in Synanon.

"As a rule, you know, I have no trouble shooting my mouth off. In
fact it's my favorite occupation. And I shouldn't have any trouble
doing so now when I have this occasion to be grateful for the miracle
that has kept me alive. But this evening I have the feeling I'm going
to be somewhat inarticulate. Because the foremost urge in my mind
is to pay tribute to the one man who accomplished that miracle, I
mean Chuck, and I'm kind of glad that he's up in San Francisco and
not here to listen to me.

"It's so difficult for me to speak lovingly of a man. Psychologists
have an explanation for that difficulty. They speak of the latent fear
of homosexuality, or some such thing. So I've never yet said to

Chuck: 'I love you.' I know I would find it very difficult to say it. In fact I couldn't possibly do so.

"But the truth is I do love him. Because he saved my life—and the life I owe to him has turned out to be a pretty full one—and a pretty good one. I like Chuck for doing what he does. I admire him for the ambition and the scope of his plans. I like to be part of him and his work. I'm grateful to him for accepting my help and for including me in his plans.

"I know this: that five years ago I was literally dying. Not just figuratively, or in a manner of speaking. I was dying, after a real honest-to-goodness attempt to destroy myself. I had made a good stab at it, but I wound up in a hospital bed, where I was unconscious for three days. That suicide attempt was no bluff. And I was just biding my time, getting up my courage to do it again, when I wandered into Synanon.

"At that time there was only one man who was grappling with the problem of lunatics like me. The problem of people whose values are so distorted, whose perspective on life is so oblique, at such a tangent, that they cannot exist without anesthetizing themselves every single waking moment of their lives.

"Chuck singlehandedly tore me loose from my drug habit. Though due credit must be given to all the others who helped create the environment in which I lived at Synanon. The fact of others being there working at the same problem that I had was of invaluable assistance. But I still have to look at Chuck as one man singlehandedly grappling with the urge that I had in me to destroy myself either in bits and stages by drugs—or as a whole by suicide—an urge at which I was determined to become a success.

"I know that he listened to me, looked after me, put up with all my nonsense, cajoled me, criticized me, argued with me, shouted at me, loved me, did everything he could to keep me from shooting dope. I'm awfully glad he did, because I think I can now say, with due modesty, that I'm a useful part of Synanon, and in a position where I can perhaps pass on to others a little of what Chuck did for me. But whatever I do will never really be my own, but merely

Chuck himself acting through me. If—as someone once remarked—any institution is only the lengthening shadow of one man, I'm glad to be part of Chuck's shadow. Chuck has saved an awful lot of lives. And I'm grateful to him. As I think every human being ought to be."

I was watching Reid as the tape came to an end, and was about to query him about some of those rather strange words to be found issuing from the mouth of a disbeliever. Words such as "miracle" and "tribute" and "love," and also various phrases about Chuck single-handedly saving his life, and that veritable litany: "I know that he listened to me, looked after me, put up with all my nonsense, cajoled me, criticized me, argued with me, shouted at me, loved me, did everything he could to keep me . . ."

But before I had a chance to argue with Reid about this aspect, Reid himself began to talk, blaming himself for not having expressed the whole truth in this speech. "The drug part of it was just a fraction of what he did. You know I might have come off dope and have still been a nobody and a nothing. Chuck made a human being out of me. It's as a teacher that Chuck is most important in my life.

"I'm thinking, for example, of the time when I had pneumonia, a very severe case, where my life was despaired of. And Chuck would come again and again to my bedside. And I was so stupid that I couldn't see this as a lesson in solicitude. I was in fact so blind that when I got well the first thing I did was to go out and shoot some dope again.

"And then, when I cleaned up, boy did I become self-righteous! Did you know John Smith? Do you remember him?"

"Of course I do. Buerger's disease . . . a colored fellow . . ."

"Yes. Well this John Smith was one of Synanon's earliest members. But an almost incurable addict. He was always splitting. Going off and shooting dope and getting himself into one hell of a mess, and then running to Synanon begging to be taken back. And Chuck would keep letting him come back. And then, what would John do but stink up the place by sneaking in pills and passing them out to everyone. I couldn't understand Chuck letting him in again and again. We certainly didn't need this guy in our club.

"And then one time when he had run off again, he got into this real big trouble. It was discovered that he had Buerger's disease, and in fact such a bad case that both his legs had to be amputated. Above the knee. And then, you know what? He still wanted back into the club.

"By that time I was more or less in charge here, in the Santa Monica house, and of course I turned him down. Absolutely not. No more of his brand of shit.

" 'Why not?' Chuck asked me.

" 'You're not serious,' I said. 'You know this guy has fucked up Synanon again and again.'

" 'He can't give us much trouble now,' Chuck said. 'He's a cripple.'

" 'All the more reason why we can't take him in,' I pointed out. 'This place is nothing but stairs, and this guy is in a wheelchair for the rest of his life. He can't even get around on crutches. How is he going to get up and down the stairs?'

" 'We've got plenty of young bloods here,' Chuck said. 'Big gorillas with nothing but muscles. They can carry him and his wheelchair up and down the stairs. Easy.'

" 'But Jesus Christ, Chuck, this guy can't even go to the toilet—'

" 'Why not? What's he need?' Chuck said. 'Some kind of special platform?'

" 'Yes,' I said.

" 'Well, can't we build it for him? Haven't we got wood and nails and carpenters?'

" 'Look, Chuck,' I argued, 'let's be realistic. We may be letting ourselves in for a lot of trouble. This guy is in constant pain. He has a medical permit for the use of drugs. Some of our animals are going to be stealing shit from him. I've told you the story of how Yla and I once kept a cripple in our home, a man with one leg and cancer of the rectum, because this dying man had a right to a supply of morphine which we kept buying from him. . . . Chuck, we'll only get into trouble with the authorities. . . .'

" 'All right, so we watch him. Where's the problem? Christ, Reid, if I had been as severe with you cats when you were breaking all the rules . . .'

"You see what I mean, Guy? Chuck didn't just stop when he had me off drugs. He had to start with me from the ground up. To teach me solicitude, compassion, humility . . ."

"Did you ever have any trouble with John Smith?" I asked.

"None," Reid replied. "This time he was cured. He became our legal secretary. He took an exam for notary public and passed it. He handled all kinds of special correspondence for us—until he died. . . ."

"I want to get back to the religious question for a moment," I said to Reid. "You say that in spite of everything that Chuck has done for you, practically creating you . . ."

"Yes. . . . Absolutely."

"You've still never felt an urge to build an altar before him, and worship him as a god?"

"Never. For my money Chuck is a great man. A very great man. I'm not prepared to say how great he may be in the context of all mankind and all history. But for my small world he's the greatest."

I was genuinely relieved to hear Reid say that, because it was a conclusion that solved for me the problem I was struggling with, namely that of holding a man in very high esteem without taxing my credulity. Suppose, for example, that Chuck really were a god, then what an embarrassment to discover in him some extremely human flaw, such as picking his nose. That would have been all right in the days of Greece and Rome, when gods were just supermen, but not since the Jewish-Christian philosophies took hold of the world.

And in the back of my mind there was always a reverberating voice —I can't remember whose, but I can remember distinctly what this person said to me: "You'll see," the voice goes, "one of these fine days your Chuck will turn out to have stashed away loads of real estate, several millions of dollars in cash, and there will be one hell of an income tax scandal. . . . You'll see, because it happens to all the founders of new religions. And it will happen to Synanon too. Bound to happen if his followers keep making a god out of him."

I talked to Chuck recently about some of these matters. And in particular how pleased I was that Reid had never fallen for any of these notions of Synanon as a religion and Chuck as a god.

"Well, of course, Reid . . ." Chuck said. "Reid—you know—Reid is awfully hung up on the matter of me as god."

"I don't understand," I said. "Reid assured me again and again that he never saw you as anything more than a man confidently stepping out in the direction of your dreams."

"Yes, yes, I know," Chuck said. "But Reid has also confessed to me that it pains him to think of me in bed with a woman. It hurts him to think of me as an ordinary person who would screw a woman. In other words he refuses—deep within himself—to put me on a mundane plane, the plane he himself lives on. You see? So where does that put me—in his mind?"

"Yes," I said, a bit shaken.

"Reid," Chuck observed, "Reid is a very complex person."

"Well how do you personally feel about all this god business?" I asked. "How do you feel about this business of being able to do no wrong. You might, for example, be able to put away a million dollars and no one would dare reproach you."

"I feel fine," Chuck said. "Of course you understand that man creates his own gods. And I just happen to have the right physical characteristics for that position. I've got the deep voice, the big chest, the authoritative manner.

"You realize that for a baby, the man of the house doesn't seem to have any real function, at least none that the baby can explain. The man is there. And then again he's not there. He doesn't nurse the child. He doesn't feed it. He doesn't cuddle it much. He's some powerful and mysterious manifestation that erupts out of nowhere and disappears again.

"Well what kind of a thing is that—that behaves that way? Why that's god. And you can see thus how the idea of a deity takes hold in the baby's mind. And never gets lost.

"This is why it's such an easy trick to play god for the grown-up children that most of the addicts here are. Psychoanalysts do it routinely with their patients. They deliberately build this bridge of transference stage until they have made the changes they want in their patients' characters. Then they cut them loose.

"But as to putting aside a million dollars, why should I? I have, on the contrary, followed the biblical injunction of not laying up treasures on earth where moth and rust doth corrupt and thieves break in and steal. But have followed the kick of laying up treasures in heaven instead. So you see I don't need a dime. And in fact I haven't got a dime. All I have is the trappings. And who wants anything else? I'm like the President of the United States. He can, theoretically, go to the movies in a battleship costing a hundred million dollars. That's the kind of a wealth I have. I have hundreds of servants here in Synanon. And don't have to pay them a cent. Because they're my family.

"Any one of them can walk out of that door tomorrow morning. But he won't. Not if he has any brains. Why should he? Hell, he's part of a rich family. If he marries, everyone of us here is involved in seeing to it that he has an apartment for himself and his bride. And a house when he has children. And if he needs a car we try to provide it for him. In his way he's as rich as anyone else here is. As rich as I am for that matter. The children of millionaires are millionaires too, aren't they?"

"And the children of God are also gods," I said.

"But if Synanon were really a new religion—instead of just a new way of living—wouldn't we proclaim a new dispensation? Wouldn't we clean out all the Catholics and the Jews and even a Mormon like Reid, and make them all members of the new religion? But we don't do anything of the kind."

"But you did create a religious festival at Synanon," I said.

"At Synanon we celebrate all holidays. Christmas and Hanukah, Easter and Passover. No matter what your religion may be, you can keep its holy days here."

"But what about your Cop-out festival? Didn't you institute that? Or was that Zev's work. It has a kind of Zev touch to it. A feeling of Zev's 'Synanon is my religion and Chuck is my god!'"

159

"No at all. Not at all. The fact is that Zev is a great Synanist, but he still hasn't snapped to the fact that Synanon is a family and not a religion, and that he would be more secure here than he could ever possibly be by working on the outside as a TV producer."

"But Zev did get you to celebrate the first Seder in Synanon, didn't he? And this Cop-out festival certainly looks very much like a Seder."

"Well, you see, at the time of Zev's Seder, he was still just fresh from New York. And all screwed up, you know. Really all screwed up. Full of this Jewish persecution bit—you know of course that he fought in the Israel-Arab war . . . had to go five thousand miles from his home to find someone who would shoot at him. That's how badly Zev needed persecution. Well, Zev comes to Synanon and sees that there are already twenty or more Jews in Synanon and decides that it's time Passover was celebrated here.

"And of course he had it all figured out in advance that I wouldn't let him. He knew in front that I was of German descent and therefore a Nazi, and he was all wired up for my refusal. And when I would give him that refusal he knew exactly what he was going to do. He was going to run out on this fat German butcher—out into the world—and shoot dope again.

"I guess there was never a more surprised man in the world when instead of being sentenced to the gas chamber, Zev heard me say: 'Crazy! By all means, let's have a Seder.' Of course he was still afraid that I had some trick up my sleeve, and not until I had put myself at the head of the table and had read the text and been asked the four questions as to why this day is different from all other days, and had explained the meaning of the different symbols, the bitter herbs and the matzos and so forth—not until then did he finally believe that there would be a Seder in Synanon—so that the ceremony was almost over before he snapped to the fact that it was actually taking place. Then he nearly wept and afterwards said to me that if only I had had a beard he would have thought it was his grandfather conducting the services."

"But the Cop-out ceremony," I said, "is modeled, isn't it, on the

Seder? The questions and the symbols and everything taking place during a meal."

"Well, why not? The Seder celebrates the escape of the Jews from their bondage to the Egyptians, and our Cop-out dinner celebrates the escape of the addicts from their bondage to drugs. But actually I had nothing to do with the details of the ceremony. Let me tell you how it all happened. I was living in San Francisco at the time, and commuting back and forth between there and Santa Monica, and one day, just before leaving for the plane I looked around for something to read on the plane and found this paperback and threw it into my briefcase. Just any old thing to read. I had never seen this book before.

"And when I got on the plane I took the book out to read—and I never read more than just a paragraph. Maybe not even that. It was a book called 'This I Believe,' some sort of compilation of patriotic and philosophic and religious statements from various important figures of our time. But all I read was just this one line about the importance of ritual and symbols in human affairs. Maybe a dozen words or so. And then I closed the book and I've never looked at it since.

"I began to think of what rituals and what symbols we had at Synanon. Our Saturday night open house. Our clean birthdays. Our morning reading of the philosophy. And it seemed to me that what Synanon lacked in this area was one good annual festival. Something that would be our very own. And the moment I began to think this way the word Cop-out occurred to me. Because that night of the big Cop-out was when the group really took on its own independent life. And also such a festival would be our very own. Cop-out and Synanon, these words belong to us.

"Naturally I didn't have a pencil with me, so I had to nudge my neighbor and borrow one from him. And I wrote on the flyleaf the one word, 'Cop-out.' And that's all. That's all I did. No details. Just one word. Of course my thought was that we could trigger some sort of folk-force here. Something that would start a tradition. Not that Synanon is a religion. But that the religious need exists in Synanon as it exists in all peoples, even those who don't profess any religion. Of course the mere fact that we need religion here doesn't make us a religion, no more than the fact that we also need transportation in Synanon makes us a bus line.

"I made no plans whatsoever. Didn't have to. The moment I broached the matter to some of the older members, it was already out of my hands. It attained escape velocity at once. I couldn't have stopped further developments if I had tried."

"It makes for a very impressive evening," I said. "I've got only one question about it. If Synanon is really for squares, and not just for dope addicts, and if, as you say, it was just by chance that it was on a dope addict that this new idea first revealed its power, then aren't the symbols that have been selected just a little too 'in' for squares? For example, what can squares make of this bent spoon symbol?"

Chuck said: "I guess most people don't know that dope addicts have a way of bending a spoon so as to make a little stand-up saucepan in which they can cook up their solution of heroin. I suppose that's as obscure to the uninitiated as let's say the holy wafer or the matzos, but the words that go with it: 'this spoon must be straightened,' that's pretty clear."

"Yes," I agreed. "The straightening out of our character deformities, that's universal, I guess. And I suppose the dark glasses that addicts wear to conceal the effect that dope has on their eyes, and the smashing of those glasses during the ceremony, could be interpreted as breaking out of the darkness, out of the dreams of dope—or out of any form of ignorance and bad habit—into the light of truth."

"And then there's the eating of the bread and peanut butter," Chuck pointed out. "That's exactly like the eating of the matzos, to remind one of difficult days in the past. And how even in those bad times we found a solution, a cheap adequate nourishment. Not manna from heaven. But bread and peanut butter from the supermarket."

"But what about this shoe business?" I asked. "The wearing of the flip-flop on the left foot and the shoe on the right. How would you explain that to people who don't know that it refers to the fact that the early members had one foot in the streets and the other foot in the club, and didn't know whether to turn their backs on their old life or on their new one."

"No matter who comes to Synanon," Chuck replied, "he's bound to come here with some doubts. He's bound to be torn between the old and the new. He may not know that in the old days in Synanon when you took off your flip-flops and put on your shoes it was a sign that you were splitting and going back to your old ways, but he'll catch on to the deeper meaning.

"Because the whole Cop-out idea has fully as much significance for squares as for addicts. In fact squares need it more than addicts. Far more. You're not going to hold the addicts responsible for the big problems of this world, are you? Is it addicts who make war? Is it addicts who are to blame for the tyrannies and persecutions of the past and the present? Obviously squares have far more to cop out on than addicts. Far more.

"In San Francisco the squares really dug this festival. There were a half dozen or more dinners organized by them—in their own homes. And each guest had something to cop out on. Or else he brought something with him to symbolize what he was giving up. One woman brought her costume jewelry. One man brought his credit card. And of course this is just the beginning. This thing will snowball. It will develop its own peculiar traditions. Not as a religious ritual. But as a profoundly philosophic and psychological ceremony that is meant for agnostics and sophisticates, as well as for Catholics, Jews, and what have you. As a way of indicating a rebirth, an end to our old ways of thinking and feeling."

10

Basically, I suppose, there's nothing more simple than Synanon. What is it after all but some people with character problems (of which dope addiction is by far not the worst) getting together to straighten themselves out by means of the Synanon game, a form of group intercommunication that has been discovered to work the stupidity out of your head faster than anything else.

It's only when you ask yourself why this works, and how it works, and what is stupidity, and what isn't, that the disputes start and tend to go on interminably. Then Synanon becomes not only difficult to explain but almost impossible.

Perhaps because in the background of any group setting out to solve their problems by this mutual garbage removal system, there are gathered the gabbling ghosts of a thousand disputatious philosophers endlessly splitting hairs and often skulls too, and the corpses of ten thousand religious martyrs and fanatics displaying their sad wounds and screaming their rival heavens and hells, and the skeletons of a million military and political bullies waving their differently colored flags before us and pointing their bony fingers to the final peace of a glorious world cemetery, and now we have in addition all the schools of scientific thought solemnly professing their constantly changing and conflicting theories.

And all this savagery and civilization forever crying into our ears their violent cross-purposes and exacting their deadly oaths of blind allegiance, so that one almost despairs that any two people can force their way through this tangle of wisdom and this jungle of ignorance—and come to know each other, love each other, and understand each other.

And only the fact that people do gives us faith in the people-curing-people method of Synanon. Because it does work. Because it has been observed to work. Time and time again. And thus justifies itself at least pragmatically.

I recall one evening a number of years ago when the red brick building in Santa Monica was loaded with a dozen or more groups all playing the game, and the corridors echoing the screams of "motherfucker" and "shit-head" (particularly from the recent members, who generally tend to be the most obscene and often the most vocal), and Chuck in his office lazily working his ivory back scratcher and saying: "Sounds pretty good. The yogurt is working."

And I remember still another occasion in that same building when a visitor asked Chuck how one would go about establishing a Synanon in some town where no one had ever heard of it before.

"Easy," Chuck said. "Just hunt yourself up a dope fiend. And love him."

And truly, so long as you stick to very simple words like "love" or "the game" or "yogurt" or "people curing people," Synanon too will seem very simple.

"I suppose," Reid Kimball said to me, "if we could freeze it, we could define what Synanon is. But then again, a frozen Synanon, that wouldn't be Synanon at all. Change is such an inherent part of it. You could, for example, say that Synanon began as a little drug addiction operation. But pretty soon people who had never used any drugs began knocking at the door and wanting to join. And I'm sure that no one, neither in nor out of Synanon, ever imagined in those days that eventually Synanon would be running a children's school. And a pen and pencil business!"

This problem of explaining Synanon is taken extremely seriously by Synanon and is so big a question that every Synanon member is eventually drawn into the act.

Synanon people are assigned a variety of jobs in a list that keeps growing from month to month. Synanon people now erect buildings and move goods and run several warehouses full of material which they "hustle," that is to say solicit and then store and ultimately distribute to their various branches or pass on for the use of some other non-profit organization. Synanon people drive refrigerated trucks and huge 20-ton rigs and trailers. They do cabinetwork, they garden, they teach school, they publish a magazine. They do book-keeping and typing, they service and repair cars, and they sell hundreds of thousands of dollars' worth of gasoline and advertising specialties and art rugs every year. So that they are now their own biggest cash donor!

But Synanon people have no job so important—nor so difficult— as trying to understand their own society, and then passing on that understanding to others. And every Saturday night, at all Synanon facilities, where the tradition of open house is observed, right after the clean birthday celebrations (when members who have been free of drugs for one, two, or more years are presented to the guests and their history told) and after some talk or some entertainment, there comes the announcement that in the library or in the living room or in some other spacious place, Synanon people will be available to answer any and all questions that guests may have.

Week after week, in half a dozen places, by some twenty or more people, this programmed job of explaining Synanon goes on and on. And discussions arise that keep visitors and residents talking excitedly until the winking lights signal that the time is close to midnight and the house must be cleared.

Chuck himself began these attempts to sum up Synanon in a paper he read before the Southern California Parole Officers in October 1958. In a cautious way he presented Synanon as an old-fashioned family-type environment that had somehow come into being at Ocean Park and which, he said, "seems to have a beneficial effect on some narcotic addicts."

How modest that statement! ". . . seems to have a beneficial effect on some narcotic addicts." And compare that primordial statement to a very recent observation by Abraham Maslow, Professor of

Psychology at Brandeis University, who declared—or rather pro-
claimed:

"Synanon is now in the process of torpedoing the entire world of
psychiatry and within ten years will completely replace psychiatry."

The truth is that still to this day no one is yet in a position to say
exactly what Synanon can do. Or can't do. Or how and why it works.
This is a matter of many further trials and ventures. So, for an in-
definite time, Synanon must remain in the posture of a man who
certainly has got something very big on the end of his fishing line—
that much is already amply evident from the commotion in the water
—but no one can yet say how big it will prove to be until the catch
is finally landed—if it ever is. For this Synanon fish only grows bigger
the more the Synanon fishermen play him.

And maybe that is the way it will always be.

Chuck sometimes seems to take a peculiar pleasure in ridiculing
his own elaborate explanations. Then he will say such things as this:
"Synanon is just a language gimmick. That's all we got." Or, on another occasion: "We're nothing but a college bull session blown up
into an institution."

Some of this, of course, is just Chuck's tendency to overstate or
understate, and thus get some sort of a free ride up and down his
own verbal roller coaster, which is not only something he does extremely well but also enjoys to the full, especially when he has a
receptive audience.

Making a mountain out of a molehill, or a molehill out of a mountain, is also part of his effort to keep himself intellectually flexible,
so that he will not forget that every word is ambiguous, that everything is at one and the same time both supremely important and
extremely unimportant, depending on whether one thinks in terms
of the immediate or in terms of eternity.

That same day, for instance, when I heard Chuck deprecating
Synanon as nothing but a college bull session, he received the visit
of some representatives of one of America's leading firms in the field
of scientific research and in the manufacture of highly sophisticated
apparatus for space exploration.

These delegates had come to Synanon because they had found character disorder permeating the ranks of their executives and hampering the efficiency of their workingmen and eventually showing up in the output figures of their plant. And having heard so much of Chuck's fantastic success in clearing up character problems by means of the Synanon game, they were thinking of introducing it into their own organization and hoping that Chuck would give them some pointers.

Of course Chuck would. Gladly. Synanon is an open book. Squares were increasingly coming into Synanon. Let their company move two or three of their executives into Synanon and in a little while they would understand everything.

How long was "a little while"?

Chuck thought that "a little while" might be anywhere from six months to a couple of years. Possibly more.

It became clear now that these delegates were disappointed. They had been expecting that Chuck would pass on to them the idea of the Synanon game in a few words. Perhaps even sell them a handy knocked-down version for easy assembly at home in one's spare time.

Chuck exploded with laughter: "How about you gentlemen explaining to us your latest rocket. In just a few words. So we can build a couple of them here. In *our* spare time."

Chuck had a right to feel indignant. He has spent the last nine years perfecting the techniques of the game. He has attended some thousand or more sessions, some of them lasting ten, twenty, and even thirty or more hours, at which startling phenomena comparable to the casting out of devils seem to have occurred.

Chuck has also participated in, or listened to, the taped records of all sorts of special games: games for couples with marital problems, all-women games, teen-age games, all-Negro games, square games, games among college students, among convicts in a penitentiary, among the mentally-ill sailors of a naval hospital, and so forth. So that it is valid to say that few people in and out of the psychological and psychiatric professions can have worked so intimately and so extensively with every conceivable kind of character disorder in every stratum of our society as Chuck has. Nor extracted such profound information about what goes on in the depths of the human soul, nor exhibited the astonishing insights that Chuck so often displays.

And yet the Synanon game seems simplicity itself. What is it after all but a group of some fifteen people who sit around in a room yelling and laughing at each other. With no authority figure such as a psychologist or psychoanalyst present.

But don't confuse it with group therapy. Because it isn't group therapy at all. It's a game. It's a contest. It's a sport. It's a vigorous workout for the mind and the emotions. It will strain your brain and your vocal cords, and for all I know your spleen too. And if it's therapeutic, as it most certainly seems to be, then it's partly for the same reasons that any sport is healthful, because it's strenuous enough to stimulate your bloodstream, raise your pulse rate, excite your senses, stir up your feelings, and leave you afterward refreshed and pleasantly exhausted.

But don't imagine that because no graduate in psychiatry or psychology is present that the Synanon game is without a leader. Of course it has a leader. Out of any group an authority figure will arise. But in the game, since no one is appointed to that post, this position is constantly up for grabs, and the more articulate one is, the more quick-witted, the more cutting one's spirit of the ridiculous, the more likely he is to dominate the game. But never for very long. Because he has rivals for that spot in all the other members of the group.

In short, the Synanon game is fun. A chance to match ourselves against everyone else and give as good as we receive. No wonder voices rise, tempers flare, and the language becomes salty. And many find that this is what they have been looking for all their lives, a chance to blow your cork in the company of people who are just as eager to blow theirs.

And the astonishing result is an occasional tear and endless gales of laughter. And some amazing insights into the depths of oneself. So that even when one is quiet, even when one is not participating, when one seems to be sitting on the sidelines, one is somehow silently involved, and undergoing a kind of self-therapy that is more effective than one first realizes.

Reporters who have to come to witness a game or two in order to write about it are prone to sum it up in such comments as this: "I get it. You people follow the attack-therapy method. I suppose that's just what hardened drug addicts and ex-criminals need. But isn't it too rough for sensitive people? Isn't this more like a verbal street fight than a session of group therapy?"

This is the impression that people who come to observe instead of to participate may derive. But the Synanon game is something to be lived, not watched. Then one will discover that it has room for every aspect of man, from gorilla growls to poetry, from girlish squeals to philosophy. And that in spite of the cataract of four-letter words it is as broad as the English unabridged and as profound as the players are willing or able to plumb. And sometimes that is very profound indeed.

Nor is Synanon to be equated with that old parlor amusement called the "truth game." Because in the Synanon game there is no compulsion to tell the truth. Of course if the truth is what you want to come out with, fine and dandy. But if you want to lie, why that's your privilege. But be careful that you make it sound like the truth, because if you're caught, the ridicule, the scorn, the laughter that will shower you from a dozen throats will be something you will not be likely to forget.

Two hundred years ago the poet Robert Burns must have glimpsed the core of the game when he wrote those two well-known lines that are to be read in his poem *To a Louse:*

> O wad some power the giftie gie us
> To see oursels as others see us!

There lies the unexpected wonder of the Synanon game. The power to see ourselves from the outside, so to speak, and not forever from the inside. The opening of our eyes to the reality of ourselves, a condition that most of us conceal from ourselves by means of a self-image with which we also hope to deceive the world.

And all those criticisms, those reprimands, and those shafts of ridicule that our fellow players pour out on us are but mirrors in which we can see ourselves reflected without the interposition of that blinding self-image that we so cherish.

This is the battle of mirrors that gives the player the opportunity of getting to know himself better.

The first smash hurts. Yes. But subsequent smashes hurt less. And as we begin to mix in the game and roll with the punches and give as good as we take, we learn that while words can excite and rouse, they can't really wound. Not really. It's all done with wooden swords. And when the game is over all the flood of words will be forgotten, and friendship with those whom you fenced with most angrily will be found to be more solid than ever.

Chuck doesn't like to see the Synanon game compared to various forms of psychiatric group interactions. He prefers to see it likened to a game of tennis, to a hot match in which you have used every trick to beat down your opponent. And nevertheless, afterward, jump over the net to congratulate the victor. With no residue of animosity, not in the least. Just the desire to lick him the next time you play.

Only in the Synanon game—and this is the most important part of it all—only in the Synanon game it is the stuff of human life that you play with, and not a thing of cotton and rubber. It's therefore a game to make you grow up. And not just swell your muscles. So that there comes a time when you discover—often to your own surprise— that you have changed without knowing it. And yet that here the cure of your behavioral problem was merely an incident in the game. In the same way that the strength and health-giving properties of a game of tennis are concealed in the stress and excitement of batting a ball across a net.

I must give here at least one example of the power of the Synanon game.

A very short time after this visit from the outer-space people who wanted to buy a knocked-down prepackaged version of the game, the Synanon club held its annual stockholders' meeting. Betty Dederich, Chuck's wife, opened the meeting before the entire Santa Monica membership.

I can still see her in my mind's eye, dark, warm, womanly, and speaking with a sincerity that I am sure must have gripped everyone as it certainly gripped me, causing me to wonder where else in the world I could have witnessed such a scene: a Negro speaking such words before a preponderantly white audience.

The words were written for her by Mike Kaiser, a square who had entered Synanon from the ranks of the advertising business less than two years before. He had been in the employ of Columbia pictures, writing exploitation copy, and, in the course of dealing with a Columbia product, namely the film *Synanon* (which was unfortunately more related to a knocked-down version for easy assembly than it was to the real Synanon), he had visited Synanon houses in New York and Westport and had become intrigued, then infatuated, and finally almost inseparable.

Until Bill Crawford, one of Synanon's directors, said to him: "Hey, Mike! You're just about living here. How about paying us some rent?" Which kind of woke Mike up to the realities and caused him to fork over a thousand or so at first, and then later some more. Then, a while later, he met Chuck and became even more attracted to hanging around Synanon. But the final step of joining he still shied away from.

Chuck said: "If I wanted to I could make up your mind for you, Mike. But I'm not about to do so. All I'm going to say to you is this: if you do join Synanon, there's one thing you never will be again."

"What's that?" Mike asked.

"Bored," said Chuck. "You'll never be bored again. I can promise you that."

Right then and there Mike was illuminated to the fact that his job as copywriter for motion picture films was really quite boring. Repetitive, false, incapable of giving him either pride or purpose. And that his only reason for sticking to it was that it paid well and was relatively easy.

Whereupon Mike decided that boredom was too high a price to pay for time on one's hands and money in one's pocket. And he joined Synanon, where you have neither one nor the other.

Here then are Mike Kaiser's words as Betty Dederich spoke them to the Synanon stockholders:

"Good evening, and welcome. In just a moment, two representatives of the management of Synanon will present to you the annual stockholders report, on what happened in Synanon this past year. However, I would like to take a minute here to call your attention to what I believe is the true significance of this annual event.

"All of you have heard directors of Synanon tell you that you are stockholders in this corporation, but I wonder how many of you really believe that this is so. None of you has a piece of paper to prove that you own a share in Synanon, and neither do I nor any of my fellow directors.

"What we all hold in common is an idea. An idea that we all keep in motion and affirm by our daily participation in Synanon. Each of us owns Synanon: for Synanon is nothing more or less than what each of us chooses to make of it. No one is going to do it for us, although many are eager to lend us a helping hand.

"No man or woman owns stock in his family, or in the family of Man, and we would feel pity for that person whose humanity demanded the evidence of a printed page. So we—you and I—are a unique group of stockholders, just as Synanon is a unique corporation."

Several times that evening I looked around the hall and thought of this new kind of consanguinity that was developing in Synanon. And that could take all these addicts and criminals and squares, these people of all races and religions and all human conditions, and bring them into solid relationship to each other. Weld them into a family. A family of financially independent stockholders, all owning unwritten shares in a family enterprise.

Obviously if Synanon is just an idea held in common, as Betty said, then the Synanon game is capable of being easily introduced anywhere. Even into this aero-space company. But here's the hitch:

once introduced into this company—or any company—would it not have to remake that company—or else destroy it?

Or would not the company have to remake the game—or else destroy it? Clearly something would have to give ground. Certainly the introduction of the game into any company where it would be falsely played could only cause more character disorder than it would cure.

In other words the basis of society, of any and all society, must become the game, so that what takes place inside of man and what takes place outside will become harmonious.

Whether this constant ventilation of the human psyche by means of the Synanon game can actually produce the brotherhood of man is of course for the moment only an article of faith, but the experiment is on its way and it is gradually forming a unique social movement that however small is something here and now for all to see and study.

"Synanon," as Chuck recently phrased it at a Saturday evening open house, "is engaged in a total war against stupidity. Which will be different from all previous wars in that the forces we lick will be eternally grateful to us for having defeated them and deprived them of their stupidity. That kind of conclusion to a war can only happen in the sort of campaign we're fighting."

Synanon's present war against drug addiction is of course only one tiny segment of this total war.

11

Chuck's usual stories about the origin of Synanon do little to clarify how all sorts of ideas and postures became mixed up in it. And I've often doubted the preponderant role which he tends to assign to happenstance.

Nor do I quite believe Chuck when he speaks of his life prior to Synanon as nothing but an endless binge punctuated by smashed marriages, hospitalizations, wrecked careers. No doubt the hard facts he gives are true enough, but the summation, for example in the quotation that Lewis Yablonsky gives in his book *The Tunnel Back: Synanon*, where Chuck speaks of himself as having "roared up and down the countryside drunk, for over twenty years," is completely misleading.

In a speech that Chuck gave at the Seawall facility in San Francisco, less than a year ago, celebrating ten years of sobriety, Chuck had his audience howling with laughter as he described the incidents of a crazy life in the grip of a huge appetite for drink. How, for example, when he parted from his second wife Ruth, who had finally grown tired of his alcoholic companionship, the two of them eventually came to an amicable settlement.

"We divided the house equally," Chuck explained. "She took the inside, and I took the outside."

How far truth is served by these good belly laughs is questionable. It seems to me that there must be a lot more to Chuck's years of carousing than a thirst for whisky. I remember being forcibly impelled to this conclusion recently when I listened to a tape made of an interview between Chuck and a recently admitted member.

It happened that a psychiatrist was present at that session, and the questions and remarks that this professionally trained man put into the tape are so utterly routine, whereas Chuck's words are so full of living insight and his little apostrophes so apt and so beautiful that one is positively transported by one and appalled by the other.

Surely one doesn't get that smart just by being drunk. But also, as proved by this psychiatrist loaded with diplomas and clichés, one doesn't get that smart by going to all sorts of schools for twenty years. So I'm not prepared to say how one becomes a modern Socrates. No one knows that. But in looking for something more solid in Chuck's past, so as to explain in a more believable manner his present ability, I ran across the following in the memoirs that Chuck dictated to Mrs. Elizabeth Dixon for the Oral History program of U.C.L.A.:

"You never know how the mind works, or what it's trying to do. The Synanon idea must have been blowing around in my noodle for many, many years without my realizing it. I read an article a long time ago. It seems to me it was maybe in the middle forties, before I was even conscious that I had any kind of alcoholic problem, and actually I didn't—I just drank an awful lot more than most people and got away with it better. I was a top notch social drinker. And as long as I never got out of hand I had no reason to think of my addiction as a problem. That's about where I was in my life when I read this article in *Cosmopolitan* magazine which discussed some things that would come out of the Twentieth Century.

"One of them was some kind of a universal credit card which would result eventually in the elimination of money as we know it today. It wasn't too long before electronic computing came in and made possible things like the Diners' Club and one thing and another. Quite possibly there won't be much money around except maybe some little change tokens in another twenty-five years or so. Money, as we know it, is on its way out.

"There were about ten things that this author discussed. Another one was a cheap and effective psychoanalysis, and this idea fascinated me. I thought about it and thought about it. Quite obviously, psychoanalysis is not much of an answer, because you'd have to have a therapist for every ten people or so, and it takes about thirty years from birth to make a good analyst.

"Well this is just too expensive in manpower and in time, so this idea of a quick and effective way fascinated me. My mind used to play with that thought. I felt that the world needed some kind of an autonomous mechanism to clean up the neuroses that develop as a result of growing up in a complicated culture. And here at Synanon that's exactly what we have. You see? The idea really grabbed me and I often speculated about it.

"When I eventually threw myself head over heels into the whole A.A. thing, I was excited as the devil. And didn't know why. Because it didn't seem to be the answer I was looking for. But at least it seemed capable of doing something that had looked impossible. It had stopped me from drinking, that was for sure. So maybe there was a mechanism in A.A. that could not only stop people from doing certain things, but maybe start them doing something else.

"Now here at Synanon some truly fantastic things are happening to people who play our Synanon game and who begin to see themselves regularly in the mirror of other people, and start examining their attitudes and their motivations and values: they get loosened up. They get happier. Things seem to straighten out for them. Their children don't bother them so much. They seem to fall in love again with their wives and husbands.

"That's what is happening right here. With squares. Not lunatic fringe people. Just ordinary people who own houses with pictures on the wall and with rugs on the floor. People who belong to the PTA and have successful businesses and so on.

"So, what the potential of this thing is, heaven only knows."

This excerpt is not the only reference Chuck has made to something mysterious in his life that might be described as a "calling." Not so long ago he talked to me about his early experiences with liquor and how one of the things that kept drawing him back to strong drink was a kind of wonderful vision, so fleeting as to be indescribable. A moment of ecstasy which no matter how brief or how long was so elusive as to leave him gasping for more. It seemed to him a glimpse into the beyond—as if a curtain had been pulled aside for a fraction of a second to give him a view into something vast and meaningful. It was the kind of oceanic feeling that once granted to a person will continue to haunt him for the rest of his life, driving him back again and again to the bottle that once had the power to give it to him, but that thereafter keeps baffling all his attempts to reach the same distant and magic shores again.

This sense of a higher purpose, of a gateway to something greater, was always with Chuck in his binges, just as it is with many alcoholics and many dope addicts. The urge toward chemicals is complex, and not all of it can be set down as a desire to escape from a drab world; some of it is the longing to recapture a precious moment of transport, some of it is a continuing attempt to get through a door that keeps closing before our inner eye just as the dazzling vision is about to be granted.

It is well to keep this oceanic feeling in mind through the stories that Chuck tells of his long stretches of drunkenness. Otherwise one may picture him as nothing but a barfly, and drunk as a lord every single night, and a pill-head at the same time, using chemicals to put him to sleep, other chemicals to wake him up, and still a third kind of chemical to keep him smart all day long.

"It would have killed anyone else," he told me, "but I had one saving habit: I was a glutton. I ate voraciously. And that prevented most of my drinking from going hand in hand with chronic malnutrition, as is so often the case."

Following his own rule that a man is not an alcoholic but just a good social drinker so long as the milk bill is paid before the liquor bill, Chuck did not consider himself a problem-drinker merely because, for instance, at a Thanksgiving dinner, he tasted so many stingers that by the time the party was ready to begin he had passed out and the bulk of him lying on the living room floor constituted an engineering job to remove.

Ruth, his second wife, saw it differently. She once called in the help of the A.A., but the sponsor who answered this call could do nothing with a man who thought of himself as only occasionally imbibing one too many. That's all. A harmless indulgence. And he continued in this generous opinion of himself and of his habit even after his wife went out to work to make sure that the milk bill *was* paid. He refused to see how liquor interfered with every aspect of his life. Interfered with his marriage, his business, his friends, and his relatives.

Until Ruth finally had enough of him.

"This kind of self-delusion," Chuck relates, "naturally had to come to a smashing end. I went on a month-long bender of such proportions that everything went to pot and I wound up all over the floor, a real jibbering idiot, with every blood vessel in my eyeballs hemorrhaging, and myself so sick with the dry heaves that I could have wished for death to release me from the agony.

"Three years before, at the time of another similar smashup, only far less intense, my wife had put in that call to the A.A., and I knew that some literature had been left around. Somehow I managed to find this stuff, and somehow I managed to read the telephone number, but the number had been changed meanwhile and it took me forty minutes to reach the club. But by chance it was the very same sponsor who was sent to help me.

"Only this time I was ready to welcome him. He nursed me through four days of horror, summoned a doctor to shoot me full of vitamins and tranquilizers, and finally on the fifth day, dragged me to an A.A. meeting in Beverly Hills, where he propped me up against a wall close to the john, so I could get there quickly. He left me with a cocktail shaker full of cracked ice and water clutched in my trembling hands so I could continue the fight against my extreme state of dehydration.

"Thus I stayed while the meeting went on, feeling totally out of the picture. Utterly friendless and alienated. Totally alone. My first wife had gone away with my son. My second wife had gone away with my daughter. I had buried my mother and had got roaring drunk at the funeral services to the disgust of all my friends and relatives, who thereafter turned their noses away from me. It was ages since anyone had rung the telephone or knocked at the door.

"I guess that can explain what I did next. I had been through a long period of silence, and apparently a great stock of unused vocabulary had accumulated just inside my vocal cords, and it had to come out. And so, suddenly, I shoved myself out into the meeting and started to harangue the audience, delivering a violent religious diatribe of which all I can remember is that it brought me bursts of laughter and finally a terrific hand, and that afterwards people swarmed up to me, congratulating me, slapping me on the back, and saying I was great.

"And I loved it!

"'This is for me,' I said to my sponsor. And he said: 'Fatso, believe me: it had better be for you. Because I'm telling you, if you don't go to an A.A. meeting every day of your life from now on— you're going to die. But fast.'

"So that's exactly what I did. I went every day. And twice on Saturdays and Sundays. I became a frantic, fanatical A.A. fellow. I lived it, I breathed it, I slept it, I ate it. For weeks I did nothing else but A.A. work. And then, when I needed money badly, I went out and got myself a job as a pattern-maker at Curtiss-Wright, but without changing my schedule any more than I damn well had to.

"Life became nothing but certain hours of financially necessary work—or what I then still considered necessary work—and then a rapid change of clothes and a quick run to the nearest A.A. house, which happened to be on 26th Street in Santa Monica. Lunchtime, evenings, every spare moment found me either there or at some other A.A. meeting sounding off on the Bible, on the Talmud, on cybernetics, even on the telephone book if no other topic was at hand. Didn't make any difference to me so long as I was doing the talking. And that schedule didn't change when my firm transferred me from Los Angeles to Santa Barbara.

"But something happened in Santa Barbara. Something very strange. A feeling of impending doom took hold of me. I couldn't understand it—I was just plain scared. Scared to death. So I never unpacked my suitcase. Every spare hour I had I spent at the A.A. And when the club was closed for the night, I huddled in my room, frightened out of my wits. And I couldn't discover why.

"I happened to have with me an old copy of Emerson's essay on self-reliance. I had read it before. As a kid in high school, and then again when I joined A.A. But it had never meant much to me. Of course I realized that it was great prose. I was even aware that it was full of the most amazing profundities, the most acute observations. But somehow I never took those wonderful bits to be anything more than Emerson showing off his genius, and of no value to me personally except as a spectator and an admirer of that genius. It was his performance, not mine. And it never occurred to me that Emerson was sending me a personal letter. Addressed directly to me.

"Nevertheless I took to carrying that little book around with me. And whenever I had nothing else to do I would take it out and do a bit of reading in it. As often as ten times a day. With some kind of inexplicable drive to read passage after passage over and over again. Until suddenly it dawned on me that this was no mere literary flight, this was a book of directions. It was as technical for the human psyche as a mechanic's manual was for the repair and running of a car.

"And what the book said was you—you, the reader—you have a piece of God in you. Why then don't you rely on your own thinking and your own impulses? Trust yourself, man! Be a convert to your own inborn religion.

"The moment I got this illumination I went to my employers and notified them that I was quitting. I was through. I no longer felt that I needed a job in order to earn my living. And I didn't. And here I am, the living proof of Emerson's manual on how to run a human life: I have never held a job since that day. And in fact never earned a penny since that day. Haven't had to.

"Of course Synanon has had some rough moments, but I don't

know of anyone dying of hunger here. At the old club in Ocean Park we used to melt down candle stubs to make new candles because we were always behind in meeting our electric bill and the company was always cutting us off. So what? We did very well by candlelight.

"And we had some difficulty with clothes too. Not on the beach, or in our clubhouse, because there any rag was good enough. But after the son of one of our early directors had got us our first speaking engagement, and we got to be in demand, we did have a problem of what to wear. At one time the whole club could muster only two presentable men's suits. One of them had been purchased for me, when Santa Monica hauled me into court and I couldn't very well appear in shorts and flip-flops—not that I wasn't convicted and jailed anyhow. And the other suit came walking into our club on the back of Jake Ross. We cleaned Jake of his addiction and stripped him of his suit. That became club property.

"The result was that we never thought of ourselves as sending out speakers to the Lions or the American Legion or to various schools and churches. We sent out our only two suits. For the suit that had been bought for me, we needed a fat guy who could fill it, someone like Arnold Ross or Jesse Pratt. And for the other one we needed a skinny guy like Jake. Jack Hurst was thin enough, but he was so tall that he had to buckle the belt around his ass so as to let the cuffs reach his shoes, while Bill Crawford was also thin enough but so short that he had to buckle the belt under his armpits to keep the cuffs off the floor.

"But no matter. We always managed to fill our two suits and thus filled our engagements. We were concerned only about the suits. Not who wore them. I remember one time going into the kitchen late at night and seeing a speaker just back from a lecture, busy fixing himself a snack while he was still wearing one of our suits. 'Why you asshole!' I yelled at him. 'You want to get mayonnaise all over our speaker's suit and wreck our whole lecture bureau?'

"The moment, up in Santa Barbara, when I realized that I wanted to spend the rest of my life rescuing drunks, my terror left me. I had no more fear. I went back to Los Angeles and got right to work. I sat in an A.A. club and took every incoming call, doing for other people what my sponsor had done for me, wiping away their tears, talking A.A. philosophy to them, cleaning up their vomit. I suppose lots of guys are living in misery to this day who might be happily drunk or happily dead, if I hadn't jerked them off some barstool.

"But I was a true believer and I wasn't going to let anything stop me. I lived in a fleabag of a room. My shoes and clothes wore out. The finance company came and took away my car. But I had the free doughnuts and coffee available at A.A. houses, and now and then people would invite me to dinner.

"I was getting close to the edge of nothing when a girl who had just put her husband on a plane walked in and drew me into a circle of people with whom I had had no contact up to that point: the beatnik crowd in Venice and Ocean Park. This girl also called my attention to the fact that I had unemployment checks coming to me.

"That decided me. I moved myself into a small room down by the beach, and made up my mind that I was going to take a year off to read all the books I should have read and never had. My room now became a branch of the public library, and I never went out except to collect my unemployment checks, get fresh books from the library, and buy myself some cans of chili, some cans of soup, some chocolate, and some cigarettes.

"That was my whole life. I read night and day. But gradually more and more people began dropping in on me. Discussion took the place of reading. My room was no longer a branch of the library but a permanent seminar. Drunks whom I hadn't cured, and drunks whom I had, would be lying all over the place screaming at me and at each other, and I would be yelling at them like a Comanche Indian, and out of all this furious talking we got molded into some sort of loose association of people who were pursuing a line of inquiry of no line. With no subject barred. And only physical violence absolutely ruled out.

"And I felt wonderful. Just great. I knew something was being born here. And when our first dope addict walked in and remained clean, I knew that this 'something' had indeed come into existence. Exactly what this 'something' was I couldn't say. Not because it was vague. It wasn't in the least vague. But it was ill defined. It seemed to have no boundaries. It seemed to want to spill out all over the place. Defining is a form of confining, and this thing refused to be confined. No matter what category you put it into, it overlapped. It seemed to want to overlap everything. It was really most amazing."

12

Synanon has remained to this day not so much undefinable as un-defined. That is, refusing to let anyone build walls of definition around it. Some pretty neat footwork has sometimes been required to maintain this free and mobile stance, particularly when Synanon moved out of storefronts in Ocean Park and into the red brick ar-mory building at 1351 Ocean Front in Santa Monica, and the ques-tion arose whether Synanon was "curing" or "treating" dope addicts, because if it was, then Synanon was a "hospital," and if it was a hospital then it was in the wrong zone, so far as Santa Monica was concerned, and it had to get out.

That was when the question of what Synanon was or wasn't be-came a matter of life and death for the organization. It caused them to go as far afield as the legislature in Sacramento to have the Petris bill passed. This Petris bill was specially written in order to define Synanon as "a place" where dope addicts might legitimately be kept free of dope.

"Of course it was just a business of words," Reid said to me. "But think of this. Before the Petris bill Synanon was really doing some-thing illegal. And I'll tell you why. Because we had no drugs at all. I mean, when an addict came here and he had to kick his habit, he had to kick it 'cold turkey.' And this was in violation of California law. Because California had provided for the following places where a drug addict could legally go through withdrawal: a city jail, a county jail, a state penitentiary, a hospital, a sanitarium. And that was all.

"Now look at what this meant. It meant that if you were a drug addict and decided you wanted to quit the habit, and holed up in your apartment, or went to your sister's place or home to your mother to stop using, you were breaking the law. Which means that if you were so unfortunate as to have formed a habit, you were actually not allowed to stop it on your own. And since it was illegal to be an addict, you were legally compelled to continue to go on being illegal!"

Chuck said: "The Petris bill was a great idea. Two bright girls, Peggy Maddocks and Mitzi Rubin, both long active in political work, conceived this thing and helped us get hold of Nick Petris, who pushed it through at Sacramento. We thought: once this gets out of the legislative hopper and Governor Brown signs it, we're saved!

"Unfortunately all governments must have categories, departments, that sort of thing, in order to make sure that their fingers are always on the controls. And so the Petris bill had to put Synanon under some kind of supervision, and it put us under the Board of Medical Examiners. Which was ridiculous. Of course. Because Synanon is nothing that doctors are more equipped to understand or handle than any other class of people.

"Looking back I wish the bill had put us under the Department of Parks and Recreation. Who also would have had no idea what Synanon was up to. Because, as you know, when the Board of Medical Examiners met to inquire into the matter of Synanon and to decide whether we were entitled to continue our work, they came up against this Santa Monica zoning thing. And the Board decided that they couldn't okay Synanon until we had settled that little matter with the zoning commission of Santa Monica; while Santa Monica decided that they couldn't let us out from under the zoning matter until the Board of Medical Examiners okayed us. And that's how they passed the buck back and forth and *we* got nothing out of this bright idea and out of all our effort."

Chronologically the Santa Monica fight begins with Synanon being ordered out of Ocean Park, where the storefronts it occupied were to be bulldozed out of existence in order to provide for increased parking space for beach visitors. The necessary land had already been condemned by the State of California.

At this time Synanon was just beginning to acquire a public image. Paul Coates had made Synanon the subject of one of his popular TV programs. And a magazine named *Inside Detective* had come down to photograph both the place and its occupants, and to do the first full-scale article ever written about them. It was to appear in the October issue, shortly after Synanon's move.

At this same time, when Synanon was being ordered to move, Ephraim Ralph, a Santa Monica real estate owner, was just losing a long-term tenant, the National Guard, who had occupied an old red brick building of his. He had seen in the papers a little notice about Synanon's order to vacate, and the thought occurred to him that perhaps Synanon might be his next long-term tenant. It seemed indeed a very happy solution, both to his problem and to Synanon's, since his big building was almost totally lacking in parking space and he would therefore have a hard time finding a tenant, while Synanon's crowd of former dope addicts, felons, and prostitutes must be facing an equally difficult problem in finding suitable space.

Ralph's building was little more than a huge brick barn cut up into various large and small rooms. It was ancient, dirty, and in bad repair. But it was vast, it was airy, and it fronted on a magnificent beach. The rental, five hundred dollars a month, was astronomical for Synanon's resources, but dirt-cheap when figured out against the number of occupants it could house. Nevertheless, in terms of the two-year lease that the owner was insisting on, and which thus came to a huge twelve thousand dollars, it was an overwhelming sum of money. I mean at that time. Six years later Synanon's total rentals, all over the United States, would come close to a hundred and fifty thousand dollars every year. And the club would reach the conclusion that they must eventually house themselves only on properties they could buy and own.

At that particular time however, Synanon had acquired some of its first important sponsors. This came about when a young dope addict we will call Frankie moved into the club and introduced Synanon to some of his wealthy relatives and friends. Among them was a public relations man. Although Synanon was never able to do anything for Frankie's addiction because the subject refused to stay in the club long enough for the program to have any effect on him, and when he did stay in the club behaved so badly that the members wanted him thrown out, his friend caught fire and kept coming around and bringing in more friends, among them several who had affiliations with the Friars Club of Beverly Hills. And he was able to get a group of these friends to pledge themselves to be responsible for the two-year rental. With this commitment to back him, Chuck signed the lease.

The first opposition to Synanon's move did not come from outsiders. It came from within the club itself. From those who felt that Synanon could do itself no good by moving out of the slums where it naturally belonged, where it had been born and where it ought to stay. These members saw Synanon as something incurably beatnik —and they liked it that way, with Tobacco Road as its permanent address. They were convinced that Synanon would be endangering its very existence by departing from its easy and comfortable way of life, unpretentious, befitting an organization that lived from the cast-offs of a more affluent world. Synanon's place would always remain with the ready-to-sour milk they got from a local dairy and eventually lost to a pig farm, the day-old bread that they got from Izzy Cohen's bakery and still get—but fresh!—the unsold sandwiches that were left over on catering trucks, and the furniture that people were ready to throw out.

Never would you fit Synanon into the Gold Coast of Santa Monica! Not the old Synanon that the members loved. Where girls in their gay wrappers were still fixing their hair or painting their nails while the morning philosophy was read, and Emerson's words could be heard resounding in a living room where there was a punching bag for Gray Thompson and a shower bath for the men to use after coming in from a dip in the ocean.

And what about the club's weekly submarine day? When every stick of furniture was moved out on the sidewalk so someone with a hose could give the inside a thorough sloshing, while the membership frolicked on the street, having a great laugh at what the local residents might be thinking of this primitive but efficient form of housekeeping.

Were they to give all that up in order to live like the bourgeoisie? Hell no!

No wonder the club approved when Paul Coates decided to emphasize the beatnik atmosphere of Synanon for his program by putting bongo drums in the hands of the girls. And bongo drums it was, for a long time after that. Now how could such a crowd be squeezed into Santa Monica's exclusive beach area where celebrated motion picture people had their fine homes?

The answer was that it couldn't. And that it shouldn't. It would be the end of Synanon if it was attempted. Half the club would light out—for sure. Certainly all the recently admitted members would split. Gutter hypes are notoriously timorous and rigid, so that sometimes the mere moving of a piece of furniture will make them flee Synanon like mad, back to the safety of their usual haunts. And as for new addicts, they were hardly likely to come stumbling into a Synanon located in that flossy area. Chuck might as well have signed Synanon's death warrant as signed that lease.

It came to some pretty hot discussions in the club.

"We don't have to be on the bottle forever," Chuck retorted. "Of course we all start life as babies, don't we? But we'd be damned fools if we considered such a beginning a good excuse for staying in our diapers forever. It's time for Synanon to grow up. Learn to live like other people."

Which met the sarcastic response: "Learn to live like other people? You mean like we should learn to hate niggers again? Is that what you mean?"

"Synanon's stand against racial prejudice remains. Of course!" Chuck defended himself. "But that doesn't mean we have to ram our tolerance down the throats of our neighbors. That might do them—and us too!—more harm than good. Inside Synanon—we'll have our usual policy. But outside—we'll have to play it more carefully. For example: there will be no more suede and paddy-chicks bumping hips and carrying on in front of everyone on the beach. That's out! See? That's out!"

"Oh, great! Synanon's policy of no policy is now finished. We now get our policy from outsiders. Is that the general idea? We're going to let their prejudices run our club? How do you like that?"

"It's not the fault of the average American that he's prejudiced," Chuck declared. "It's not *his* fault. That's just the way he happened to be brought up. He's got to be reeducated. Of course. But not insulted."

"In other words, we got to live like they do, just to spare the feelings of these fucking whities? Is that how it's got to be?"

"And that's another thing!" Chuck shouted. "Our language! We're going to have to clean it up! In public. I don't care how you talk in our games, but when strangers are around, we're going to conform!"

Privately Chuck guessed that Synanon might lose as much as a third of its residents, as a result of the move. And that would be bad. But there would be a good side to it: the way would be opened for Synanon to grow again. Something that had become impossible in Ocean Park.

On an evening when Synanon was having a luau on the beach, back of some newly constructed public restrooms, Chuck appeared before the membership and invited them for the first inspection of their new quarters. With the move thus initiated as the climax of a jolly evening when everyone was in gay spirits, the whole thing came as something of a lark. And when Chuck opened up the empty building, they all rushed in, racing through the darkling edifice, laughing and yelling, exclaiming over the size of the bathrooms, disregarding the antique and dirty fixtures that were ready to break down, and joking about the number of people who could be accommodated.

"Here we can pee in line, instead of having to line up to pee!" they shouted.

Perhaps no one experienced this move from Ocean Park to Santa Monica quite so profoundly as Ricky Volkman, a young and attractive woman who was then involved in a marriage that was rapidly going to pieces. She managed nevertheless to earn her living as a full-time teacher while at the same time studying for her master's at U.C.L.A., concentrating on criminology, and it was through a young delinquent with whom she was working that she was led to Synanon, then still in its early stage in the storefronts of Ocean Park.

"I was thunderstruck," Ricky told me. "Literally. The spirit of this little group! The sense of dedication. The tremendous vitality and purpose of these former felons, these former drunks and prostitutes and dope addicts, all crowded into a couple of rooms. They impressed me as being completely visionary, and yet at the same time hardheaded and real. And I was determined that I was going to be allowed to experience one of those fabulous group encounters of theirs which they still called 'synanons with a small s.'"

But Chuck insisted that one experience would be of little value, one must make a routine of it. So Ricky Volkman became the first square to go into the games whole hog.

"I found them tremendously exciting," she told me. "But of course totally meaningless so far as I was concerned. In the first place I had never had any character problem. Never used drugs. Hardly touched alcohol. And in the second place I was far above the level of these people. Intellectually, I mean. After all I had studied for years all sorts of psychological and sociological courses, so I had the notion that the members would be very anxious to hear what I had to say. As for their being of any help to me, that idea never occurred to me.

"And I laughed at the attitude of Synanon people who thought they were going to straighten *me* out. I thought that was both presumptuous and ridiculous. But gradually I began to see that all my knowledge had never been of any benefit to me personally. That it had never had any connection with my real feelings and my private life. That it was just so much brain stuff that I kept accumulating, good for passing exams and eventually for earning a living.

"It wasn't easy for me to come around that far. I suffered. And had no idea what I was suffering from. I never dreamed that I was going through the pangs of withdrawal. How could I even imagine any such thing when I had never taken any dope?

"But gradually I began to understand that I had been taking a certain kind of dope all my life. And that this dope habit had to be kicked. My drug wasn't heroin. It was my false self-image: the image of a lovely and highly educated girl just stuffed with sweetness and light. And when, in the games, the members would begin to slash at that self-image, I couldn't stand it. Life, stripped of all my old and beloved illusions, was too difficult to bear. I found myself aching to get back to my stash. Just like any other dope addict.

"And again and again I would get into my car and drive off—to get as far away from Synanon as I could. And then suddenly it would occur to me: 'You're splitting. Exactly the same as if you were one of the muscle-brains in the animal pen. Absolutely no different!' Then I would remember that HANG TOUGH motto that one of the addicts (who himself later proved unable to hang tough enough) had painted on a ship's life preserver, and I would swing the wheel of my car hard around and drive right back. Determined to see it through."

Ricky also encountered that other problem that everyone faces in Synanon: how to explain the place. How to explain it to relatives, to friends, to her fellow-teachers. Mostly she just kept quiet about it. That was so much simpler. But she knew that it would get around, and she felt that it would be the beginning of endless misunderstandings and endless attempts to clear them up.

There was one person however to whom Ricky felt she had to talk, and that was the principal of the school where she worked. She did not want her connection with Synanon to come to this woman as a rumor or a surprise. Fortunately this happened to be a person of great wisdom. After she had listened to Ricky for a long while, she said: "What you're describing to me is a school for living. That's exactly what your Synanon is. And you must stay there and write your thesis about it. That may be your biggest contribution to the field of education."

So Ricky stuck it out. Through many moments of joy and many moments of crisis. For example, when the pressure from the surrounding community began to manifest itself. And one day an agent from the company that had insured her car visited her and asked embarrassing questions and finally informed her that his firm would not issue her another policy because of the criminal element she frequented.

"It came as a shock to me that I was being spied on," Ricky said. And worse came when the club moved to Santa Monica, and Ricky decided that she too would move from Ocean Park to some apartment that would be near the new Synanon. And discovered that no landlord in the neighborhood would rent her a place. Word had gone out that she was an undesirable. Landlords had heard of the crowds of foul-mouthed men and women who would flock to her premises three evenings a week and yell bloody murder into the wee hours of the morning.

Once again she faced a choice, and this time it was either move in altogether, or get out. Any halfway position was now impossible. She chose to move in. But when Chuck told her how much Synanon was going to charge her for room and board, she felt hurt and angry. Despite all her Synanon experience she still pictured herself as graciously stooping to mingle with people beneath her in class and education, people who ought to be grateful to her for coming to live with them instead of arrogantly asking her to pay.

It was painful to be compelled to acknowledge to oneself that the truth was that she had been receiving free treatment from Synanon long enough, and even now was only being charged for bed and board. And nothing at all for some of the best therapy in the world. There could be no question of who ought to pay whom. Besides she had money—and they didn't. . . .

"I had still another shock that first week in the club at Santa

Monica," Ricky said. "While all the members were busy hustling old furniture, pleading with local merchants for discarded plumbing supplies and cans of discontinued brands of paint and so forth, and working like mad to give the old barn some semblance of livableness, certain citizens of Santa Monica were organizing to get rid of this monstrous thing that had suddenly moved into their midst.

"I was terribly upset by the things I heard and that I read in the papers. And I remember asking Chuck: 'What can they do to us?'

"Chuck said: 'Kick us out—if they can.'

"I said: 'There's going to be a meeting at the City Council. Don't you think the club ought to go there . . . ?'

" 'And let half our population be frightened out of Synanon?' Chuck asked.

" 'Then you at least must go,' I said. 'You must talk to them. Explain Synanon to them.'

"But Chuck shook his head. 'Throw pearls before swine and they will rend you apart.'

" 'Then I'll go!' I cried.

" 'Go ahead,' he said. 'But on one condition only. That you don't speak a word. Just listen. And report back.'

" 'I know shorthand,' I said. 'I'll take notes.'

"That's how it happened that I was the only member of Synanon present that evening when the Citizens Committee made its first move. And what I saw and heard frightened me so that I felt like someone who had sneaked in under false pretenses. I tried to take notes as surreptitiously as possible. I was scared of being thrown out bodily.

"I can still remember a man getting up and yelling: 'Do you want your daughters raped in broad daylight on the streets of your city?'

"And another man shouting: 'Until Synanon is kicked out of Santa Monica, I'm keeping every door, every window in my house locked. Day and night!'

"And one woman getting up and ranting that dope would soon be peddled openly in Santa Monica. And thousands of drug addicts would come swarming into the city. . . .

"And then came property owners who declared one after another that if Synanon remained in Santa Monica, land would soon be totally without value there. 'You homeowners will lose your entire investment because all decent citizens who have any concern for their welfare will move out! What American family would want to raise its children in the midst of jailbirds and prostitutes?'

"I don't know how I managed to keep myself from shouting out loud: 'But it isn't true! None of it is true! I know Synanon. You don't have to be afraid of them. I'm living with them. The girls in my room—I often wake up at night and hear them crying to themselves in the dark. Because they miss their children. Synanon wants these mothers to be with their children—but funds are lacking. . . .'

"That's what I would have screamed out if I hadn't been so scared. It was a nightmare to sit there and hear Santa Monica's City Attorney declare: 'I promise you, citizens of Santa Monica, that I will do everything in my power to remove Synanon from this community. There are legal ways to do it. We have codes here. We have a health and welfare code, a zoning code, a fire department code. We don't have to submit to this. Synanon can be forced out for the violation of any of these rules and regulations. Our office is looking into the matter right now.'

"When I heard this plan for the legal lynching of Synanon being applauded by this mob I couldn't stand it any longer and I ran out and came back to Synanon almost in tears, to tell Chuck about the meeting. But Chuck stopped me in order to call a general assembly so that I could read my notes to the whole membership.

"And Synanon's reaction was beautiful. But just another one of those things that always sets Synanon apart.

"It was immediately agreed that every effort would be made to encourage all citizens of Santa Monica to come to Synanon and see for themselves what it was that they were so afraid of. It was also agreed that any and all visitors would be treated as distinguished guests and Synanon residents would try to supply them with all the information they wanted.

"That was the kind of response I should have been able to bring to that gathering of angry citizens. To be able to say to them: 'There! Look! Compare your behavior to that of the people whom you are trying to kick out of town.'"

What Ricky actually did was to write the first scientific study of Synanon for her master's thesis, a paper that has been published and republished, and is still available in two different college texts. She herself has gone back to the world of squares, is now re-married and is Professor Rita Johnson of Los Angeles State.

She still loves to talk Synanon to anyone who will listen, and to conclude: "I was reborn in Synanon."

But what could the club do about citizens who didn't want information? What could they do about the Santa Monica *Outlook*, for example, which apparently never had any real interest in finding out what Synanon meant. It became that paper's practice to follow the name Synanon with their own interpretation of what Synanon was. They would put in parentheses, like this "(Sin Anonymous)." And Chuck was invariably styled "self-confessed alcoholic."

That helped spur the hysterical rumors about Synanon being some kind of criminal or sex cult. Or perhaps both. Santa Monica's chief of police, Otto Faulkner, told a reporter: "We don't like the type of people Synanon attracts to this community. It attracts felons and narco's."

Any documentation, any verification of such charges? Any statistics of arrests proving it? None. But that never caused this chief of police to withdraw his statement, which was printed and reprinted in the Santa Monica *Outlook*, and harped on again and again by their columnist Louise Randall Pierson.

And in the midst of all this furious verbiage came the repeated assurances of City Attorney Cockins that Synanon would soon be cited for four misdemeanor counts of violations of the California state code regarding hospitals, namely the illegal operation of an establishment for the care and treatment of the insane, the operation of a hospital without a license, the treatment of addicts in a place not specified in the state code, and for violation of the fire prevention rules set up by the state fire marshal. And for good measure one additional violation: that of the Santa Monica zoning code.

What is striking about these charges is of course the hypocrisy involved, because it was obvious that these accusations had nothing to do with what was really troubling these alarmed citizens of Santa Monica. I mean that no citizen was actually afraid that this building constituted much more of a fire hazard with Synanon in it than it had been when the National Guard had been there. And surely only a minimal number of these citizens could have had any serious concerns over the fact that Synanon did not have a regulation hospital license.

All this is too clear to require much discussion.

It is also open to question just how many of these angry citizens were really big property owners, afraid of a drop in the value of their extensive holdings. No doubt, of course, that some few of them were. But hardly a great proportion of them. Thus there was displayed here the ugly fact that a sizable section of a so-called wholesome American community could sanction the use of the rankest kind of hypocrisy by bringing Synanon to the bars of "justice" on cooked-up charges. That getting Synanon out was the main thing. No matter how.

What was it that weighed so heavily on the hearts and pocketbooks of the Citizens Committee and roused them to such a pitch that they decided any stick was good enough to beat down this dog? Was it because Synanon was a place where Negro and white lived in harmony, as if skin color didn't already furnish a sure guide for choosing one's friends and companions? Was it because Synanon was a place where former criminals and non-criminals were so closely mingled that it was impossible to tell who was a jailbird and who wasn't? Was it because Synanon was a place where the sexes sat down together to argue out their most intimate problems without lies or shame?

Perhaps what really bugged these people was the fear that Synanon would expose them to the realization of having wasted their lives in narrow meaningless pursuits that must eventually bring them to an unhappy old age with nothing to show for the years of their existence. While here in Synanon were people living on two dollars a week for total spending money and nevertheless full of elation and spirit because they had freed themselves from the burden that so many of us choose to carry around all our lives, superstitions about sex and skin color, religious bigotry and commercial rat-racing.

In any case Synanon aroused in these citizens some obscure fear that they did not know how to verbalize except in rumors about a horrible sex cult practiced behind its red-brick walls.

This rumor of a nasty sex cult in Synanon was no doubt the reason—at a time when a prominent actor was visiting the place to satisfy his mind about it through personal inspection—why his wife, completely under this bordello illusion, came barging in, half-drunk, swinging her purse like a weapon, and running through the building yelling for her husband. And when she discovered him in Chuck's office engaged in peaceful conversation, she smashed him in the face with her pocketbook so hard that blood dripped from him, and then she went barging out screaming insults to everyone, to leap into her car and drive madly off. And later to take an especially active part in the fight against Synanon.

This actor was just then up for an important part in a scheduled production. And Chuck thought any legal action at this point might injure his public image and cause him to lose the role. So Synanon let the matter pass.

Chuck's query of how Synanon could be a bordello and still file articles of incorporation with the State of California, and also register itself as a non-profit organization with the Income Tax people so as to get official permission to solicit tax-deductible donations, thus apparently hoodwinking hardheaded bureaucrats up and down the United States, this intelligent query seemed somehow to make no impression whatsoever on those who were determined in advance that Synanon must be vile.

Nor did it make any impression on some of these citizens that Chuck repeatedly expressed the simple fact that in Synanon people behaved about sex precisely the way people behaved about it elsewhere. That is to say they fell in love, they fell out of love, they married, they divorced, they had children.

Doesn't everyone?

But because of these persistent rumors that Synanon had some special sex angle, curious visitors always warmed themselves up to the prize question, and this would so infuriate Chuck that when he had heard someone ask for the thousandth time: "What do you do about sex?" he bellowed:

"What do we do about sex? Why we screw! What do you do?"

If Chuck ever expected anyone to reply: "We chop off the sex organs," he was doomed to disappointment. Because invariably what happened was that people blinked for a moment and then had to admit that they handled their sex problem exactly the way Synanon did.

"We're not running a penitentiary here," Chuck would say. "We don't see any reason why people who want to get rid of their drug addiction should be separated according to sex and thus nudged towards homosexuality. Nor are we running a Sunday school. We leave such stupidities to the experts who run this nation's jails and asylums."

In spite of the fact that sex figured in none of the charges against Synanon, it seemed to be the dominating motif of the trial that dragged on for a couple of months in the Municipal Court of Santa Monica, with Judge Hector P. Baida presiding. Judge Baida should obviously have limited the testimony to matters bearing upon the supposed violations, but he overruled the objections of Synanon's lawyer to the sex question, saying: "It may not be pertinent, but it's interesting."

Which wasn't what one can call jurisprudence. But at any rate completely honest. Not hypocritical. And also exactly what the Santa Monica community had indicated that it wanted.

Synanon's lawyer was the best that could be had at the moment, namely one of their own former addicts, a tall, gaunt man who had become a hype while still in high school, but had nevertheless been a good student and had eventually passed his bar. Feeling, perhaps,

that the judge's good will was worth something, he did not fight His
Honor too hard on this issue, even letting him get by with such
notions as this:

"Where women are living on one floor and men on another, something is bound to be going on."

The prosecution was of course more concerned about the sex thing
than any other aspect, and had managed to discover a number of
former addicts who had left Synanon for one reason or another.
Among the most important of these was a man I will call Abe, who
had actually been on the board of directors of Synanon for a while.

Abe claimed that Chuck had often referred to his institution as an
"insane asylum" and had used such words as "Oedipus complex" and
"negative transference," thus lending weight to the charge that Synanon "treated" addicts as "patients" by psychoanalytic methods. And
therefore fell into the hospital category.

But the most important part of his testimony concerned the famous TV room of the brick building. This room, so he claimed, had
been set aside for sex relations. And sex, so he said, was part of the
"treatment," some couples being ordered to stop their sex relations,
while others were urged to indulge. And for this purpose there was
this TV room of moderate size, furnished with couch, draperies,
carpeting, and king-size bed. And also with a TV set which had no
tubes or working parts and was a mere cabinet.

This highly damaging testimony became the sensation of Santa
Monica, where, for a long while, the TV set without any tubes
seemed to be justification enough for any measures the community
might take.

Chuck, who has a kind of sneaking admiration for his dope addicts,
has ever since denied that Abe could be classed as one of them. "He
was no hope-to-die heroin addict," I've heard Chuck say. "Didn't
have the guts for it. Oh, he was addicted all right, but totally without the courage to feed his habit. Among the real hypes he was
despised as a 'dirty cotton boy,' a man without the guts to go out
and steal for himself."

I had never heard that expression before and it intrigued me. "What in hell is a 'dirty cotton boy'?" I asked.

Chuck said: "Well you know how addicts heat up their solution in a bent spoon that makes a kind of tiny saucepan. And then, in order to guard against impurities, use a bit of cotton through which to draw up the solution into the needle. Well it seems that some of the more timid addicts hang around the genuine drug addicts when they are fixing, and beg for these bits of cotton, which they later boil up in order to give themselves a kind of weak fix. A sort of second pressing of the grapes. A near-beer kind of thing. Of course boss hypes despise 'dirty cotton boys,' and tack that expression on people who may or may not deserve it." (But other members of Synanon have told me that Chuck and Reid invented the category of "dirty cotton boys" just to vent their feelings about such betrayers as Abe.)

Another one of these Synanon runaways used by the prosecution was Art Bandler, who gave the same sort of testimony as Abe. And it was so plain to the members of Synanon who were in court that day that Art had just taken a hefty fix that despite the damaging testimony he gave Chuck nudged him in passing, saying: "You'd better get yourself back to Synanon."

Basing himself on such suspect testimony, the mayor of Santa Monica was led to say—on a Tom Duggan TV program—that Synanon was conducting a house of prostitution, for which Synanon promptly sued him for two hundred thousand dollars.

On a rebuttal program Tom Duggan asked Reid about the mayor's contention that since Synanon has only one woman for every three men, the board of directors regulates all sexual activities, and Reid replied: "The mayor is following the testimony of some disgruntled runaway addicts. One of them, for example, Art Bandler, was actually loaded while on the witness stand."

This statement made Tom Duggan furious. He demanded from Reid an immediate retraction. "You can't know whether this Art Bandler was loaded with dope when he was on the witness stand. You can't possibly know that. And you're jeopardizing the license of this station, and putting me in danger of losing my program, by naming someone on the air as a using drug addict!"

Reid insisted: "But he was loaded . . . !"

Which only made Tom Duggan all the more boiling mad and all the more insistent that Reid must immediately withdraw this accusation. Whereupon Reid said: "Well, then, may I rephrase what I said? And put it in the form of things that no one can question."

"You'd better!" said Tom Duggan.

Reid then said: "There can be no doubt that Art Bandler was on the witness stand and that he testified against Synanon. Testimony to which the mayor of Santa Monica obviously gave complete credence. Shortly after that, within a period of a couple of hours or so, this same Art Bandler came to Synanon's door, crying and contrite, claiming that he was forced into the position of having to testify against us, and begging us for our help.

"We decided that Art Bandler needed our immediate attention no matter how badly he had behaved just a couple of hours before. If he was not actually a using drug addict, he certainly gave every indication of being one, and in fact was then going into what certainly looked like withdrawal. I mean he sweated, he vomited, he trembled, and complained of hot and cold flashes, he had diarrhea. . . . If all this was just acting, it was one of the most convincing performances ever put on."

All Santa Monica seemed convulsed with this question of sex in Synanon.

Jeanne Camaño, who was at that time the only member of Synanon capable of acting as a legal secretary, was very worried about the way things were going at the trial, and the way feeling in the community was being built up against Synanon.

"All this sex exposé!" she said to me. "We should be doing something to stop it."

But Synanon's lawyer kept reassuring her: "Sexual misconduct is not what we're being tried for. So it can have no possible bearing on the outcome."

But of course it did. For it made it practically impossible for the judge, no matter how favorably inclined he may have been, to let the club off completely. You can't trifle with sex in the average American community. Sub rosa, yes. But not publicly.

On the occasion of his own inspection of Synanon, Judge Baida went around making such comments as this: "Well, it certainly doesn't look like a hospital here." And evidently it didn't. There were no hospital beds or hospital equipment and nobody that looked like a patient or needed a nurse's attention. In fact there were no nurses or orderlies, or bedpans or anything like that in the place.

And then Judge Baida sniffed the air and said: "Doesn't smell like a hospital either." And obviously there was no reason why it should. Everybody was busy working around the place, and no one was under any medication.

But then the judge wanted to know about the members: "You're curing them, aren't you?"

Chuck replied that the club was simply doing its best to furnish the members with an environment that would keep them from wanting to use dope.

To which Judge Baida replied: "Well that's what I would call curing them, wouldn't you?"

Chuck said: "We try to keep them free of drugs."

Judge Baida said: "Exactly. So you must be a hospital after all."

"The whole thing is just a battle of semantics," Chuck said. "Define hospital one way, and of course it will include Synanon. Define it another way, and of course Synanon is not a hospital."

What Judge Baida did was find Synanon guilty on two counts. And not guilty on three. The usual attempt to appear impartial while being anything but. What mattered was that Synanon was found to be treating dope addiction in violation of the state code, and was therefore operating a hospital without a license. And as such was ipso facto guilty of violating the Santa Monica zoning code and the judge thereupon gave Synanon until May 10 to vacate.

This victory in court encouraged the forces arrayed against Synanon. And Synanon's lawyer got busy with steps for a retrial. But an unexpected fatality made it impossible for either side to have a transcript of the proceedings. The two sides therefore had to get together to prepare what is called an "engrossed statement," that is to say a mutually agreed upon version of what had taken place at the trial.

"I just couldn't understand why our lawyer allowed so much of that sex testimony to be put into the engrossed statement," Jeanne Camaño told me. "But he still kept insisting that we were being tried for being a hospital, and that was the only thing that should concern us."

He was wrong. Because no sooner was the engrossed statement ready than the Citizens Committee had a hundred and fifty thousand copies reproduced and mailed to every resident of Santa Monica! The whole town now had documented evidence of Synanon's sex habits.

Self-styled authorities on Synanon now began to pop up all over Santa Monica; for example, one expert who made the startling discovery that both Synanon and syndicate began with the same three letters S, Y, N. What better proof, he inferred, did anyone want that the underworld syndicate had a hand in the formation of Synanon, and that this was the opening wedge for syndicated crime to come into Santa Monica.

Thus equipped, this profound research scholar took to the lecture platform, and in reply to a question from someone in his audience, hazarded the guess that Synanon might be getting some of its financing from the use of its female members for erotic purposes. It happened that a gentleman had come to the meeting with a tape recorder and the speaker had cheerfully agreed to its use. This gentleman then gave his tape to Synanon for the club to do with it as they might please.

Synanon chose to sue, and this self-made authority's lawyer had to advise his client to abandon the lecture platform and subsequently to settle out of court by paying Synanon a substantial sum.

But that took a number of years.

And meanwhile the finances of Synanon, poorly supported by the syndicate, and even more poorly by its erotic girls, went from bad to worse.

"Of course our girls," Chuck said, "deserved respect, not calumny, since they had been earning fancy livings on the outside, but had voluntarily chosen to accept poverty in order to clean themselves up. Apparently a lot of Santa Monicans didn't see it that way.

"Meanwhile we lived from minute to minute," Chuck told me. "Poverty was killing us, but we refused to die. In fact poverty was a weapon that some Santa Monicans used against us, hoping it would force us out of business. For example there was a wealthy motion picture actor who had a fine beach residence not far to the north of us. He was also a member of the Friars Club and learning that a group of people who met at the Friars had got together to guarantee our five hundred dollars a month rent, he influenced them to break their promise.

"This group of sponsors simply quit. Kicked their promise into the gutter. Didn't even have the courtesy to inform us of their decision. So there we were, in our club, straining every nerve and muscle to feed our people, and not even aware that we had been abandoned. And as the rent became due and then overdue, and no money reached us, I tried to get in touch with these gentlemen, but they were unavailable. I telephoned, I wrote. All I got was a secretarial runaround. And finally not even that. Just a complete blackout.

"We have around the club a phrase about dope addicts, that they will always burn you. I discovered that so-called gentlemen addicted to nothing but money could do that too.

"All sorts of misfortunes piled up on us. For example, one of our sponsors, on whom I could always count for a few dollars to pay utility bills and so forth, went out on the town for a good time one night and took it into his drunken head to visit Synanon in the middle of the night. With a couple of whores on his arm! You can imagine what the appearance at that ungodly hour of a white-shirted gentleman from the gay outside world did to my poor frightened addicts and prostitutes. And what might have been the actions of the police if they had come in at that moment. Naturally I had to throw him out fast. And of course never got a penny from him again.

"The five hundred dollars a month for rent became a problem almost too huge to contemplate. The first thing I did was break it up in two installments. Our landlord was a bit suspicious, but he took the two hundred and fifty and expressed himself as willing to wait another couple of weeks for the rest.

"The next thing I did was canvas the joint to see what members we could send out to earn some money for us on the outside. Herman went out to work for a meat-packing company. Pete went out on another job. Some of the girls got jobs in local department stores on the sales force.

"It was a dangerous practice. We really didn't have any members yet who were so secure in their new clean life that we could trust them to pick up a sizable check at the week's end and not rush off to see their connection. And those few members who were really solid, we needed them inside, because it was their ability that we depended on to run our foundation. After all we had a cageful of monkeys. Somebody had to help take care of them. I couldn't do everything myself. But that was the chance we had to take. We needed those salaries. Desperately.

"You've got to remember that we had not yet developed the cohesiveness that we have today. A cohesiveness that—at least partially —we owe to the fact that we can give some of our best members some reward beyond mere freedom from their old habit. I mean things like a private room, better furniture, the use of a car. Reflect that despair had already played a great role in driving these people to drugs and to crime, and if we remained forever unable to give them anything else but more despair, inevitably the weaker spirits must be driven back to the street. And to the spike.

"You've no idea how frightened addicts are, and how necessary the feeling of security is to their effort to throw off their habit. And here we were, living amidst terror. A lousy write-up in the press, or a medical man openly expressing the opinion that our methods were medically unsound and even harmful, would sweep through the club like an invasion of monsters from Mars. Everyone was convinced that the club's last hour had struck. That the place would be pad-locked by the police. And invariably such bad news would be fol-lowed by some members running off. With the result that our population refused to grow. The best we could manage was to keep it fluctuating between fifty and seventy. We just couldn't break that number seventy.

"In spite of the many friends who came to our Saturday nights—and too often these were our same old supporters doggedly demon-strating their loyalty by coming back week after week—the club felt that it had on its back the whole social structure. The Department of Corrections was after us. The newspapers. The courts. The City Attorney. The police. The lunatic fringe. All the supposedly nice-smelling people."

13

Jeanne said to me: "I don't think Chuck ever slept during those terrible months. He was so worried about the club. Every night he would report to us what had happened and then invite questions. And at the noon seminars he would lecture to us about our Synanon philosophy. Or about anything. Just to keep up our spirits. I remember once that he had us going for a whole week on the question of firing a bullet from a moving train. And whether it would go just as far if you fired it in the direction of the locomotive as it would if you fired it in the direction of the caboose.

"And I remember him saying: 'Well that's a much more important problem than the reactions of the citizens of Santa Monica! One is sense and the other is nonsense.'

"I remember too how every week he would summon a general meeting and he'd predict how many people would leave. And he'd end up saying something like this: 'Well, if I'm left with only ten people, Synanon must go on existing. And right here in Santa Monica!' "

"Of course it wasn't quite as black as Chuck pictures it," Reid told me. "I mean it was rough all right. But we could always get a laugh out of the antics of these nice-smelling people. Now I don't want you to get the impression, Guy, that Synanon doesn't want people to smell just as nice as they can, but people who are concerned only with how nice they smell and not at all about how their behavior stinks—that's what I'm referring to.

"For instance—and I'm thinking right now of this question you've been discussing: of how you explain Synanon. That's all right when you're talking to people who are trying to understand. But suppose you're dealing with people who are resolutely determined not to understand. What then?

"I recall, for example, a time when the Citizens Committee had scheduled another Synanon discussion at the Santa Monica City Council. You know it was no problem to do that. The City Council met every Tuesday evening, and all you had to do was put yourself on the agenda.

"The Citizens Committee had already had five such evenings and I can't imagine why they should have wanted another, but I went there with Vince, just to see what would happen. I remember the room was crowded and we sat in the back and I do believe that if we had let ourselves go, Vince and I would have ended with belly-aches, the proceedings were so excruciatingly funny. Of course it was painful too, because our image as residents of Synanon was involved. And that image was getting mangled.

"The Citizens Committee was represented by some seven or eight people, and since I lived in the club almost twenty-four hours a day, and since I never forget a face, I can say with almost one hundred percent assurance that only two of them had come to visit the club, and neither of them had stayed there more than a terrorized ten or fifteen minutes.

"One woman, who if she didn't wear tennis shoes, ought to have done so to conform to the pattern, got up and declared that she was a nurse. 'I'm a registered nurse,' she kept repeating. 'I'm qualified to understand such places as Synanon. Now let me first tell you how Synanon got its name.'

"Vince and I waited breathlessly. 'It comes from the state of Sinaloa, in Mexico,' she explained. 'Synanon has huge plantations of poppies, opium poppies, in Sinaloa. Vast fields growing nothing but poppies. And when these poppies are in bloom, the petals are gathered and then crushed and made into a paste . . .'

"Vince and I thought we'd die suppressing our laughter. But she went right on describing the process of packaging this paste and shipping it to Synanon, where the pure heroin was extracted, and then turned over to agents who distributed it all over the city of Santa Monica to school kids.

"Guy, I swear to you, that this incredible nonsense was terminated by thundering applause from all the councilmen and the visitors. A real ovation. And of course, what could we do? What could we do but applaud along with the rest. And even louder. Because we had never heard anything so excruciatingly ridiculous.

"More nonsense followed. For instance I can still remember one venerable gentleman who rose to announce dramatically: 'I've been there. I visited that place. I was taken on a tour of their establishment. And what I saw!'

"Then he sat down. Please believe me. He didn't say anything else. Just that: 'And what I saw!' And another thunderous ovation.

"There was a general hush when another member of the Citizens Committee described how he had walked past the place at night and had seen the lights turned down low, and how he had realized then that these people were up to no good.

"One woman felt that she must get into the act and rose to explain that she lived at—I forget what street and what number, but I remember rapidly figuring out that it was at least thirty blocks or more away from Synanon. And yet she began to bemoan the good old days of Santa Monica before Synanon entered this paradise. 'On nice evenings,' she said, 'I used to enjoy going for a walk, out in the fresh air. I can't do that anymore. That's finished. We'll never be able to do that anymore.'

"She really—I swear to God—got a tremendous hand. The crowd overflowed with sympathy for this poor old woman deprived of her former innocent walks by the presence of Synanon—two miles away from her home!

"And that's when I had to get up. I was so aroused that without consciously willing anything, I just surfaced like a swimmer and hot words began to pour out of me.

" 'I've never heard of such insanity!' I exclaimed. 'I'm absolutely appalled. I really am. I want to inform you good people that I was a dope addict for twenty years. Yes. Right here in this community. And the police never bothered me. Never! I mean, not once.

" 'I could take you people out, right now, and show you twenty or more dope peddlers carrying on their business within a few blocks of here. And without any interference by the police. And with innocent people walking the streets by the dozens and totally unaware.

" 'I bought my first supply of heroin on the grounds of the John Adams Junior High—here in Santa Monica. And twenty years later I bought my last dope on the campus of the Santa Monica City College, a mile or so from here. And during all those years as a dope addict, when I had at times a habit that cost me as much as five hundred dollars a day, I stole every nickel of it from good citizens such as you—and never once did I see the inside of a Santa Monica jail on a drug addiction charge. Never once!

" 'And now I want you good people to contrast the unfettered and undisturbed life I lived as a drug addict, in Santa Monica, with my present life—in Synanon. I never steal now. I'm absolutely free of any drug addiction. I'm a law-abiding citizen. And what is the result of my reform? The result is that I've never been in such trouble with the law. Our club is threatened every day with eviction. I am attacked in your press. I am maligned right here in your council chambers. And a respectable old lady tells us that she is afraid to stick her nose outdoors—now—now when I'm living clean—whereas before when I was robbing right and left and loaded with dope— this woman felt absolutely safe.

" 'I can only conclude from your attacks on Synanon—that you are all in favor of my returning to my old life as a dope addict. And that if I should do that, you'd all feel much more comfortable. And this lady could then go back to her evening strolls with a complete sense of security. Is that really the impression that you want to leave with me?'

"I sat down amidst total silence. And I want to say this, Guy: it was not the silence of shock. Definitely not. These people were not shaken out of their beliefs, not for one moment. Their silence was simply the silence of people who had patiently suffered an interruption in their talk, as if, for instance, a noisy airplane had temporarily prevented them from conversing. And now that I was finished, they could resume their own kind of babble. The kind they wanted to speak, and to hear spoken.

"I was so put out, I can't tell you. Because all the while I was thinking of myself as coming through with a historic oration. I was Thomas Paine reborn, trumpeting out the truth, with all the fervor of righteous indignation. And the reception I got was more than embarrassing. It was humiliating."

Since the Santa Monica zoning battle did not succeed in destroying Synanon, though it came awfully close, some members have occasionally conjectured that a number of good factors may have come out of the struggle. In the first place, of course, the publicity. What started out as an almost purely local issue, by the flames it generated, drew the attention first of Los Angeles, and then of the whole nation. This could hardly have happened—at any rate not so soon—if Santa Monica had paid no attention to the new tenant in their midst.

The Los Angeles *Mirror* with four articles by Art Berman, and then the Los Angeles *Times* with another series, started such national magazines as *Downbeat, The Nation, Time* magazine, and so forth, to publish their own reports. With the result that a group of some sixty people in this small town became far more important than its numbers would seem to have merited at that time.

And this happened not only because Santa Monica was opposed to Synanon, but also because Santa Monica was *for* Synanon. "We could never have come through this battle if Santa Monica had been one hundred percent against us," Chuck said to me. "Naturally Santa Monica also supported us. Merchants gave us food and supplies, citizens offered us their old furniture, a couple of dentists volunteered their services.

"But that doesn't mean that the benefits outweighed the harm," Chuck argued. "And that Synanon is therefore always spoiling for a fight, as some people seem to think. We gave up in Westport when we saw that it was going to be a long-drawn-out affair. We got slapped down there in another zoning fight. Our lawyers had figured out a smart angle for carrying on the fight, but we said, 'No! We're pulling out.'

"We were invited to come into Detroit and when the same battle began there, I phoned Jack Hurst to pick up his marbles and come home. The result was that the city authorities quickly solved the zoning problem for us.

"We don't crave hostility wherever we go. We had it in Santa Monica, then in Malibu, then in San Francisco, and then in Tomales. We're tired of hostility. And now it's started up in this little town near San Diego where a hundred and fifty people have got together to stop us from buying St. John's Seminary which the Catholic Church is planning to abandon, and for the purchase of which we had just gone into escrow. I said immediately: 'Let's call the bishop and tell him we're no longer interested in the deal. That we have no intention of having our Synanon children exposed to the hatred of the surrounding community.'"

No matter how many years have now passed since the Santa Monica fight, Chuck can still feel the scars of those first two terrible years, and still cannot forget that he is probably the only man in the United States who ever had to go to jail for a zoning violation. That honor was reserved for the head of Synanon.

"I had never been locked up before," Chuck told me. "I was treated very nicely, but I couldn't take it. I regressed right back to infancy. I was literally terrorized. I caught the heaviest cold I ever had in my life and coughed myself into such paroxysms that I ripped the muscles of my groin and got myself a hernia that I eventually had to have surgically repaired."

If it were possible, however, to strike some sort of balance of good and bad in the matter of Synanon and Santa Monica, Dr. Bernie Casselman would certainly count as one of the fortunate assets that Synanon acquired as a result.

"I read the pro-Synanon articles in the *Independent*, and then the anti-Synanon articles in the Santa Monica *Evening Outlook*," he told me, "and they were so different, so opposed, so inconsistent with each other that I decided I had to find out for myself."

Bernie (if he hasn't recently lost weight) is as round as a balloon and as impishly gay as a fairy-tale hobgoblin. And he considers his Synanon experience the greatest thing that ever happened in his life.

"All I did was reach for the phone, get Synanon on the wire, and ask to speak to Chuck," Bernie said. "I said to Chuck: 'Look. I want to find out for myself which paper is telling the truth.'

"And Chuck said: 'Well come on down and have lunch with us.'

"That's how easy it was, Guy. Just a phone call. Anyone could have done it.

"I was working then with the Ross-Loos Medical Group in Santa Monica and Synanon was only a hop, skip, and jump away. And I can't tell you how impressed I was. The place was just tingling with vitality. So full of inner strength and conviction. I don't have words that can express it.

"And these people still had no doctor. No medical attention whatsoever was available to them.

"I went back immediately to the Ross-Loos place and picked up everything that was lying around, I mean in the way of bandages, ointments, tape, and I said to Chuck: 'Give me a room, and I'm your official medical man.' They quickly set aside a room for me that was later to become as famous as the TV room. And there, at stated hours, I opened my clinic for Synanon people.

"It wasn't so much at first, but eventually it began taking up half of my time. And I had a living to earn. Because Ross-Loos severed me from their payroll the moment they heard I was having anything to do with Synanon.

"So it was kind of rugged. For me. But never was there anything so exciting. I had more experience and more practice in a few years than most doctors can boast of in a lifetime. Everything except money.

"But I loved it. And the stories I could tell you. Of people who came into Synanon behaving like animals, and were gradually turned into human beings.

"And the problems of the recovering addict. How he goes through all the degrees of coming back to life. For example, he's been anesthetized so long he has lost the experience of feeling water passing through his urethra when he micturates. Now suddenly he feels— I mean really *feels*—the sensation of urinating, and it frightens him to death. Quick he's got to consult Dr. Bernie! Every itch, every pimple—with them it's like it was their last agony. Such hypochondria!

"And cyclothymia! One minute they're on top of the world. The next minute they're at the end of their rope. It's all over.

"And I could still cry when I think of Morris Hodges walking into my clinic and saying: 'Do you mind treating a colored fellow?'

"Oh, Synanon was guilty, of course. You know that. Why I myself, just for fun, one day counted forty-five electrical connections on one line. Everything they did with that house was illegal. They never took out a single building permit. Couldn't. Didn't have the cash. That place was just jammed with building code violations.

"But it was a wonderful practice, Guy. And I enjoyed every minute of it. Such crazy, wonderful people."

"But I understand that you have now severed your connection with Synanon. I mean medically," I said.

"Guy, I couldn't take it anymore. For years I was their only doctor. And there was so much to do that I finally had to close the clinic and let Synanon bring their sick to me at my office, where I had the proper equipment. Which would have been fine if Synanon hadn't grown. It got so I'd open up my office in the morning and there they were. The whole waiting room was filled. With these non-paying patients. And the people that pay, seeing my waiting room so crowded, would leave.

"To save a little money and make it possible for me to go on being Synanon's doctor, I gave up my apartment, moved my bed into my office. And as you see, I still live here. My office is still my home.

"But just as soon as Synanon began to have some other medical volunteers, I started cutting down my Synanon practice. But never completely. Not to see the old Synanon bunch coming to my office, why that would mean losing contact with the most meaningful experience of my life. No. I'll never do that.

"It's been trouble and it's been fun, and I've loved every second of it. You know of course that no doctor's office in town has been broken into so often as mine. Did you know that? Why where else would an addict go looking for drugs when he splits from Synanon because his craving has gotten the better of him? What other medical office does he know as well as mine? So here is where he comes, at night, looking for opiates. That's why you see all these locks on my doors.

"Some of these crazy splittees even think they can come back here and get free treatment from me. Just like they were still in Synanon. But I won't permit that. I tell them: 'Go get yourself reinstated. Then I'll look at you.' And you know what? Some of them have done precisely that. Just on my say-so.

"Look at these files. Just look at them. Synanon patients. Nothing but Synanon patients in all these drawers. Look. Drawer after drawer. Packed. Why, Guy, you could spend the rest of your life here. There's enough material here for a hundred novels. Oh, the stories I could tell. And the problems!

"Like removing tattoos. From the girls. You know that addicts have themselves tattooed to hide the marks of the hypodermic needle. Later, when they clean up—the men don't mind so much— but the women! Especially when they expect to get married—and they want respectability. I've taken off any number of tattoos. I've made myself a kind of expert in removing them without leaving a visible scar. A lot of Synanon girls are very grateful to me for that. A lot of them. Ask Arline. She'll tell you.

"Yes, the craziest stories. From people like Jack Kovner, for instance. Do you know Jack?"

"Of course I know Jack Kovner," I said. "Nice guy. Very bright. And articulate. I've heard him give a talk."

"Wasn't that way when he came to Synanon," Bernie said.

"Frothed at the mouth. Body shook like a leaf. Limped. Was always falling downstairs. Or knocking himself against tables. His body was a mess of bruises. And he was coming in to see me every day.

"Finally I said to him: 'I'm committing you to the County Hospital. Unless you stop this drooling and this shambling and keeling over. One more bruise and out you go!'

"He stopped. Just like that. Straightened out. Wasn't going to let anyone take him out of Synanon. Oh, I could go on forever. . . ."

And Bernie very nearly did. For over five hours he talked and laughed about his Synanon experiences while I took notes frantically.

"I've just scratched the surface," he said finally, "but if I don't stop talking I'll work myself into a real nostalgia for my Synanon days, and I'll go right back there, and then I'll be in the same soup I was before, not knowing if I'll make enough to pay the rent."

But that final word didn't stop Bernie from talking Synanon to me all the way out to my car, telling me about an imaginary sexual condition that seems to trouble almost all Synanon men. "But don't you go using that in your book unless you've checked with Synanon," he warned me.

"Oh, no problem about that," I said. "The world's been full of secret societies, but Synanon is the world's first absolutely anti-secret society. That's what makes it such a radical new departure."

"Synanon," Bernie said, "is Chuck. Because Chuck founded it in Ocean Park and because Chuck saved it in Santa Monica. So you check, and don't get me into any trouble with the best friends I've got."

Whether the zoning fight in Santa Monica can be considered as compensated for by such devotion as Bernie's, I don't know. But there are others who can be thrown into the scales. "Dede" Harvey, for example, Reverend C. Mason Harvey, minister at Santa Monica's huge First Presbyterian Church, whose nickname doesn't come from his being a Doctor of Divinity, but from his having been born in China where he was his parents' second son, and in China the word for second is *dede*.

During the height of the attack on Synanon, he invited members of the club to come and speak to his Sunday school classes, and had them meet members of his congregation. And he returned these visits by bringing his Sunday school students to sing carols at Synanon on Christmas Eve.

When Art Berman interviewed him for the Los Angeles *Mirror*, Dede made the following statement to him: "There is a very effective whispering campaign here against Synanon. The testimony in court was from people who had been to Synanon and left. And they had an ax to grind.

"I think I know what is going on there. Whenever you get people of both sexes together, there is bound to be some sexual promiscuity. But if I've got to start kicking out of town all the people having illicit sexual activities, I'm afraid my congregation would be sadly depleted. And you may quote me."

Several times Dede preached sermons on Synanon, even though he had in his congregation many inveterate Synanon haters. Efforts were made by the board of elders to pry Dede out of his ministry—which caused Synanon to describe Dede as a lion being devoured by Christians.

When he heard the oft-repeated pronouncement of the chief of police, that Synanon attracts felons and narco's, Dede said: "I hope my church will attract sinners. There's no percentage in preaching to the converted."

At one time, during the struggle, the Democratic Club of Santa Monica scheduled a panel discussion on Synanon at Roosevelt High, with Chuck, Reid, Dede Harvey, and Bernie Casselman on the platform. And Synanon people had set up a table in the rear with some of the club's first literature, which consisted of reprints of favorable articles that had appeared in various magazines.

No sooner had the meeting started, than a tree-trunk of a man leaped up and boomed: "The flag! You forgot to salute the flag!"

Another bull-necked gentleman immediately swept the Synanon literature from the table and started wiping his shoes on it, yelling like a banshee.

Reverend Harvey quickly sprang to his feet and started to lead the audience in the salute. Whereupon this bull-necked individual began scrutinizing everyone, and suddenly screamed for the proceedings to stop.

"Wait! Wait! There's a man over there who isn't pledging!"

The whole hall was compelled to pause and to look around to see who this traitor might be who was deliberately exhibiting signs of not pledging.

"You! You over there! You weren't pledging!"

A gentleman feeling himself indicated, spoke up: "You mean me?"

"Yes, you! I been watching you. You didn't have your hand on your heart!"

"Oh, really? I wasn't aware of it."

"Come on, now. You can't get away with that! What are you doing here anyhow?"

"I live here. In Santa Monica."

"You live here? And what do you do?"

"I'm a professor of history. American history. I teach at U.C.L.A."

It was this kind of super-patriotic madness that troubled Dede Harvey and caused him to wonder if it might not be leading to some sort of mob violence. Which he therefore sought to head off by publicly announcing that he and his wife and children were moving into Synanon to reside there for three months. And they did.

It was another step in the development of a warm relationship between the Presbyterian minister and Synanon that eventually—four or five years later—led Dede Harvey to ask for an indeterminate leave of absence from his church so that he might join Synanon in a more official capacity as head of the San Diego square game club, a club that now numbers three hundred players, mostly from the nearby colleges, and has an exploding waiting list of people who cannot yet be accommodated.

Present that same evening was Jack Roberts, co-owner of a prosperous Los Angeles advertising firm. It happened that a neighbor of Jack's in Malibu was Professor Donald Cressey, the criminologist who had become Synanon's first honorary dope fiend.

Professor Cressey drew Jack's attention to the struggling organization whose club he passed every day when going to work, and Jack was immediately attracted to the Synanon program and the fascinating characters who were dedicating themselves to keeping it from being crushed.

"I felt that I could be of most help in the field I knew, that of publicity," Jack told me. "I designed for Synanon its initial S, and afterwards I coined the phrase 'Help Synanon Help.' I also began the S.O.S. group, that is to say the Sponsors of Synanon, and among the people I involved was my friend Fred Nicholas."

It was this Fred Nicholas who, at that same meeting, watched in dismay as one woman screamed that Synanon people were human garbage, and that she did not want to live in a town where there was human garbage.

"I'm against garbage!" she yelled. "I'm against communism! I'm against Synanon!" And she worked herself up to such a pitch that she finally burst out: "I'm against everything!"

"I got really upset about this human garbage talk," Fred said to me. "And after the meeting I went up to Chuck and I said: 'I'd like to help.'

"Chuck said: 'What's your line?'

" 'I'm a lawyer,' I said.

" 'We need you,' Chuck said. 'Desperately.'

"That's how I got involved. And Synanon did really need some fresh thinking in their legal case. Which was chaotic. Their own addict lawyer was a good enough man with an adequate grasp of the law, but I saw right away that what was needed was not more law, but less.

"And another volunteer lawyer, Al Matthews, who had given generously of his time and talent, was also pushing—as I saw it—in the wrong direction.

"It seemed to me that the first necessity was to gain time. I trusted that with the passage of time the local population would get used to Synanon and recognize that their fears were unfounded. I therefore applied for a zoning variance. This was after all the normal thing to do. I knew of course that we would be denied, since the zoning board was not about to clash with the rest of the governing bodies of Santa Monica. But we had the right to use permissible provisions of the law to stall off things for a while.

"Then the Building and Safety people got into the fight with a two-pronged attack, listing violations of their code and giving us the choice of either bringing the clubhouse up to code or getting out. They also filed suit to abate a nuisance, declaring that Synanon was illegally running a hospital.

"To bring that ancient building up to code would have cost a fortune. I replied to these threats with a cross complaint, asking for an injunction to stop the board from harassing us, citing the Fourteenth Amendment to the Bill of Rights, which guarantees equal protection of the laws to all. We also filed a motion to consolidate both charges against Synanon and have them heard before a judge. This was granted.

"When inspectors began to swarm through the club to specify violations, I responded by pointing out that such violations existed all over Santa Monica and that it was clearly prejudicial to single us out when similar conditions elsewhere were being ignored. I demanded that all Santa Monica be subjected to the same scrutiny.

"That did it. Property owners became alarmed. The Building and Safety officials withdrew their charges. And the scheme to get rid of Synanon by this method fell through.

"That didn't mean that Santa Monica was giving up. In fact about this time Chuck had to go to jail. But meanwhile I was getting ready for another delaying tactic. I went to see Attorney Cockins for a friendly talk, and told him frankly that I had come to work out some arrangement. I told him that I could well understand the kind of pressure under which he was working and that I wanted to get both of us off the hook. If the city would give Synanon enough time, Synanon would get busy to relocate itself.

"Attorney Cockins agreed immediately that if Synanon would submit to the city a bona fide plan for its relocation outside of Santa Monica, he would see to it that the authorities would give us ample time.

"I quickly found a site near the Nike base on the hills above Malibu where we could lease twenty-five acres. And we immediately opened an escrow on the property with a check for a thousand dollars, the deal of course contingent on obtaining a permit to build there. . . . Remember Charlie Beckham?"

"Yes, of course," I said. "The architect who was in the very early square games."

"Exactly," Fred said. "I had him draw up for us plans for a group of buildings, and I took these plans and perspective drawings to City Hall in Santa Monica. I explained that we were obviously not going to build there and then find that we couldn't occupy the place because we were out of zone. This area had actually been zoned for residential purposes although nobody in his right mind would want to put up his home there. So we were applying to the Los Angeles Zoning Board for a variance. And I asked Attorney Cockins to let us have four years time to make our move. He cut us down to two.

"You were there—at the Malibu rezoning hearing, weren't you?" Fred said. I nodded, and he went on: "Then you remember that it was the same old Citizens Committee stuff, except this time the citizens were from Malibu.

"So we lost. And our Malibu plans were out. But it didn't throw us back to where we had been. Because we had demonstrated sincere efforts of trying to relocate. And whenever Santa Monica would start harassing us again, I could come back with some sparring action to hold them in check.

"Meanwhile time was doing more for us than the law. Since business remained good, and real estate in Santa Monica kept going up and up, the fury against Synanon began to die down. And over the years Synanon made a number of moves that helped soothe the situation. For example: when Synanon was invited to open a branch in San Diego, it was decided that no addict would kick in Santa Monica. Kicking addicts would have to go to the San Diego facility.

That stopped all the nonsense about 'cold turkey' and the cruelty of it, and the accusation of being a hospital in a wrong zone.

"Synanon also stopped the use of the red brick building as a dormitory and began to operate it more as a clubhouse and office building, a place where members could eat and hold meetings. Inasmuch as the beach area is full of clubhouses, the zoning department couldn't very well object to us on that ancient basis any longer.

"It was never anything but a very raucous minority that had fought us in Santa Monica," Fred concluded, "and now they find themselves running out of steam. In fact I think Santa Monica rather likes us now. Admires us for our guts. For having fought our way through. Even the chief of police now has to agree that Synanon does not constitute any hazard to the community. Because of the better feelings established, we dropped our libel action against the mayor for the remarks he made about us on television. I won't say that everything is sweetness and light, but the Santa Monica *Outlook* has certainly moderated its fury against us, and I think I can describe the situation as calm and likely to remain so."

Chuck had the same feelings. He hadn't forgotten how he had once been shoved into jail in Santa Monica, but he too thought that passions had abated. Indeed he was so convinced of it that when the possibility began to be bruited about that Synanon might acquire possession of the big Del Mar Club building, one of the largest and handsomest properties on the beach, Chuck said that he expected no trouble because the lunatic fringe had lost the hold it had once exercised on the citizenry and the power structure of Santa Monica.

The truth was quite the contrary. The anti-Synanon forces hadn't given up in the least, there had just been no occasion for them to erupt. For several years Synanon's growth had been concealed from Santa Monica because the expansion had taken place in San Francisco, in Detroit, in New York, and so forth. Now that growth suddenly manifested itself dramatically right in the heart of Santa Monica when Synanon took over a building whose value was being estimated at three and a half million dollars. And once again one could see the truth of the old saying that the Bourbons (or their miniature equivalents of today) never learn and never forget.

Immediately the Santa Monica *Outlook* screamed out huge headlines. And once again that paper's editors and columnists began to denounce Synanon as a fraud and an unwholesome blight on the family community of Santa Monica.

The July 19, 1967, edition contained the following editorial paragraph: "In announcing his acquisition of the Del Mar Club, promoter Charles Dederich said he doesn't anticipate any hostile reaction from our community, because the 'lunatic fringe' that opposed Synanon in the past has largely disappeared. We would correct Mr. Dederich; what has disappeared is another chunk of Santa Monica's good character."

The old Citizens Committee bounced back to life and quickly scheduled meetings with the City Council in order to slaver against Synanon. And City Attorney Cockins was once more on deck to hold out the promise of a legal lynching, just as he had done years before, but this time he couched it in the form of a demand that the state Attorney General's office launch "a full-scale investigation into the Synanon Foundation's status as a tax-free non-profit corporation."

And Mayor Pro Tem Kenneth Wamsley invited the enemies of Synanon to spy on the organization. He assured them that "if you know their people are breaking the law and tell us, we'll hit them where they hurt. But that's part of your responsibility, to help the police get the proof." Thus he implied that the guilt was certain, only the crackdown would have to wait until the people brought in the necessary evidence.

This public branding of Synanon as a quasi-outlaw came at a meeting where there was much screaming against Synanon as a "bunch of freeloaders" who are thumbing their noses at society while flooding the town with "drug addicts, deviates, prostitutes, and similar undesirables." The result was to encourage all the hooligans of the neighborhood to perpetrate at will a series of harassments against the club. Homemade bombs began to be tossed on Synanon property, and one night drunks deliberately broke into the apartment of some Synanon residents and terrorized them with switchblades. But when Synanon called the police for protection, the latter (evidently taking their cue from the well-publicized attitude of their superiors) openly refused to intervene and even threatened to run in the plaintiffs instead of the violators.

The stage was thus set for the enemies of Synanon to use the whole city apparatus in a willful attack upon Synanon. In a move that Mr. Wamsley freely admitted was a *coup d'état* designed to bypass the halls of justice "where Synanon might have obtained an injunction" (his own words), some thirty Santa Monica police were specially detailed to guard the invasion of Synanon's newly acquired beach area by a private contractor equipped with bulldozers and other earth-moving machinery, who quickly set about ripping away fences, smashing down cabanas and other beach fixtures, and driving a new fence squarely across one of Synanon's paddle-tennis courts, using jackhammers to cut holes in the concrete for the necessary posts, while the police dragged off members and directors of the Foundation who dared to protest, tossing them bodily into paddy wagons and hauling them off to the police station where they were frisked, fingerprinted, and mugged as if they were the criminals caught in the act of trespassing, when the crime was actually the work of the police.

Chuck, at a quickly assembled press conference, had this to say: "We are taxpayers . . . but we are being treated like second-class citizens and criminals. It is quite possible that my city has fallen into the hands of mad dogs. We don't know who they are. We will flush them out in the courts."

Friends swarmed to the defense of Synanon. Commentators declared that it was nothing less than the ugly visage of Nazism that had shown itself in Santa Monica. Lawyers gathered to volunteer their skill in laying the groundwork for a massive legal action against the city. And Mayor Yorty invited Synanon to move to Los Angeles.

Meanwhile, Santa Monica, seeing how the wind was blowing at the moment, tried to throw up certain excuses for its behavior, in particular the notion that this piece of land was in dispute. When I spoke about this to Chuck he said: "Anything is in dispute if you want to make a dispute about it. Suppose I lay claim right now to the Washington Monument. Then obviously the ownership of the Washington Monument is in dispute. Of course I wouldn't dare go to court with such a claim. I'd be thrown in the nut house."

Even Santa Monica was aware of the emptiness of its dispute. And a few months after its Synanon fracas, it demonstrated how such "disputed" matters are properly handled. Synanon's nearest neighbor on the beach to the south, is the POP amusement park. It hasn't paid any rent on its land leased from the city for a number of years. It is $17,000 in arrears. Did Santa Monica summon its armed police? Did they call forth bulldozers and jackhammers? Of course they did nothing of the kind. A hearing was held, a hearing at which the city presented its case and asked for permission to be *"allowed to proceed with a lawsuit against POP."* And this permission having been granted, the city will only now begin to institute such a suit.

Contrast this behavior with the city's action against Synanon. At *two minutes before midnight* of Friday, September 15, 1967, Synanon was notified by mail of the city's position respecting land leased to the Del Mar.

Seven hours and seventeen minutes later, at 7:15 A.M. Saturday morning, September 16, the city moved in with its bulldozers and thirty armed cops.

"This kind of forcible entry," Norman Heering, Synanon's resident lawyer, said, "went out with the fourteenth century. Questions of who owns a piece of property, and who has the right to occupy it, have been, ever since, matters that are up for adjudication by the courts."

John Wallace, editor of *The Synanon Scene,* a semimonthly newspaper, declared that "Synanon exists only by virtue of teaching good citizenship. It teaches respect for law and order, often to people whose life on the street taught them to hate cops' guts." He concluded that Synanon's job has been made more difficult by this demonstration of government behaving immorally and lawlessly.

But on the other hand, as Reverend Scott Beach of the San Francisco Synanon pointed out: "Santa Monica's lunatic fringe may have made one of the most valuable contributions the foundation has ever had. For they have provided the fuel for a fire that will surely burn the name of Synanon more deeply than ever into the structure of American life."

14

Speaking from a purely theoretical standpoint, there can be, I suppose, no valid reason why a good anti-Synanon study might not be written. But the trouble with the people who hate Synanon and would welcome such a treatise is that the haters refuse to devote the necessary time to investigating their subject—which incidentally might cure them of their hatred. Thus a local medical doctor, some years ago, went into copious criticism of Synanon because, so he claimed, it was neglecting the one area where it should have been most active, namely the Negro element where drug addiction is especially high.

The doctor did not of course trouble himself to research this question to any extent. He certainly did not look into the efforts being made at Synanon to handle this matter. He just took it for granted from a glance at some Synanon population figures that it wasn't being done. Nor did he retract any of his criticisms when he subsequently must have noticed how city after city in America was turning into a laboratory demonstration of the extremely complex nature of this problem. He apparently continued to think that Synanon was a fraud and a failure because it wasn't immediately solving what the rest of the United States wasn't solving either.

Meanwhile, in Synanon, the Negro population was nevertheless growing, and two Negroes rose to become members of the board of directors, years before the United States Senate had a single Negro member, and the Supreme Court its first Negro justice. So that recently the Black Muslims of San Francisco voted to remove Synanon from its list of White Devils in an almost unprecedented accolade saluting Synanon's ever more successful attack upon the greatest problem this country faces.

It is not only in this connection, however, that I had the following conversations with Chuck and Betty. And with their daughter Jady. And Reid Kimball. Each of them separately and alone.

Chuck had this to say to me about his love life: "I just didn't see any necessity for rushing into a marriage. I had had two marriages under my belt already, and both of them failures. Betty had had three. And without success. So between us there were close to half a dozen failures to chalk up against these affairs. And mind you, all of them with that precious piece of paper. That signed piece of paper that says you're properly married. That piece of paper that you afterwards fold up and put away and can't remember where you put it."

"Well yes," Betty told me, "I guess I did very much want that piece of paper."

But when I talked to Chuck he pointed out that Betty was close to forty at the time, and he was close to fifty, "and neither of us could cast ourselves as romantic figures. We were long past that," he added.

"No," Betty said to me in the privacy of her office, "Chuck isn't romantic. He doesn't hold hands. But sometimes I catch a look in his eyes. Kind of soft and misty. And I give him a big smile. I guess words would be out of place."

"If there is anything I pride myself on it is my gift for the proper timing," Chuck explained to me; "I have an instinct for that. And I knew that for the average American, and certainly for the average Santa Monican, Synanon already spelled total rebellion. Add an integrated marriage—and who could say what violent feelings might not have been aroused in that community."

Betty told me: "When I first came to Synanon I thought of Chuck as my grandmother. Because he kept after me to read and improve myself, just the way my grandmother had done when I was a child in Oklahoma. But Chuck of course seemed far more elevated to me. In fact when I would be cleaning, or scrubbing, or painting in Synanon, I would always arrange it so that someone else did Chuck's office. I wouldn't have dared step into his place. His things, his furniture, his walls, seemed somehow sacred to me.

"Like almost everyone in Synanon," Betty continued, "I split. And went back to drugs. And then came back to kick again. And then had to leave once more when the County Probation office pulled me out. That was a very angry period of my life, when I went to jail many times, fortunately not for long sentences. I suffered from an ulcer too and of course always went back to dope.

"Until one day I called up Chuck and said: 'How would you feel about my coming back?'—He said: 'Where are you?'—I told him, and he said: 'Then I'll see you in an hour.' I had only six weeks left on probation and Chuck arranged it so that I was able to spend them in Synanon.

"That was about the time that Chuck broke up with his girl friend and she left. And afterwards I thought Chuck often looked lonely."

Chuck said to me: "You know, Guy, I come from a prejudiced Middle Western milieu. Intellect and education gave our people a certain liberal cast, but it was all surface and no body. In fact until Synanon began I had never had any relationship whatsoever with any Negro. I mean any personal relationship. I knew them as waiters, porters, doormen, servants. My first man-to-man association with a Negro was with Jesse Pratt, one of our first addicts.

"As for a man-to-woman relationship with a Negro, that just never occurred to me. It was the furthest thing from my mind. Until I became aware of Betty."

Betty told me: "The only association I had ever had with white men before was with those who were deliberately looking for a Negro woman. Of course I had many of that kind, and I had no idea that Chuck had never touched a Negro woman. And if he had told me I wouldn't have believed him. Because with Jesse Pratt he was like a brother. They had a wonderful friendship.

"In fact, later, when he did tell me, I, sometimes, involuntarily hated Chuck for ever having thought that because of my color I was different from other women."

"Well, yes," Chuck admitted to me, "it did come as a distinct surprise to me that a Negro woman was just like a white woman. I kind of resisted the idea. But I couldn't help eyeing Betty. I admired her posture. Her gentleness. And I knew she was smart. I knew too that she was not a cabin Negro, that she had come from an upper middle-class family. But of course there are these clichés, which are so difficult to get rid of. For example when you speak of Frenchmen you never visualize a coal miner or a steelworker. But Frenchmen do dig coal and do work in steel plants.

"So eventually I kind of took another look at the whole situation. And for the first time in my life I copped to a sexual attraction for a colored woman."

Betty told me how she saw Chuck one night when she was working late. He was alone, and she thought he wanted companionship. When he walked out onto the balcony overlooking the beach, she took her courage into her hands and walked out too.

"I started to talk to him about Synanon affairs, just to make conversation," Betty said. "And he answered my questions and explained things to me, and then he began to talk about Synanon's future. He thought that Synanon might some day have its own radio station. And even a TV station. He went on for about an hour and a half, while I kept pretending that I too saw that kind of grand and glorious future, but of course I didn't. How could I with all this fuss going on around us, and everybody acting like they wanted to throw us to the dogs? I thought we'd be lucky to survive."

"I guess," Chuck said, "that she was setting her cap for me. In these matters it is always the woman who is in control. And I figured that she was kind of looking forward to the day when she could get into bed with the chief."

Betty said: "One evening I passed him in the hallway, and he stopped me and said: 'I'm going to take a walk on the beach. Want to come along?'—I said: 'Great. I'll get my coat.'—That's the evening that he kissed me for the first time. Not a real kiss. Like what I would call a high school kiss. I figured maybe he was just trying to find out if my lips were like other lips."

"When Betty and I became lovers," Chuck told me, "a whole new world was opened up to me. I had never known a woman who was so much a woman. It seemed to me that just instinctively she knew what I wanted and when. All the white women I had known had been in competition with me. I think Betty saw me much more as her child."

Betty said: "He began to hang around the kitchen where I was working. Began to lend me books and talk to me about them. Our love affair was really mostly philosophical talk. But how my heart would beat when I would see him! I really had a terrific crush on him.

"But it didn't sit well with some. In fact for a while the whole club seemed to have nothing else on its mind but why Chuck, if he needed a piece of tail, had to pick himself one of the animals just out of the gutter. The Negroes in the club resented it most of all. One person in particular whose deep hatred for whites has revealed itself again and again in our games, resented me more than anyone. Sometimes when I would come into one of the rooms, where he was, he'd get up and walk out and signal all the other Negroes to follow him. He felt I had disgraced myself by falling in love with one of our oppressors. That hurt.

"And at the games, I was really put through the wringer. By the men. Because the girls wouldn't even talk to me. Their attitude seemed to be: 'Who the hell did I think I was?' Maybe I'm exaggerating. Perhaps I was just far too sensitive at that time."

"Now and then I got hauled over the coals, in the games," Chuck said to me. "About my not living up to my own ideals. Not being a proper role model, as we now say. But I'd explain my position. I'd explain the problem that I had in representing Synanon in a community that was—by and large—opposed to integration, and the necessity of coddling rich sponsors and facing the press with its enormous power for good or evil."

"I was about ready to give up," Betty told me. "I said to Reid once: 'Chuck is just screwing over me.' And asked Reid about the possibility of my going down to San Diego and getting busy at the club there, and letting Chuck loose."

"I had other questions that I had to ponder," Chuck said. "Betty had split once, and the Probation Department had pulled her out once. And both times she had gone back to drugs. And to shoplifting. The whole mess. Then she had gone straight for three years. But not outside. Only here in Synanon. So how solid was she really? Synanon had already experienced a number of three-year members who had nevertheless gone back to dope. So I thought: let's watch it for a while."

Reid Kimball said: "I finally had all I could take. I said to Chuck one day that I had a bone to pick with him. He said: 'Save it for our next game.' And I said 'No.' I said, 'I want this talk with you alone. Belly to belly.' And I said: 'I want to talk to you honestly, Chuck. I'm losing my respect for you. It's common knowledge that you're shacking up with Betty . . .'

"He wasn't offended, Guy. He just paced back and forth, while I kept arguing. I said: 'Now I've heard a hundred times about Santa Monica, and integration, and about your ability in social planning and in correct timing . . .'

"Chuck didn't argue back. He just kept saying: 'Yes, yes, you're right. You're right. In God's name, you're right.'

"But I didn't stop until finally he said: 'Oh hell! Call her up then, and tell her we're going to be married.'"

Chuck said: "Of course that was a mistake. To have Reid call up Betty and propose to her for me. But really, Guy, there were no unconscious implications to be deduced from it. I was awfully busy. I had no people like Chester Stern then, no dog robber, no Lois Folsom, to run my routine office work for me, and take everything off my shoulders except that which absolutely had to be handled by me. I was swamped. Day and night."

"When I get angry," Betty confided to me, "the first thing that pops up in my mind is this high and mighty white plantation owner sending his overseer to fetch his colored slave out of her cabin and bring her to his mansion."

"Oh," Chuck said to me, "I suppose it does still stick in her craw. But really, to still get all googoo about a situation that was already so established. Of course I did make a mistake in having it a double wedding. But I had already arranged for this Arline-Gary marriage, so I thought why not get some extra mileage out of the same ceremony?"

"Of course I didn't turn him down," Betty admitted. "But I wasn't too pleased. Although I didn't lose any time running out at once and buying myself a gown. But why did I have to be married at the same time as Arline? She had a right to her own ceremony. And I had a right to mine."

I said: "I heard you in a game some time ago, Betty, and it seemed as if you would never forgive Chuck, for the way in which he offered you marriage."

"Oh, Guy, please don't let anything in your book give that impression. How could I feel any genuine resentment towards a man who sat up all night long on a hospital bench without sleep, when I was so close to dying of pneumonia. I knew he was there. And everybody in that hospital knew that this man had a wife in that room. A wife whom he cherished.

"But I did want our marriage to be perfect, if only because everything else about our relationship is so perfect. But of course very human too. He knew for example, the profound psychological problem that every Negro has with his race and his color. And for that reason he wanted me to share an LSD experience with him. And there's one moment of that trip that will haunt me all my life. Chuck was sobbing and holding me. And I was looking into a mirror and watching my face changing over to the white race. But Chuck was saying: 'Wasn't it more beautiful before?'—And I cried and said: 'Yes, yes. I like myself just as I am!'

"And I remember a moment in one of our dissipations when someone started to worship Chuck as a god and kneel before him and ask his forgiveness. And then everyone started to do that. And I became alarmed and I cried, because I didn't want him to be god. I wanted him to be a man to love and kiss and go to bed with and cook for.

"And he consoled me. He said: 'Here. Feel. I'm real. I'm no god. All this is just symbolic.'

"I know Chuck loves me. And he knows I love him. I'm sure of this because it is to me he turns to first when some new idea comes to him. He wants my comment. He tries it out on me. I become his bouncing board. And he listens to what I have to say.

"We have a rich life together. Becasue of all we're trying to do, and because of all the many people we meet. And it is because he shares all this with me that I have developed to a point where we can both give each other love and mutual respect and increased strength."

"What's this about your not wanting to go see your father when he was in prison?" I asked Jady, who is seventeen years old now, but was only ten at the time when Chuck had to serve his sentence for a zoning violation.

"Everybody was using me," Jady said, "because I had the right to see Daddy every day, and somebody could accompany me and get in on the visit. But I didn't want to go to that jail every day. Don't forget, Daddy and Mother were divorced, and Mother—you know she was Jewish—after the separation we went to live with *her* mother. And Grandmother always felt that Mother's troubles would be over now that she was being divorced from that goy and could settle down with a nice Jewish boy.

"Well that's exactly what she did. And I guess the only reason she did it was for my sake. Only I disliked my stepfather right from the start, and more and more as time passed. He was Jewish, yes, but nice he wasn't. He wouldn't work. He had a laundry at first, and then he sold insurance, and sometimes he didn't work at all.

"And he wasn't anywhere near Mother's intellectual level. And Mother was lonely—and she used to go down to Synanon not necessarily to see Chuck, but, for companionship. And then finally she had had it, and she separated from my stepfather and filed for divorce. And this even though she was going to have a baby. Which infuriated my stepfather. He got so mad about it finally, that later, after the baby was born, he waylaid Mother just when she was coming out of the doctor's office, with the little one in her arms. And he shot her.

"I saw him rushing at her out of the corner of my eye. But I didn't see the actual shooting. I just heard the shot, and then the commotion and people yelling: 'Somebody's been shot,' and I could just see something laying on the ground and the crowd pressing all around her. And then the police came and took me away. And later Daddy brought me to Synanon.

"Then there was the trial, and if I disliked my stepfather before, I hated him now. With his little moustache and his high forehead, he looked like the devil to me. And I'll never forget my grandmother sobbing . . . it was she who took the baby. . . ."

"He was recently released, wasn't he?" I asked.

"Yes. He's out on parole. But if he tries to see me, I'll call the police."

"How did you like going back to live at Synanon?"

"It was horrible. I was going through a bad stage. I didn't like Betty and Daddy living together. And I hated myself. I dreamt of nothing but having pretty dresses, and having a mummy and daddy like other children.

"I was especially uncomfortable with Betty. And maybe even more so with Daddy. All I could remember of him from long ago was his being drunk. Always drunk. But now, when he wasn't drunk anymore, he still frightened me. He was so big and loud. And when I would hear him yelling in the house, at some poor dope addict, I would tremble. Really, he scared me to death.

"I was a funny little fat kid that had temper tantrums. I didn't understand what was going on, and I didn't know what to do with myself. I would hang around the front desk, with some of the girls who were members. I was no good at school either. I was, in fact, a mess."

"Like many a good therapist," Chuck said to me, "I was no good at all when it came to my own family."

"I remember," Jady said, "when Herb Williams took me to live with his family, and I would cry with envy, when I'd see how warm Herb was to his daughters. And I recall once that in passing, he slapped one of his daughters on the rear. You know, just an affectionate pat. And I almost cried thinking: why didn't my daddy ever do that to me?

"Living with Herb Williams was the greatest thing that had ever happened in my life up to that point. They had a nice home and I had a real taste of square living, and I thought it was wonderful. But after a while Daddy and Betty, who had been in Westport, came back, and we all went up to live together again in San Francisco. Also I lost some weight, and I did just a little better in school.

"But then I developed another reason for hating myself. Because when I graduated junior high I had the right to bring two people to my graduation and I didn't want Betty to go. I didn't want to be seen there, by all my schoolmates, with Betty. I didn't know how to handle it, but my unhappiness must have been so plain that Betty caught on, and didn't go. . . ."

"I felt it was time for a talk," Chuck told me. "I asked her if she realized how much she had hurt Betty. I asked her if she realized how much her Jewish mother would have been ashamed of her behavior. I asked her if she knew that her mother had found it difficult to get work in New York at one time because she was Jewish."

Jady said: "He insisted I must apologize to Betty. And I did. But it was just a formal sort of apology and Betty knew it. And I knew that I had just hurt her again.

"For years I was unhappy about this. Betty understood the reason why I never brought any girl friends home. Not to Synanon, and not to the bungalow we called Wuthering Heights. And not to our home in San Francisco. And not when we moved to Tomales Bay. And it wasn't only Betty. It was also the fact that I was Jewish. . . . I had a mezuzah on a chain around my neck. I owed that to my mother and grandmother. But I had the mezuzah under my dress.

And once I was terribly embarrassed because in jumping I had made it pop out. And once some kids called me a dirty Jew. . . .

"Just about everything embarrassed me. My being Jewish, my living in Synanon. And Betty. And in the teen-age Synanon games at Tomales Bay, I used to get it from everyone about my refusal to face reality, about my being a snob, about my practicing all kinds of deceit so I wouldn't have to bring my girl friends to Synanon. It wasn't until I came from Tomales Bay, back to Santa Monica, that finally Betty and Chuck called me into the office one day. It was the first really emotional talk we had ever had together. And Betty was wonderful. Not bearing any grudge, saying she understood. . . ."

"I had bought her this dress she wanted," Betty said, "and she put it on and loved it. And I said: 'Well, don't I get something for it?' And she threw herself into my arms."

"It was the first time I kissed her," Jady said to me. "I felt so much better."

"I still have a hard time," Jady said. "Even now. In Hamilton High. Which is such a snob place. But things are opening up. I even brought a girl friend home."

"What was her reaction to Betty?" I asked.

"Oh, she took it fine. No shock at all. It still hasn't sunk in completely. But I'm improving. I'm becoming so proud of Synanon. In fact there's nothing annoys me so much now as when I see blank faces on my schoolmates when I tell them that my father is the founder of Synanon.

"And then they stare at me and say: 'Synanon? What is that?'

"How frustrating!" Jady said to me. "Trying to explain in a few minutes just what Synanon is. So my girl friends don't go thinking of it as some kind of a jail or hospital. So they'll get at least some notion of its warmth and spirit, and something of the great social movement that is coming out of it. I'll talk fast and try to compress and wish that there was some way that one could sum up Synanon so that people don't go off with the impression that it's just some sort of a nuthouse for dope addicts."

I thought there was some kind of implied challenge in Jady's remark. As if I ought to come up with my own explanation of Synanon. But I wasn't going to let myself in for a discussion of what Synanon is. Not at that particular moment.

15

What I wanted to discuss with Chuck the other day was the subject of imitation Synanons such as have been cropping up more and more lately. Only recently, for example, I had seen the following quite brazen invitation in the form of an ad:

"Wanted: men and women to join in a Synanon-like association."

I knew that it was nothing uncommon for people who had had some Synanon experience, and who, for one reason or another, had then left the club, to dream of having a little Synanon of their own. Or at least a little game club.

The only quasi-Synanons that merit attention today are the open and deliberate attempts on the part of certain officials in the State of New York to form Synanon-like places for the treatment of drug addicts with the very liberal grants appropriated under the four-hundred-million-dollar Rockefeller program. Dropouts from Synanon, as well as Synanon graduates, have become well-paid administrators in some of these attempts, among which Daytop Village on Staten Island seems to be the most successful, and which also enjoys the advice and counsel of Dr. Daniel Casriel, the author of the first book about Synanon, *So Fair a House*.

Dr. Casriel is that already mentioned authority on addiction whose experience had taught him that there was no possible solution for the addict except to lock him up in a jail or hospital for the rest of his life, or else give him all the free dope he wanted. And that continued to be Dr. Casriel's opinion until he happened on Synanon and immediately dropped a projected vacation trip to Hawaii in order to remain in Santa Monica and study this amazing actuality that contradicted all his former conclusions.

This matter of present and future imitation Synanons was one that I had touched upon before, but rather fleetingly, in my discussions with Chuck. And on several occasions I had urged upon him the registration of the word Synanon as a trademark. I had adduced the case of Mark Twain as an illustration. Not that I thought of Synanon as making any profit out of leasing the use of the word Synanon, but merely in order to put the club in a position to prevent a word which had been invented by them from being defamed by being indiscriminately used for operations only distantly resembling the real thing.

(By registering the name of Mark Twain as a trademark, Samuel Clemens himself, during his lifetime, and the executors of his estate after his death, had obtained a permanent hold over anyone who wanted to print or film or otherwise use the author's works. And this despite the fact that the copyright eventually expired on all of Mark Twain's writings, thus throwing them into public domain, with anyone free to print what they pleased. Only not with the by-line Mark Twain. Because those two words remained under the protection of registered trademarks and this keeps the Mark Twain estate in perpetual control against any demeaning usage of the author's writings.)

But Chuck's attitude was different. "We don't want to patent Synanon," he said to me. "If anybody wants to imitate us, I say: 'Go right ahead! Crazy! But the question is how do you imitate something you don't fully understand? You can't come here for a few weeks like Dr. Casriel did, dash off a little book, and then establish a Synanon. Consider, for example, what we're doing with the game here. We've been playing it for nine years, and I'm just beginning to formulate its basic rules. Just beginning to think of compiling a manual on some of the more tricky aspects of how to become a good game player—after nine years!

"How can someone steal from us something we ourselves still don't quite understand, and which a thief must obviously understand even less than we do? Isn't that ridiculous? To steal something which is still in the process of development, and which you'd have to come back to steal again, year after year, as it keeps growing?

"These imitation Synanons, if they can actually help an addict, why great! More power to them. But you see—they can't. Not really. Because if imitation is your policy, then how can you have a policy of no policy? In short, Synanon can't be stolen. No more than you can steal Notre Dame or the Boy Scout movement. Of course not.

"Don't you see that something you can always become a part of can never really be stolen? Because anybody with any honesty would simply join us. And anyone so dishonest as to want to steal what we've got instead of joining up would only be demonstrating that he lacks the absolutely indispensible moral base to do anything vital with the Synanon he has stolen.

"Study the letter that Reid wrote the other day to Sargent Shriver and you'll see what I mean."

I did study that letter. Reid wrote it to the man appointed by President Johnson to head the Office of Economic Opportunity. It concerned a thirteen-week experimental counseling program that Synanon Foundation had agreed to run in the State of Nevada for expelled high school students. Synanon was to receive three thousand dollars for its services, and Fred Cebrowski and another Synanon person had been detailed to travel from the Tomales Bay facility across to Las Vegas once a week to hold a meeting with 25 youngsters in an "Operation Back to School" project.

Synanon carried out its part of the contract by sending its two representatives on this thousand-mile trek. But the authorities in Las Vegas did not produce the 25 youngsters, excusing themselves by adducing that a rock and roll musician happened to be in town and all the kids had naturally flocked to hear him.

Reid's letter was a cancellation of the contract. He wrote that the officials in Clark County, Nevada, seemed totally unconcerned about how and what Synanon might be doing to earn those three thousand dollars.

Synanon, however, *is* concerned, and although $3,000 is a relative pittance in a government program as vast as the Office of Economic Opportunity, Synanon, by its very nature, cannot be party to this type of irresponsible spending.

I trust you will appreciate our position in this matter, particularly when I point out that Synanon, for internal reasons if no other, must demonstrate to its own members a posture of unremitting honesty. This is probably the largest single factor of the Synanon ethos. I might add that those same members, almost without exception, have been at one time or another pawns in the various games played by individuals and agencies whose only expertise and success lay in their ability to elicit grant money. They realize more clearly than anyone that this shameful nonsense has done more to perpetuate and even worsen the problems of crime, delinquency, and addiction than any other single factor—including poverty.

Perhaps at some future negotiations a way will present itself whereby the Economic Opportunity Board could avail itself of Synanon's experience and knowhow; namely, its success in dealing with people who have behavioral problems and absorbing them into the responsible society. I certainly hope so.

It was precisely in order to explore more fully this whole area of where Synanon with its "unremitting honesty" stands with respect to the social milieu in which it has its being that I would drive up again and again to Chuck's new home on the outskirts of Beverly Hills. The Tree House is one of Synanon's latest acquisitions of real estate, a kind of fortress of glass and steel with a swimming pool curving around like a castle's moat, a structure originally dreamed up by a multi-millionaire as a flamboyant love nest for a famous Hollywood beauty, but soon abandoned after the usual squabble.

Chuck had long felt the need for a residence befitting his rank and stature, a place that would be both a home and an audio-visual psychological workshop, one that would be sufficiently far removed from Santa Monica so that none of the facilities could claim that Chuck by residing in one branch or another was playing favorites. And the different branches forced back on their own resources would thus be compelled to learn to run themselves independently of Chuck, under the supervision of the new president of the club, Jack Hurst.

The Tree House not only had the proper location, but with its huge fourteen-inch steel I-beams, its artificial grotto done with concrete sprayed from a gun, its elaborate jungle landscaping, its bomb shelter with secret escape tunnel, and its view over the width and breadth of Los Angeles from the sea to the mountains was big enough and solid enough and magnificent enough to make a setting for any man—even for a Chuck Dederich.

"I like big things," Chuck once confided to me. "Big cars. Big rooms. Massive furniture. Women with big behinds. I'm crazy for size."

It shook me therefore, the other day, when I reached Chuck's new office to learn that the Tree House was being offered for sale. "Why you just moved in," I said. "Matter of weeks."

"We have an attractive offer right now," Chuck said, indicating some papers on his desk. "We picked up this place for practically no money down. It had been vacant for many months and vandals had made a shambles of it, ripped up the rugs, busted all the mirrors, stolen all the fixtures, wrecked the garden and the swimming pool. But that was no problem at all for our Synanon boys. We hustled new rugs. We cleaned up the garden and the pool. We soon had this place restored to palatial condition. But now I see a hundred thousand dollar profit for us by trading this property in for an apartment complex where we can house two hundred or more Synanon people. You don't suppose we're going to turn that down, do you?

"You know that Synanon always lives as far out on the edge of its means as it can. For us money simply constitutes so many more square feet of living space in which to house the flood of youngsters who are waiting to step into our club."

"But what about your audio-visual laboratory?" I asked.

"We'll set that up somewhere else," Chuck said. "And maybe make ourselves another hundred grand. If we're lucky again . . . But for the moment, at any rate, we've given Synanon another chance to expand. We really have no desire to be rich in money. Our aim, as always, is to be rich in people getting well."

Chuck went on to describe how different Synanon's attitude was compared to the average project, set up simply to achieve a grant, and where the addicts who were eventually to be involved were just so many guinea pigs. And the experts seemed always more interested in the next lecture they were preparing about their latest effort than in the human material upon which it necessarily had to be based.

And one conference paper or another has to be dreamed up again and again in order to furnish a reason for the continuous round of narcotics festivals. According to Chuck these festivals are a joke. It's always the same people meeting each other in different places. One year in Toronto and the next in London. So that you hear on all sides Dr. X saying to Dr. Y:

"Why, hello there, Joe. Haven't seen you since our conference at Tallahassee."

"Since all this traveling," Chuck pointed out, "is paid for by public money, or else comes out of grant funds, naturally none of the boys want to miss out on them, even though they have absolutely nothing new to report. You can always dress up an old project to look like new. One man is working with four addicts and another man with seven. One is doing group therapy and another is doing individual analysis. One is using methadone in orange juice and another is using it in tablet form. One is able to report that two of his addicts stayed clean long enough to go back to work and to last ten days on the job. And another can report no cures. Which doesn't make any difference, since it's all in the name of science.

"I went to one such conference at U.C.L.A.," Chuck said, "where all the papers put together did not concern one half—let me repeat that—all the papers put together did not concern one half the number of people whom we had living clean at Synanon. And yet when

I got up to report about our hundreds of addicts, many of them living clean for five years and more, and with no substitute drugs and no use of coercion, there was no unusual interest in what I had to say. It was listened to with the same weary politeness that had greeted all the other papers. And when I told them that Synanon was open to them for inspection no more than fifteen minutes away, in Santa Monica, it was only a couple of these experts who gave themselves the trouble of dropping in on us for a brief look. They weren't looking for cures, they were looking for science, and they therefore had no more interest in our place than in some other place whose failure rate was one hundred percent."

Despite the importance of what Chuck was telling me, and despite the rapidity with which I was taking notes, I could not keep my mind from wandering and reviving for me some recent conversations I had had with one of Hollywood's better-known character actors, whom I'll call H.D. Because these conversations concerned the very same subject, namely the question of unremitting honesty.

H.D. had been a very close friend of Synanon, back in the early days when Synanon direly needed a good friend. But then something had happened and he had broken with the club. But apparently without ever losing his profound interest in it. And to this day the memory of Synanon obviously remains with him as one of the more meaningful episodes of his life.

I happened to speak to him about the Tree House, and told him that only recently Chuck had mentioned that he would be glad to hear from his old friend. Besides H.D. would now be seeing Chuck surrounded by a frame that suited him, an exciting house combining the severely modern with tropical lushness.

"Did he buy this house?" H.D. wanted to know.

"Synanon bought it," I explained. "To be Chuck's home."

H.D.'s comment on that was startlingly unexpected: "Oh! So that's where all the money goes? Well now I understand everything."

H.D.'s introduction to Synanon was as follows: Years before, during a period of unemployment, H.D. used to notice at the office where he collected his weekly unemployment check a man so strikingly like a pirate from the Spanish Main that he was impelled to ask him if he too was an actor.

"No," the man said.

"Well, what is your business?" H.D. asked.

"I'm a dope addict," the man said.

This man was George Antar, otherwise known as George the Turk; that's how H.D. got to know Synanon. George was just then residing in Synanon in order to clean himself up after many years of addiction. Incidentally, he did.

H.D. was immediately attracted to this crazy and wonderful group of people, and was soon on the friendliest terms with all the top boys such as Jack Hurst, and of course Chuck. And he became one of the club's first sponsors, contributing forty dollars a month. And then once, during the bitter Santa Monica zoning battle, when Chuck had to go to jail, H.D. said: "It just occurred to me that you might be able to use a whole year's checks in advance." And then and there he wrote them out a check for five hundred dollars.

It was shortly after this that something must have happened, for H.D. was seen less and less frequently, and finally no more.

I asked him about that once, when I was visiting him at his home. Telling him that at Synanon that lordly check of his was still remembered with gratitude. "People wonder why they never see you around any more," I said. "You should really drop in on them."

"I'd love to see the old bunch again, Guy," H.D. said. But then he reconsidered. "No," he said, "I wouldn't. Not really. It would be too painful. The contrast. To see them as they now are. With Chuck like a god. Surrounded by his admiring disciples. And all that luxury in which he lives. When I think of how it was in the old days. When I think of the vision that Synanon once was. . . . No. It would really be too painful."

"Nothing has changed," I said, "only that the place has grown. And growth has naturally brought a lot of problems that have had to be met in various ways. But the old spirit, you don't have to worry about that. It's still there. All of it. Intact. Go down and see for yourself."

But H.D. continued to shake his head. "No. I want to remember Synanon as it was when I knew it. When total wrecks would crawl out of the gutter and be welcomed in. With no questions asked. And no money demanded. Wild animals who would eventually turn into wonderful human beings. That's over with, Guy. It can't possibly happen now. Not today when you have to pay heavily to get into Synanon. Not when addicts who haven't got the cash for a substantial donation just aren't wanted. Not when Synanon has become far too expensive for the ordinary gutter-hype. . . . And God help an addict today if in a moment of wretchedness he should split. He's lost everything. That poor fellow will never see the inside of Synanon again. Never."

This was a matter that I had to bring up before Chuck and Reid.

Chuck asked me: "Doesn't H.D. still live in that very beautiful home of his?"

"The same," I said.

Chuck said: "Well, it's a pity he won't come around. He and I used to hit it off so well. I really loved that guy. But I never begrudged him his wonderful home, and I really don't understand why he should begrudge me mine for as long as I'll have it."

I turned to Reid: "H.D. remembers you when you were nothing but a quivering blob. He says he watched you with amazement, the way you gradually turned into a man with wit like a firecracker and intelligence like a razor. But he claims that if you were to try to get into Synanon *now*, looking just the way you did *then*, you wouldn't have a chance. They'd never let you in today. Not totally broke the way you were. Not totally smashed. You'd first have to raise some dough. A thousand dollars or more."

"There's that ridiculous money rumor again!" Reid exclaimed angrily. "Now let's see if I really have this intelligence like a razor, Guy, and if you will put this in your book, maybe we can finally clear this thing up. Of course Synanon wants money. How the hell are we going to house an addict, bed him, feed him, clothe him, entertain him, educate him, restore him, if we can't lay our hands on some money? But are we going to get this money from the average addict? Obviously not. Most addicts are broke and have no other source of income than petty crime or prostitution. And no sooner do they manage to lay their hands on any money than they turn it into dope just as fast as they can.

"But when we take the history of an applicant, and we discover that time and time again he was able to have bail put up and to hire lawyers to defend him, and we learn that he has a family that he keeps running to whenever he finds himself in a really bad spot, we don't see any reason why we shouldn't run to this family too. Why not? What's wrong with that? If this junkie has been able to squeeze money out of his people before, to pay bail bondsmen, let him squeeze some out to pay Synanon. Why not? For God's sake, why not?

"That will make it possible for us to bring in a couple of addicts who have no relatives and who genuinely can't raise a dime. They ought to have their chance at Synanon too. Wouldn't we be criticized even more if we behaved stupidly in these money matters, and thus reduced the number of people we could take care of? Our rental bill alone now comes close to thirty thousand dollars a month! That's money that has to be paid! And that keeps increasing all the time.

"But now what happens when a story gets around that so-and-so's people have had to cough up a thousand bucks to get their kid into Synanon? With everybody gossiping about Synanon, naturally some hype who has no intention whatsoever of breaking his habit hears about it and finds this a great excuse for blaming his condition, not on himself, but on Synanon. So he starts whining around about how much he would like to clean himself up, but of course with Synanon the only place one can do it, and with Synanon now charging so much, that avenue is closed to him.

"In the good old days, so this stoned idiot will keep repeating, when Synanon was still a great vision, he could have come here and we would have accepted him. But now it's useless. Hopeless. And so he goes on blabbing lies about Synanon, so his wife or his family or his friends won't keep harping Synanon to him any more. And of course the more he talks that way, the safer he feels of being left alone to continue his habit.

"People are constantly coming to us with these rumors about Synanon now being only for the rich. And maybe if you get this into your book, that will be the end of this nonsense."

While I had Reid hot, I brought up one of H.D.'s other points. About splittees. About their never being allowed back into Synanon. I knew that this was untrue too, but I had heard it not only from H.D. but from various other people, so I wanted to hear what Reid had to say about that.

"Now how the hell shall I answer that one?" Reid exclaimed. "Suppose, for example, we announced that it was Synanon's policy to take all splittees back. Wouldn't every crazy gutter-hype who comes into Synanon be tempted to take advantage of that? And split as often as the impulse came to him? Already certain—in front —that we'd always take him back?

"Now wouldn't that be a totally insane way for Synanon to handle this problem?

"Or take the opposite. Suppose we announced that no splittee could ever return, and then some dope addict in a moment of imbalance splits, and knowing that he can't come back ever, when remorse overtakes him, he falls into despair and kills himself.

"Isn't it clear that at Synanon we can't say that we *will* take splittees back. And we can't say that we *won't*. Is that really so difficult to understand? Isn't that just our old Synanon policy of no policy?

"But what I can't understand, Guy, is why, if H.D. has all these questions in his mind, why the hell he doesn't come here and visit us. Does he really expect us to take the whole Synanon story separately to every person who has some mental doubts about us? Isn't that why we have our open house? For just exactly this sort of question. To keep people constantly informed?"

I said: "H.D. insists that Synanon doesn't really want him around any more. Not since he had the temerity to criticize Chuck. 'They loved me there so long as I admired everything that Chuck did' is what H.D. told me. Then what happened was this: one of

Synanon's members who was attending Santa Monica City College, and had permission to use one of the foundation cars to get to his classes, was so unfortunate as to be handed a speeding ticket. And, according to H.D., here's how Chuck reacted: 'You've just finished your college career, Buster! That's out! You start mopping the toilets again.'

"H.D. was overcome at the cruelty of it. He argued with Chuck that to cut a student off in the middle of the term just for a speeding ticket was entirely too severe. In fact inhuman. But Chuck stopped him short, saying: 'I'm handling this. And I know exactly what I'm doing.'"

I added: "Chuck has already told me that he has absolutely no recollection of such an incident. But he is quite willing to admit that he might have behaved that way. In fact it is very likely that he did. Can you recall anything about it?"

Reid said: "There have been several thousand nuts around here, and each one has had his share of incidents of one kind or another. That just happens to be one that I can't remember either. But I'm not saying it didn't take place. On the contrary it sounds very much like what might have happened. So what? Here's this former drug addict whom we've cleaned up and are now sending to college. And this ass-hole is driving to school in one of our cars and what does he do? He brings us back a speeding ticket!

"Well, screw him! We're lucky he didn't wreck our car while he was at it. Very likely Chuck realized that this imbecile wasn't ready yet for college. If he has no more judgment than to go speeding in a car that doesn't belong to him—a car that belongs to all of us—then he needs a lot more work done on his moral attitude before he starts studying chemistry and metallurgy. Because what's a guy of this stripe going to do with chemistry and metallurgy if he has no moral base? Why he's going to use his knowledge to blow up a safety deposit vault. Obviously. There are already too many educated criminals in this world without Synanon adding to their number."

"Well, anyway," I said, "that's H.D.'s story. He claims that for daring to charge the master with cruelty, he was blacklisted at Synanon."

"Of course that's utterly without foundation," Reid said. "Why H.D. could enter this building right now, and everyone would be only too pleased to see him back. My guess is that what actually happened was that for a while we were all just too busy to sit around and bullshit with him. And he got to feeling neglected. And all the rest of it took place in his own mind. Typical elaboration of an incident of no importance when it's locked up in the brain of someone who refuses to air it. Surely H.D. knows enough about Synanon methods not to keep harboring a grievance but to bring it here and lay it out on the table for everyone to have a look at.

"And as to cruelty—well you know that Chuck has never posed as St. Francis. You know that. We do some very cruel things here, now and then. We don't deny it. In fact we take pride in it, when it's for the good of someone. Emerson nailed it down: 'When the doctrine of love pules and whines, then the doctrine of hate must be preached.'

"Not so long ago there was an addict who entered our San Diego facility. The usual stinking mess. Utterly smashed. Underweight to the point of starvation. Teeth neglected for so long that they had to be removed. All of them. And it just so happened that right at that time a dentist had volunteered some free work for us, and we were able to assign this idiot to him.

"In short we worked with this cowflop as hard as we could. But he kept fighting us. And the moment we punished him, he'd split and get himself strung out again, and then come begging to be taken back. And we kept right on taking him back.

"Finally Wilbur Beckham, our director of the San Diego plant, called him into his office. Asked him if he really wanted to come back again. When he said that he did, Wilbur asked him to take out his teeth. Wilbur took the dentures and locked them up in his desk. 'That's two thousand dollars worth of teeth,' Wilbur told him. 'And that crockery was not a gift to *you*. It was a gift to

Synanon. And until you learn to stop walking off these premises with our property in your mouth, those teeth will stay in my desk and you can live on mush!'"

After a moment Chuck said: "Well, of course H.D. is right. He's right in one respect. He knows—and we know—that Synanon has nothing going for it except its moral stance. He knows that if we've lost that then we've lost everything. His point of view is absolutely correct. Absolutely correct. But you see, his behavior leaves much to be desired because if he has doubts about us—or about me—why doesn't he come here and face us? We've got games going all over the place. All the time. In fact we're the only society in the world built on the idea of total confrontation. So why does he go around spreading his misapprehensions? Why?

"Someone ought to tell him how many hundreds of thousands of dollars we've turned away because I wouldn't have my boys and girls peeing in a bottle. Someone ought to tell him that!"

"What's this about peeing in a bottle?" I asked.

Reid said: "This is a chapter of your book that you should title: 'The Pee Flows in Brooklyn,' or else 'The Great Kidney Caper.'"

Chuck approved those titles. "They're disrespectful," he said, "and that's exactly the posture of Synanon. We stand for total irreverence! For all sacred cows. Synanon will never bow down and worship urine, just because that seems to be the thing that's done. We leave that to certain physicians and experts in drug addiction. They worship the piss of dope addicts as if it were sacred water from the holy river Ganges."

"Will someone explain this to me?" I asked. "What has urine got to do with drug addiction?"

"Millions!" Chuck exclaimed. "All manner of clever and stupid projects for the study of dope addiction have received grants of money from the government or else from some of the big private funds. And the question is never whether you've cleaned up an addict or not, but whether you can present scientific evidence of it. Either way, you understand. I mean it makes no difference whether your method works or not, just so long as it's scientific. And the best scientific minds will accept only one testimony as to that, namely urinalysis.

"But you see, at Synanon, we're crazy! We're absolutely mad. We let our urine go right down the drain. Along with all that money. That's what we think of piss, here. But of course at those projects, they save it. Naturally. They pile it up in their archives. Why New York must be full of bonded warehouses stacked to the rafters with non-refillable fifty-five-gallon steel drums full of dope addicts' urine.

"Why not? If it can get you two million dollars from the Rockefeller Foundation, or hundreds of thousands of dollars from the National Institute for Mental Health, because your project is scientific, whether it cleans anybody up or not, you're not going to chuck that piss down the nearest sewer, are you? Of course not. You're going to frame it. You're going to drape it around your walls. Or at least let it ripen to perfection in kegs of genuine kiln-dried oak.

"Of course these lovers of the kidney secretion can't really do the dope addict any good. Obviously not. How can they when they're so much more interested in his ability to make water than in his ability to keep himself free of heroin. I suppose these urine-worshipers have heard of our trust system by which we test human beings instead of testing their pee. But they wouldn't know what to do with our method. Because you see trust is something you can't put into a test tube. You can't take it to the laboratory and get a chemist to certify it for you. You can't keep a medical record of it. So it's no earthly good to these projects whose main product is paper, not people.

"So what happens? Well can there be any doubt about what happens? It is exactly what always happens between people who have no trust in each other. They certainly can never do each other any good. The doctor will continue to scratch around for his grant-money. And the addict will continue to scratch around for his dope. And both of them will go right on cheating each other. Naturally.

"And of course Synanon can't ever get in on those juicy grants. Because I won't have my people making weewee in a bottle. That's something that you can force upon prisoners or upon patients. But we don't have any prisoners or patients in Synanon. You see? We have only members. No staff! So I and my wife would have to pee in a bottle too. No! Synanon will never go into the business of manufacturing piss. Not for anyone! Synanon is in the business of manufacturing human beings. And that's the business it's going to stay in!"

16

I talked to Professor Lewis Yablonsky about this pee business and he laughed. "The funniest part of it," he said, "is that it's so damned true. Synanon did lose anywhere from a quarter of a million dollars on up to millions because Chuck will never accept this urinalysis business.

"I was part of the original situation," Lew continued. "In fact it was I who started Chuck on the idea of getting some of this grant money. I told him of the huge sums that were available and something about how you go about getting them. Because that's a special art, you know. There are people who have a real talent for it. There's even a word we use for it. We call it grantsmanship. Don't laugh. There are people who know just how to design a program, just how and where to go applying for it, and just how to draw up the application. And they can hit it just about every time. Of course such a talent is worth a fortune. Whether the resulting programs are worth anything or not."

Lew Yablonsky is still the only Ph.D. who has not only studied Synanon but actually attached himself to the club. Ricky Volkman, of course, was the first university-trained person to probe Synanon. And in a way she was instrumental in bringing Lew there.

Here's how that happened: after a year or more of urging she finally induced her teacher, the noted criminologist Dr. Donald Cressey, to pay Synanon a couple of visits. Despite the shortness of these visits Dr. Cressey was genuinely and deeply impressed by the little band of former dope addicts, and when he went abroad to teach in England, and there met Dr. Yablonsky, who was attending the 1960 United Nations Congress on Crime and Delinquency that was being held in London, he told the younger man about this strange and stirring group.

And subsequently, when Dr. Yablonsky temporarily took over Dr. Cressey's place at U.C.L.A., he made it his business to drop in on Synanon, which was only a ten- or fifteen-minute drive away. He began by making friends with Chuck and the residents, and had soon established himself as Synanon's sociological theoretician and eventually as the author of a penetrating book about the club called *The Tunnel Back: Synanon.*

Lew told me: "I guess I came to the club with the same preconceptions about dope addicts that everyone has. I mean that there was no hope for them. And even when I corrected myself, I was still left with all the ambivalence and all the vacillations that so typically affect the squares who come to Synanon.

"Let me give you a very personal and intimate illustration. You know that I fell in love with one of the girls there. With Donna. You know how beautiful she was. And still is. But perhaps you don't know for how long I refused to think of my relationship to her as a real love. After all, I couldn't forget that she had been a dope addict. I couldn't ignore the kind of life she had led on the streets, while scratching for dope. Such an affair, I said to myself, couldn't possibly be the big and all-important love that a man looks forward to in his life.

"Donna understood my feelings. She didn't like them. But she understood them. And I guess both of us suffered as a result of my doubts.

"Then, as my studies of Synanon progressed, and I gradually came to believe more and more strongly that Synanon was a totally new and an unusually powerful form of human environment, and that this new society, as I could see with my own eyes, was capable of raising everyone of its constituents into a better and fuller life, I found myself faced with this dilemma: either the book I was beginning to write about Synanon was true—or else it was false. If false, why was I writing it? If true, what basis had I for thinking of Donna as being less influenced by Synanon than other members?

"And thus I noticed, after a while, that my relationship to Donna was a kind of indicator of my faith in Synanon's capabilities. And when we had a falling out, this would carry over into my thinking about Synanon. I would begin to doubt. . . .

"Rumors about my affair with Donna eventually reached my colleagues at the university, and I heard queries about my intentions. I couldn't really be contemplating marriage to an ex-dope addict, could I? Did I have any idea of the recidivism among dope addicts? Yes, I knew that at Lexington and Chino and elsewhere the relapse of drug addicts hovered close to one hundred percent. I tried to convince myself that Synanon was totally different. But I remained torn. For an additional reason: because as a professor who was hoping to rise in the academic world, I had a duty to guard my career against gossip and scandal.

"But then I asked myself whether I wasn't a sociologist first, and a professor afterwards? And if I was a sociologist should I not have faith in my specialty?

"And so, in time, my love for Donna became the justification of what I was writing. And therefore the justification of my career. And when I would go to those meetings of the Citizens Committee in Santa Monica and I would hear this slavering against Synanon, I felt that it was the woman I loved who was being reviled, conspued, outraged. And I couldn't stand that. I wanted to go out and fight on the barricades!

"I remember once walking along the beach with Donna, on a foggy night, and noticing how the dim light gave her beauty a kind of unearthly quality. For some unconscious reason I asked her: 'If you hadn't happened into Synanon, what do you think you'd be doing now?'

"She said: 'I wouldn't be doing anything. I'd be dead.'

"I will always think of that moment as the one when I realized how much I loved Donna, and how strongly I felt about this sociological breakthrough that had been accomplished at Synanon and its ability to heal severe character disorders that our society is generally unable to cope with. I mean that I no longer saw any boundaries between my love for Donna and my love for Synanon. And I felt I had to marry myself to both of them. And protect them both.

"This was at that crucial period when Synanon was really in a very vulnerable condition. Chuck was in jail. The fury of the Citizens Committee was at its height. And I dreaded some overt act on the part of the Santa Monica police, who might for example, have driven up some night with four or five paddy wagons and arrested everyone on suspicion of using dope, and carted off the entire membership to the hoosegow.

"At that time there were only sixty people in residence and the sheer terror this would have spread into the ranks of these recent addicts, and from them to all the other hypes on the street, might have killed the idea forever.

"I remember exactly when it was that I first broached to Chuck the idea of getting some of this grant money. It would be a difficult day to forget. It was the evening when Chuck had to report to jail to serve his sentence. We had a discussion lasting some three or four hours.

"We agreed that Synanon would suggest the following project to the National Institute for Mental Health, which is a branch of the Department of Health, Education and Welfare, and in charge of distributing millions to various worthy projects, particularly in the field of juvenile crime and drug addiction. Our idea was to run one hundred youthful offenders convicted of drug addiction through the Synanon program.

"We would choose these young people from cases convicted by the courts of New York, and would avoid marginal offenders, picking our hundred samples from the roughest and toughest. The money we would ask for would cover only minimum costs of food or shelter in Synanon, with no significant sum asked for staff. All we wanted for these hundred subjects over a three-year period was two hundred and fifty thousand dollars. Which was thus less than a thousand dollars a year per person. A little over two dollars a day to house, clothe, feed the kind of men who were costing society as much as fifty times that sum when in prison or out on the streets.

"I doubt if ever there was a more modest request, and I was convinced that the N.I.M.H. would jump at the chance to test out the flamboyant claims of Synanon at so small a price."

Chuck said to me: "Lew was still very inexperienced in the matter of drug addiction. He still did not fully accept the verdict of Professor Alfred E. Lindesmith, of the University of Indiana, that the last and toughest monkey on the addict's back will be the bureaucrat.

"Reid, Jack Hurst, myself," Chuck continued, "all of us, in Synanon from the very beginning, have had so many encounters with the Establishment, with the people who have the diplomas, the people who have the government appointments, that we were not at all surprised to be turned down. Not at all.

"Of course we did have more hope than usual, because this time we were not just a bunch of junkies wanting to have a go at curing ourselves—of course that's forbidden, you know. It's forbidden to cure yourselves when there are a lot of people around who have spent many years training themselves to cure you in the expectation of making a good living out of it. That's only human.

"But this time we had on our side Dr. Lewis Yablonsky, a man with all the recognized diplomas. A man who was teaching sociology at a great university. So we did think that this time we had a foot in the door. Of course we were wrong.

"Look at it this way, Guy, and you'll see what I mean. Imagine a street. And two buildings. Two buildings on opposite sides of this street. That is to say, you think they are on opposite sides of the street, because they face each other. And in fact they glare at each other, as if they hated each other. And they do hate each other. But at the same time they are partners and really on the same side of the street.

"Let me explain. In one of these buildings there lives a connection. He is making a very good living out of the drug problem. He's fat and sleek, and there's only one threat to his fortune. Namely that someone will eventually discover the solution to the problem of addiction. That will be the end of him.

"And on the other side of the street, in that other building, there is a government appointee who is charged with eliminating the drug addiction problem in that community. And he gets a good salary for it. And is provided with an office, a secretary, assistants, and government funds. So he too is fat and sleek—due to the existence of the same problem that keeps the man on the other side of the street equally fat and sleek. But notice that he too has only one threat to his fortune. And it's exactly the same danger that threatens the man across the street. Namely that someone will eventually discover the solution to the problem of addiction. Because that will be the end of him too.

"In other words, deep inside, they both dread the same thing. Obviously. But of course it wouldn't do for them to join hands. Not openly. After all, one of them represents the world of crime, and the other the world of law. . . .

"But one action they can both wholeheartedly agree on: Synanon is a fraud and a failure."

Reid jumped into the discussion. "I think I can illustrate this situation for you, Guy, so that you will see there's an area here where it becomes so to speak undignified to support the Synanon method in the face of the opposition of the so-called trained and professional opinion.

"About six years ago Governor Brown wanted the whole question of the treatment of narcotic addicts in this state reviewed, and he appointed for that task a young lawyer whom I'll call B. out of charity. This young man got all the usual trappings that go with such an appointment, I mean a psychologist to assist him, a secretary, that sort of thing, plus the usual allowances for office and travel and incidental expenses. I mean they really set this guy up in a cushy way. And he was a kind of dapper fellow, very hip, a real charmer.

"Naturally we wanted to get in on this act. And we invited B. to come down to Santa Monica and investigate our work. And eventually he did pay us a visit. And immediately fell in love with our whole approach. Why not? All he had been seeing so far were hospitals or prisons, places where nobody was having any fun. While Synanon was full of cheerfulness and activity, and life there was a genuine ball. We don't see anything wrong with that. Why shouldn't life be a ball? Isn't that healthier for everyone?

"Now of course there was one additional reason why B. took such a fancy to us—and her name was Tammy. She was a cute little former whore and addict, and our friend B. really went for her. But that didn't bother us too much. Because B. was giving us plenty of his time so we could fill him in with our ideas and our ways of handling the dope problem. And he seemed to be genuinely excited by everything we told him.

"And as for Tammy, she had been a pro long enough to know how to take care of herself. We didn't worry too much about her.

"But what bothered us was that our good friend B. wasn't making any moves in our behalf. And we needed real support. Money in particular. Or anything that would give us status and enable us to reach out and get community help. So we could rent more space. And bring in more people. And give our members something better than food that was already halfway to the garbage can, and something better than two-story bunks in a crowded dormitory. And we dreamed of introducing our methods into one of the state projects for dope addicts, which would then serve as a showcase of what we were capable of.

"Because you see, we're monomaniacs. Forever busy with the job of straightening out character disorders.

"But we couldn't get anywhere in that direction with B. He just wouldn't budge. And we began to suspect that maybe he never would. We guessed that after all he was from the right side of the tracks, and Synanon would always be from the wrong side. That our ways would always be too unprofessional, and that he'd be a fool if he didn't hesitate before taking a bold position for us, because we had nothing to give him. In short, the way we toted it up, he had nothing to lose by ignoring us, and everything to risk by proclaiming us.

"And meanwhile, there we were, teetering month after month on the edge of bankruptcy.

"But what was there to do?

"Then, one day, B. wanted to know more about our Synanon game. And of course we discussed it with him. Openly. Telling him that we ourselves weren't quite sure just what the game was. An encounter. An interaction. An experience. Something very difficult to describe in words. It was total freedom of speech and total elimination of physical violence, and thus offered the kind of release of emotions that some people never get in their whole lives. One's hostility in the game could be genuine or pure sport. Nothing prevented one from indulging in exaggeration, vituperation, sarcasm, ridicule, and directing it towards anyone in the room.

"We suggested that he might think of it as a kind of game played in a huge bed, with everyone trying to snatch the covers from everyone else, and everyone trying to hold on for dear life. And really there was nothing funnier than this kind of verbal striptease. No better release for shouts and laughter. And afterwards a feeling of having enriched oneself, of having taken deeper stock of oneself, a feeling of something accomplished and something more still to be done.

"Just how or why the game could be a moment of truth in depth to almost everyone involved, and just what it thereby accomplished, all this was so various as to make it impossible to put one's finger on exactly what went on. But sooner or later most, if not all the players, could certify that they had been benefited. That they had shaken out some of their rigidities. Obtained new insights into their own nature. And were now enjoying life more than ever before.

"This explanation did not satisfy B. It merely piqued his curiosity. I'm not going to deny that to a certain extent we did want to lure him into a game. Because we wanted to level with him. And we wanted him to level with us. But it would be false to say that we rigged up a special game for him."

At this point Chuck took over from Reid: "The fact is," Chuck said, "that I warned him. I told him that our Synanon game was sometimes more than just the screams and the laughter and the obscenities that one could hear in the corridors on game nights. The game could really get quite rough. Girls, and sometimes even men, would break into tears, and run off to their cots. Of course it was all verbal. And no permanent harm. . . . Still I suggested that he might prefer to be only an observer.

"But no. He kept insisting that he wanted to be a real player in a real game.

"Okay. If that's how you want it," we said, and we set one up for him. We had Jack Hurst, Jesse Pratt, Reid, and myself plus several other members of Synanon. And a couple of professional people who just happened to be there; for example, a psychologist and still another doctor, this one a medical man, and our friend at the time from the parole department. . . . They all wanted to be in on a game too.

"One of these two doctors claimed he had had some experience with group therapy and he kind of wanted to take charge and so we had to argue it out with him, that our game was not group therapy, even though it might be considered therapeutic and even though it involved a group. He then accused us of quibbling about names and we got into a real hassle, but eventually the game got started.

"It began kind of harmless. You know, the usual sort of kidding around, people sort of probing each other out and having a pleasant time. And nobody smelling blood yet. Not yet. But of course it had to come out. I mean our feelings about B. He would later yell about having been seduced into a trap, which was ridiculous. Our game just happens to be permanently rigged against pretense and phoniness. It's the greatest enemy hypocrisy and self-delusion ever had in this world. That's part and parcel of the nature of this kind of verbal encounter. In the freedom of it. So that when the communication lines get hot, the phonies are right away in trouble.

"Because hypocrisy and self-delusion can't find anything in the truth with which to defend themselves. They have to reach out for lies. Fabrications. Excuses that won't hold water. And the more of that kind of stuff one reaches for to defend one's unreasonable position, the more rotten becomes the foundation one stands on. The whole structure has got to collapse and engulf the hypocrite, or else —to save his hide, he has to run out on the game.

"That's exactly what began to happen when our game got around to the point where I asked B. if he had not convinced himself that at Synanon he was seeing something that was not to be found anywhere else in the United States, or indeed in the whole world, namely close to a hundred hope-to-die heroin addicts living clean of their own free will. Not a lock on any door, no substitute drugs, no monetary rewards for the members, in short nothing to hold them in Synanon except the kind of human environment which we have created here.

" 'You're aware of that, aren't you?' I asked B., 'that it is only our method of handling people that keeps them here free of drugs and crime.'

"He said that yes, he was fully aware of it. And it was marvelous. He had seen nothing like it anywhere.

" 'Well that's great,' I said. 'But now what are you going to do about it?'

" 'What am I going to do about it?' he asked. Not really asking, of course. Just fencing.

" 'Yes. What are you going to do about it?' I repeated.

" 'Well what exactly do you mean, what am I going to do about it?'

" 'I mean precisely that. Aren't you appointed to be the eyes and ears of the governor? Aren't you supposed to nose out everything that might interest him in the way of treatment for drug addiction? Isn't that what you were commissioned to do? So why do you ask what I mean?'

"B. said: 'Well, you know what I'm going to do. I'm going to write a report for the governor.'

" 'Yes, so I understand,' I said. 'But what about that report? Are you really writing it?'

" 'Certainly I'm really writing it. But you know that my report isn't due until December,' he said.

" 'Well, December, that's quite a long way off, isn't it? Over three months.' "

"That's when I got impatient," Reid spoke up. "I felt I had to get in on the action. I turned to this guy and I said: 'Now let me get this straight, B.,' I said. 'Here you are, spending all this time with us, and convinced that you have seen something so unusual that the like of it isn't to be found anywhere else on the surface of this globe, and all you propose to do is to write your report in several months—and meanwhile not say a word to anyone or do anything . . . ?'

"B. got kind of annoyed. 'I've told you already I'm writing my report. And that it's due in December,' he said.

" 'Well do you mean to tell me,' I said, 'that you are actually so bound to the letter of your commission that even though you've discovered here the most significant advance in the treatment of dope addiction ever—yes, ever!—you're not going to do a single thing about it until the last second of the deadline? Is that what you're saying? Is it really? Because if you are, I must tell you I find it difficult to believe.'

"That's when B. began to bluster. 'Well, yes!' he said. 'That's exactly what I'm saying. I'm running this commission. And I have my schedule. And I know exactly what I'm doing.'

" 'Great!' I said. 'But just for a moment let's look at it this way. Just by way of analogy. Suppose your commission had been set up to investigate—well, let's say cancer, the treatment of cancer in California. And suppose that you had a brother who had cancer. And then you ran across a place like this, where cancer was being relieved like nowhere else on earth. Would you still say, would you still insist that you had your schedule and that you were going to keep quiet about this until December—I mean in spite of your brother—and just so you could spend your time playing grab-ass with one of

the pretty patients who was being cured of cancer? I mean exactly
like you're doing here at Synanon with Tammy? Would you do that?'

"'That's a hell of an analogy!' B. yelled. 'Dope addiction and
cancer!'

"'I think it's a very good analogy,' I yelled back at him. 'My wife
killed herself because she knew of no cure for her drug addiction.
Just as your brother might also kill himself because he felt there
was no cure for his disease—and meanwhile you're here, keeping
silent, and maybe some hype on the street is just preparing to do
away with himself . . . just as I once attempted to do away with
myself because there was no way out . . .'

"'I'm not keeping silent!' B. shouted. 'I'm writing my report. And
it's going to be ready in December!'

"'Of course you could write it a lot faster if your hands weren't
too busy with Tammy's tits to go to a telephone and call up the
governor or the Department of Mental Health . . .'"

Chuck broke in: "That's when one of the doctors present
jumped to his feet and said: 'I've never seen anything so destructive
in all my life. This is no game. This is no pastime. This is no
therapy. This is naked brutality. It's beyond belief.'

"And he went on to advise one of our women residents to get out
of Synanon as fast as she could if she valued her life. Whereupon
this former alcoholic and pill-head felt it incumbent to switch to
the side of the Establishment by appearing to be just as shocked
as they were, and went around the room busily apologizing to everybody whose feelings might have been hurt. . . .

"So the whole thing broke up. With B. screaming that the game
was a setup, a fraud, a plot to coerce him. . . .

"But the meat of the coconut," Reid pointed out, "is this. We
never saw B. again. But he kept to his word. He did bring out
his report in December. I remember it well. A yellow-covered
booklet of over a hundred and twenty pages. And I want you to
guess, Guy, how many pages of that report he devoted to Synanon.
I mean how many paragraphs. Or rather, how many words. You
know the answer. Not one! Not one word. We just didn't exist.

"While doctors—some of whom were trying out silly and useless methods on three or four patients, and charging them fees ranging up to a hundred dollars a day, and having no results to show for it—people like that got fully mentioned. But Synanon, with nearly a hundred successes at that time? Not even in the Index! Now think that over! It's as though someone would go halfway around the world to see the Eiffel Tower or the Taj Mahal, and then he'd report that he saw a wastepaper basket on the corner, and a dog chasing a cat, and two children playing leapfrog, and not one word about a monument that wasn't to be seen anywhere else in the world. Not one word!"

Chuck said: "That's not by far the most ridiculous part of it. Listen to this. At the same time that the governor and the citizens were putting out all these thousands of dollars for a report that didn't mention us, the governor could have walked out of his office in Sacramento and gone to the newsstand, and for thirty-five cents—for just thirty-five cents!—he could have picked up a copy of *Time* magazine, which hit the newsstands just about the same time as the report came out. And saved himself and the state perhaps a hundred thousand dollars.

"Because there was *Time* magazine giving Synanon a full-page treatment! You see the journalistic media have never had any trouble discovering that Synanon was good news for addicts. Something the State of California could not discover with all that money!"

"I bumped into this doctor," Reid said, "the one who had declared that he had never seen anything so destructive as our game—I bumped into him several years later at one of those narcotic festivals, and I said to him: 'You know we now have not just a hundred clean addicts living at Synanon, but *four hundred*. And every one of the fellows who was at the game with us is still living clean. And I've been wondering if you still think of our game as the most destructive pastime you've ever seen in all your life.'

"And he snapped right back: 'I certainly do!'"

"And we had the same experience with the Dodd Committee," Chuck pointed out. "Senator Thomas Dodd, as chairman of the Senate subcommittee to investigate juvenile delinquency was another one who discovered us. He stood up on the floor of the Senate and delivered a thundering oration about the work that Synanon was doing for drug addicts. He referred to Synanon as 'a miracle on the beach at Santa Monica, a miracle that I feel can benefit thousands of drug addicts.'

"He went on to say that he was bringing this matter to the attention of the Senate because he wanted to pay tribute to the founding members of Synanon and to give its present and future participants some of the encouragement and recognition which they have often been denied until now.

"Senator Dodd even went so far as to direct the National Institute of Mental Health, that has all those millions of dollars, to provide Synanon with funds for the expansion of our program and for the introduction of other Synanons in other high addiction areas of the United States.

"What Dodd had to say about Synanon, when it got back to us in the newspapers, had us going around on clouds, convinced that at any moment the phone must ring and it would be long distance from Washington telling us that there was all this money for us from the N.I.M.H.

"But of course the phone never rang and we never got a cent. Not one cent. Since then Senator Dodd has been pilloried for careless handling of money. As if everyone else in Washington was absolutely scrupulous about the expenditure of every dime.

"And then we had the same thing when the California Assembly Interim Committee on Criminal Procedure investigated us. That committee loved us. And took their time studying us thoroughly. And when they issued their two-hundred page report, Synanon took up seventy pages of it. Giving us the feeling that now we had finally arrived!

"Here, I'll read you some of what they had to say. Listen to this: 'Recognizing the failure of standard treatment approaches to the narcotics addict, and the magnitude of California's narcotic problem, we urge that every possible approach to rehabilitation be explored.

Government does not, and should not, have a monopoly in the field of narcotics rehabilitation. We welcome any effort that offers promise of some success in rehabilitating narcotic addicts. We believe that Synanon's program is one of the most promising yet developed in the United States. . . .'

"And hear this, Guy. '. . . the most promising yet developed in the United States. *It deserves the helpful, non-directive interest of the people of California.*'

"In other words this committee was saying to California: 'Don't try to change Synanon. But give them help.'

"But how did the bureaucrats feel about it? Study this report and see how the big shots of the Department of Corrections weaseled out of that recommendation. Here's their state director saying: 'If Synanon develops techniques and programs which appear to work, our department certainly will evaluate them. . . .' Which translated into plain English means that the Department of Corrections could not see as yet anything to interest them in Synanon, but that in the future if something of interest should occur there, they would look into it. Incidentally, to this day, they never have.

"And here's the chief of the Department of Corrections bringing up again the old business of the Santa Monica zoning violation. Saying: 'It would be illogical to ask a state agency to approve the operation of an organization which has been found guilty on two counts.' Think of that, Guy. At no place in the report of this Interim Committee was there any suggestion that the Department of Corrections should approve our *location*, or approve our *building*, but that they should help our program! It would have been no problem for the department, with their funds, to relocate us so that we could have no zoning problem.

"Such are the expressions from the people who were then operating the California treatment for narcotic addicts. The people of whose work the committee had said: 'Recognizing the failure of standard treatment approaches.' But that didn't faze these bureaucrats one bit. They weren't going to give up their lucrative posts no matter how great their failure. Never. Their state director said: 'I'm sure no one expects a state department to turn its thousands of parolees over to an uncontrolled, unresearched private agency.'

"You see? You see. Completely disregarding the fact that this legislative committee had just exhaustively researched Synanon. And they had therefore no right to use the word: 'unresearched'! And then this attempt of theirs to cover up their hostility towards Synanon. By lying if necessary. Which came out during the questioning of one of these medical bureaucrats, where the investigator had to point out to the doctor that he was using the term 'illegality of operation' again and again.

"The investigator said: 'Would you agree with me, Doctor, that that term could be changed to the question of the legality of the location rather than illegality of operation?' Now how about that, Guy, for a subtle verbal distortion? Ballooning our supposed violation of Santa Monica's zoning regulations, into the charge of conducting an illegal operation.

"But to be brief about it, just as we got nowhere with Senator Dodd's urgent request that the N.I.M.H. help us, so we got nowhere with the Interim Committee's request that the Department of Corrections help us. We had a solid wall of bureaucracy against us all the way from Sacramento to Washington. And we still have. We still have."

Lew Yablonsky told me something of his early attempts to interest the National Institute of Mental Health.

"When I first fully realized what a fantastic sociological discovery was coming out of Synanon's work, a discovery that I'm convinced must eventually revolutionize man's whole approach, all over the world, to crime and delinquency as well as to all other behavioral problems, I saw that the only thing holding it back was severe financial undernourishment.

"And naturally, at this time in the United States, I thought this was something for a government grant. And I knew where the available millions were. The N.I.M.H. had them. I've told you already how I discussed this with Chuck the night he was preparing to go to jail. We sat in his office and talked about it for two or three hours, until the Greek, who later ran the New York Synanon house on Riverside Drive, popped his head in and said: 'Time for jail, Chuck.'

"I swear to you, Guy, I had to think of Galileo. Galileo put under arrest for saying the earth moved around the sun. Sounds fantastic, but that's the way I felt.

"Well, you know of course, that we got nowhere with the institute. Our exchange of letters was slow and vague. They refused to come to the point, and I didn't know how to make them get off the dime.

"And then, finally, we got a letter that wasn't vague. It was a letter rejecting our appeal. Nothing vague about that. The institute was willing to admit that our proposal had certain merits. But there were other aspects of it which they could not accept. However they would soon send a team of investigators out to Synanon for a personal inspection.

"Chuck was determined that no one was going to accuse him of having made up his mind in advance about these experts. He called us all together and told us that he wanted these men to see every angle, every nook and corner of Synanon, no matter where it might be and how much they wanted to poke around in it. And their every question was to be answered fully and honestly.

"And so finally the team arrived. All men of the highest scholastic attainments. Representing all the important scientific fields bearing on addiction: medicine, sociology, physiology, psychology. All dressed in the neatest, finest suits, and all carrying matched luggage. And pipe-smokers every one of them.

"Obviously Synanon was going to get an in-depth examination. So we thought. But the fact is that we couldn't move them out of Chuck's office. We just couldn't. Chuck kept urging them to take a tour and see everything for themselves, but they wouldn't budge.

"I'm convinced that they had no difficulty realizing that here something new and different was being done. But instead of welcoming it, instead of eagerly examining it, they recoiled from it. I had the impression that it made them uncomfortable. Chuck, of course, would always interpret this as the natural stance of the Establishment sensing a threat to itself in the Synanon program, and instinctively shrinking away from it. Here were these people who had already spent millions and would be spending additional millions on tired old repetitious projects that never turned up anything worth a damn so far as addicts or criminals were concerned. And this never bothered them. Here however was something new, here was an unknown quantity, and it disturbed them.

"They couldn't figure me out. They kept wondering how I had got mixed up in this. What was I, a man with a Ph.D., doing with these Synanon executives who didn't dress the way the staff of an institution ought to dress, neither in a white doctor's smock, nor in a Madison Avenue suit, but more like guys taking it easy on a Saturday afternoon in their own homes. Guys meeting in an office that didn't look like an office. It was all far too irregular.

"A couple of them took me aside at one point to whisper to me: 'You realize of course, Yablonsky, that we can't give money to an operation of this sort.' And the way they said it reminded me of the old line: 'What's a nice girl like you doing in a place like this?'

"And whatever discussion we did have didn't seem to want to get off the ground. Because these inspectors not only didn't want to inspect, they didn't want to concede that there was anything here that should excite or interest them. With the result that conversation languished. What could one reply to such dismal comments as this: 'Oh yes. That is very similar to the sort of thing that is being done at the Philadelphia (or Boston) halfway house.' Thus implying that it was all old hat to them. Even though neither Philadelphia nor Boston could possibly come within miles of matching what Synanon was actually achieving with addicts. How then could it be the same thing? How could it possibly be?

"Or they would say: 'Of course we're always on the lookout for new projects to give money to.' Which was a kind of gentle caress on the head that was almost insulting in its patronizing effect.

"And one of them actually said—quite seriously: 'I see in your proposal that you have asked for four typewriters. And then I notice that down here your budget calls for salaries for only two secretaries.' He said this, Guy, as if he had really put his finger on the phony in our application. And it was obvious that he still had some reservations about this even after our explanation that the club itself would be able to furnish two unpaid secretaries out of its membership, and that we had deliberately eliminated practically all staff expenses in order to keep our budget as small as possible. Of course this too was suspicious, and even challenging, since the usual project stipulated by far the greater part of the budget towards the salaries of doctors, sociologists, psychiatrists, in short one's own kind of people. While our project seemed to be saying: 'We have no use for your kind. We do better without you scientists and experts.'

"Thinking it over later, I guess our attitude toward them was just as negative as their attitude towards us, but at the time it made me boil. After all, the main object was to clean up drug addicts, wasn't it? So what the hell difference how we did it? Since the orthodox method didn't pan out, why not give the unorthodox a chance to prove itself? And anyhow, to query the matter of four typewriters, when so many more important issues were involved! So what if we used the extra two typewriters for doorstops? What the shit did that have to do with Synanon's ability or lack of ability?

"I tried not to let my emotions run away with me. I tried to think of the possibility of our being granted funds in a future application. And I made an effort to pull out of them some guidelines so that we could couch our next proposal in more acceptable terms. But it was as if they had their own secret that they were not too willing to share with us. I can't explain it, Guy, except to say it was like they had some sort of exclusive country club and they weren't going to let us slum-dwellers into it. In effect we were being blackballed.

"Chuck would sum it up later saying: 'Here we were ready to talk Synanon philosophy to them, explain to them our Synanon techniques, and these ass-holes were worried about paper clips!'

"But I guess what distressed these Madison Avenue boys most was the fact that Synanon had no urinalysis program. Several times they came back to question us regarding our certainty that our addicts were really keeping clean. And to the subject of what sort of scientific control we had instituted. Naturally we tried to explain to them our philosophy of trust, and how it had led, long ago, to a reversal of values, from the code of the streets to the code of Synanon, but obviously even the word 'cop-out' made their hair bristle. It was a word so far removed from the domain of science that one could feel them squirming when we used it.

"And so, after a while, we kind of gave up. They were anxious to catch a return plane, and we were anxious to get this ordeal over with. As Chuck would later say: 'After this experience, let's have enough sense not to waste any more of our time with these guys who are only looking for piss in a bottle. Let's let them know at once that if they're after urine they'll have to crawl down our drain.'

"And, still smarting from this interview, Chuck asked me: 'Have you any idea, Lew, how much money was appropriated for this boondoggle?'

"I did a little quick figuring of what the plane fare, what the fees for five such experts might be, and came up with an estimate that ran anywhere from five to ten grand.

"Which really stuck in Chuck's craw. Five or ten grand was money just then so badly needed by Synanon that it would have been manna from heaven if the N.I.M.H. had denied us our application and just sent us the sum appropriated for the five inspectors. Which led Chuck to this comment: 'Those bastards should have been trying to find ways to give us money. Not forcing us to scratch around for it at their feet.'

"I'll tell you this, Guy, a visit today of people like that group would never even reach Chuck. They'd be handled by a second or third string of Synanon executives. With over eight hundred people now living here free of their old acting-out problems, we're beginning to rank with the biggest institutions of the country. We don't have to take that kind of crap any more. Not from anyone. We don't have to explain ourselves. Eight hundred addicts living without drugs and without barbed wire is the only explanation we need."

Dr. Elliott Markoff, a psychiatrist who spent some time during his training years studying Synanon, feels that Synanon has misinterpreted that episode of the visit of the scientists from N.I.M.H.

"I happen to know at least one of that group of five quite well," Dr. Markoff told me. "I can state it as a fact that they were really deeply impressed. Both by Chuck and by Synanon. One of them even put it this way: 'Synanon is a project that cries out for scientific validation.' Well, Chuck has it in his power to grant science that validation."

"You mean a pee-in-a-bottle program?" I asked.

"It doesn't have to be called 'pee-in-a-bottle'!" Dr. Markoff objected. "It's 'urine chromatography.' Why does Chuck keep up his constant fight against the Establishment? Why does Synanon have to pose as if it were some kind of beatnik operation when it's nothing of the kind? Why does Synanon have to create an impression as if it kept no records, when as a matter of fact it keeps excellent records.

"When I was studying Synanon," Dr. Markoff continued, "I tried to convince Chuck that his records were not only admirable but that the results they showed were highly favorable to Synanon. But Chuck was very possessive about those records. Sometimes I wondered if he really knew how favorable those records were, he was so cautious about letting anyone see them.

"Chuck seemed to be saying to the men who had the law plus the moneybags on their side, he seemed to be saying to them: 'Just give us the dough and we'll give you clean addicts. Take it or leave it!' "

"You're not implying, are you," I asked, "that the Establishment doesn't actually have any bias against Synanon? For example the California Department of Corrections. . . ."

Dr. Markoff admitted the existence of bias there.

I said: "Didn't you yourself have an agreement with the Department of Corrections to act in a consultative capacity for one day a week at the Corona Rehabilitation Center? And wasn't that agreement suddenly canceled when the department learned that some time before you had written a paper called *The Dynamics of Synanon*, highly complimentary to Synanon and to its methods?"

"I'm convinced of it," Dr. Markoff said. "The people at Corona apparently took the position that anyone writing a paper in praise of Synanon must be against the methods being used at Corona. So they combed me out. In fact they detailed one of their men to find flaws in my Synanon paper, but he only succeeded in making an ass of himself. . . ."

"When you were on the stand at the Faucette trial," I said, "you testified that the Department of Corrections considers Synanon a hotbed of vice. In fact you quoted one of the top officials of the department as refusing to investigate the merits of Synanon because he was afraid of being raped."

Dr. Markoff laughed. "I actually named that official in court, Guy. He has never yet visited Synanon, but that hasn't prevented him from reaching the conclusion that it is nothing but a whorehouse. You have to understand that some of the top men at the Department of Corrections are moral prigs. They hate sexuality."

"What about homosexuality?" I asked.

"Of course you're bound to have homosexuality at a place like Corona where you make a practice of separating the sexes," Dr. Markoff said. "But that's different. Because homosexuality is a sexuality that you can fight, whose existence you can deny or punish, whereas to mix the sexes as at Synanon is to accept sexuality as part and parcel of the human condition and this they refuse to do. They have to battle it.

"You see, they look at things their way. For example they will tell you with a straight face that they think Synanon is cruel towards addicts because Chuck delivers those terrible verbal castigations that Synanon calls 'haircuts.' And they point with pride that nothing of that kind would be permitted at Corona. Now go and tell the department that putting a man dressed in a crazy uniform behind barbed wire is far more cruel than any haircut Chuck ever gave, and they won't even know what you're talking about. They won't have the faintest notion. That's how far out they are."

Dr. Markoff went on: "I'm convinced that Chuck would have no problem winning an almost total victory over all other methods of handling dope addiction in this country, if it weren't for that massive ego of his. Now really, what's so terribly wrong with urinalysis? Except that Chuck has once and for all set his face against it with a thundering NO!

"And of course he's right. But having made his point, why keep stressing it? If all it takes to bring the scientific world over to your side is this little business of peeing in a bottle, then why not? We live in a scientific age, an age that demands this kind of validation, so why not? Really now, Guy, why not? I happen to think that Chuck is doing himself a disservice by his rigid position, and holding back Synanon from the great role it is entitled to play in the field of rehabilitation."

Before closing his interview Dr. Markoff wanted to tell me the story of a meeting of the American Psychiatric Association that was held in New York in May of 1965. "I gave a paper there, presenting my favorable evaluation of Synanon. Apparently the California Department of Corrections had got wind of it because one of their men was ready to follow me with a vicious attack on Synanon consisting largely of ugly sexual innuendos.

"But what happened was this: no sooner was this scathing anti-Synanon paper over and the meeting opened for questions from the floor, than a young man got up in the audience and introduced himself as an editor scouting for material and for authors for the publishing house he was connected with. 'I happen to be a former drug addict,' he explained, 'and a graduate from Synanon. And I can honestly say that I owe my life to their program.'"

"That must have been Jake Ross!" I cried. "He's my editor at Doubleday!"

And I told Dr. Markoff the story of the origin of this book.

17

As I drove away, late at night, from Dr. Markoff's home, I began to wonder about all the people who had in the past year or so said to me: "Synanon saved my life." And I asked myself: what about those who leave other treatment centers? Don't any of those people say: "Manhattan General saved my life?"

Is the fault in me? Is it because my ear is almost constantly glued to Synanon?

I do know this, that Dr. Casriel, after all his years of studying the dope addiction problem, came away with the conviction that the dope addict was incurable. He himself, therefore, never saw a patient who could say of any institution that it had saved his life. The story of Riverside Hospital in New York is well known. This lavishly funded place spent millions in what turned out to be such a flagrant fiasco that the operation had to be closed down several years after its opening.

John Maher, one of the rising junior executives of Synanon, declares that it isn't true that Riverside Hospital couldn't cure dope addicts. "In fact Riverside cured me twice. I was also cured at Bellevue and again at Manhattan. The reason I've been cured so often is because none of these cures lasted any longer than it took me to reach my connection once I was discharged as cured."

Almost everyone I've interviewed at Synanon has had a history of many "successful" treatments. Among the more curious being the electric and insulin shock treatments of a girl I will call Estelle.

Estelle had been through all the usual places treating drug addicts and finally came into the care of a private psychiatrist who gave her several courses running up as high as thirty shocks per course, and each shock costing Estelle's mother twenty-five dollars or more. At the end of which this doctor declared that Estelle was incurable. Which was of course only his own egotistical conclusion that since he couldn't cure her by shock treatment, no one could cure her by any method. This psychiatrist therefore advised Estelle's mother to take her daughter to England, where she could register herself as a drug addict and no longer have to steal or turn to prostitution in order to buy her heroin. This is in line with the popular American delusion that England has solved the addiction problem.

Estelle's mother, tired of her daughter's endless idiocies and imprisonments, decided to follow the doctor's advice, at the same time warning Estelle that this was the end of the road. That all she would get was a one-way ticket to London. In other words: "Go there and die!"

It happened, however, that someone overheard some of this conversation, someone who had a relative in Synanon. This person brooded about it and finally managed to get in touch with Estelle's mother and urged Synanon instead of England.

And thus it was in Estelle's office in Synanon Industries where she supervises the work of eight girls that I heard her say: "Synanon saved my life."

And there's Timmy Culligan, who tried to clean himself up again and again. At Manhattan General. At Metropolitan. At Central Islip. And by private therapy too. "I was never clean," he told me, "longer than four hours after any one of these treatments. Never!"

But now, acclaimed by *Look* magazine and by the *New Yorker*, and supported to the tune of millions by the Rockefeller Foundation, we have still another cure: the methadone treatment for the cure of dope addiction. Of which John Maher says: "This one is the pinnacle of human stupidity; in a field in which there is plenty of competition for the spot."

The *Look* magazine article of November 1965 displays a huge caption: NEW HOPE FOR DRUG ADDICTS. And a sub-heading tells how "a teaspoonful of medicine taken daily in a cup of orange juice is changing former dope addicts into decent law-abiding men."

Great! Except that the body of the article explains that this so-called "medicine" is really a German-invented synthetic narcotic! "As a pain-killer," so the article states, "methadone is not as effective as morphine, but a lot cheaper." And it goes on to say that "methadone's effects are not quite so potent as morphine's, but they last longer." Which of course means that in one respect at least they are actually *more* potent! But that would give the show away, wouldn't it?

So we now have this new and powerful synthetic 'morphine' magically lifted from the rank of dope to the classification of a "medicine," by nothing more than a slight semantic operation. A few letters of the alphabet do the job. And since the addicts who take this treatment get their "medicine" for nothing, and are even lodged and fed, why of course there's no call for them to go out on the streets and steal. They get all the dope they want handed to them. So they become "law-abiding," but of course without any basic improvement of their character or their disposition.

"Giving drugs to drug addicts," as John Maher once said, "is like passing out children to child molesters. Bank robbers can also be made law-abiding by opening up the banks and shoveling out the money to them. Using that method all the criminals in the world can become law-abiding citizens by tomorrow morning."

"What I discovered," Zev Putterman told me, "during my two years on methadone, was that it is in fact an excellent addictive drug. In many ways better than heroin. It reaches the market not only in tablet form but also in a liquid, and that's how I took it, by mouth, thus dispensing with needle, bent spoon, tourniquet, and so forth. In the second place the dose can be made hefty enough to last a good twenty-four hours, whereas heroin soon gets out of hand with the frequent fixes one needs, which in some of the older addicts results in a condition where they can no longer find a healthy vein in their bodies in which to shoot it. That's why you see some crazed old-timers putting a tourniquet around their neck in order to get a vein in their neck or forehead to swell up and allow the insertion of a needle. In the third place, since methadone is a cheap synthetic, there's no black market for it—not yet at any rate—and no cutting with sugar or milk, which makes the heroin you buy such a gamble, where you're never sure whether a fix is going to be great, or just good, or absolute garbage. With methadone you're right in there. Every time.

"Methadone is really a drug addict's dream of the cheap and long-lasting fix," Zev concluded.

Reid Kimball didn't quite agree with Zev. "I don't know what year Zev is talking about, but today there is a tremendous black market in 20 c.c. bottles of methadone. In fact, it's a real seller's market. And the solid methadone, called kick-pills, will sometimes go for as much as five dollars a pill."

The big objection to the methadone habit, according to Zev, is that it is so difficult to stop. "That's when you're in trouble," he said. "In serious trouble. If a heroin habit takes you eight days to kick, a comparable methadone habit will take you as many weeks. The physical manifestations will stop, but the sense of discomfort will hang on. Kicking methadone is a real psychic smasher. There's nothing so difficult and nothing so demoralizing. It nearly drove me out of my mind."

Reid took some exception to that too. "Zev talks as if kicking heroin was no more difficult than kicking Post-Toasties. I had a methadone habit that lasted several years. And I will admit that the feeling of depression, the sense of impending doom, the despair constituted an excruciating torture. But I couldn't see any great difference in the length of time it took me to get off methadone compared to getting off heroin."

Chester Stern, who is the recently appointed director of the New York Synanon house, also kicked a long-standing methadone habit. His experience was more in line with that of Zev. He described it to me as an almost intolerable sensation of having the marrow of one's bones screaming with pain for weeks on end.

Zev said: "Kids on the streets of New York are scared shitless of the methadone program which is building itself up to become the legally approved attack on the problem of addiction. These kids have heard how difficult it is to detoxify your system from methadone, and the terrible tortures one has to go through.

"But of course," Zev added, "you're not supposed to stop methadone. Not ever. I know Dr. Marie Nyswander, who developed this cure. She is a dedicated, hard-working woman. Her theory is that drug addiction is a disease. A disease like diabetes. And in the same way that insulin is the ideal relief for diabetics, so methadone is the ideal relief for the addict. And just as in the case of diabetes, the patient must be prepared to rely on the use of this drug all the rest of his life."

John Maher said: "I've been clean now for five years. In Synanon. With no drugs whatsoever. So how can a doctor claim that drug addiction is like diabetes? That's ridiculous. Just recently, while back in New York I ran into an old dope addict friend of mine named Freddie Lash. Kind of a middle-aged crumb, a petty thief, sort of a caricature of myself as I would have been if I had never hit Synanon.

"To my amazement he told me he was living clean. In fact he had been living clean for eighteen months.

"I couldn't believe it. To me he looked loaded to the gills. 'How come you're managing to stay clean?' I asked him. 'What are you doing? Dropping pills? Getting stewed?'

" 'No,' he said. 'I'm on methadone.'

"That explained it. Because it was so obvious that here was the same alienated, terrified, isolated human being—the same mindless animal that I had been while on heroin. Nothing had changed in him except that he had switched his drug. And his commitment to society, his usefulness to his fellowman appeared to me to be precisely the same as before: I mean totally nil.

"And it upset me to think that it should be permissible for doctors to freeze this wretch in his wretchedness and consider him healed, just because this freezing program would raise them to the status of experts on drug addiction and enhance their careers."

Zev said: "It's a fraud. And an illusion. All done with verbal trickery. Where a drug suddenly becomes a medicine. And you're clean just because you're loaded with methadone instead of heroin. And where you're considered a useful member of society because you can tote urine to the laboratory, like the guy is doing in the *Look* magazine pictures. Because of course they've got a pee-in-the-bottle program and that's about all this zombie can do. And the article admits as much. And his fellow-patients can't achieve much more. Some of them manage to function as nurse's aides, others try to help the janitor, a few go to school.

"When I came to Synanon and saw what was being accomplished here with no drugs, with guys like Frankie Lago and Oscar Camaño turning into talented artists, I composed a glowing letter to Marie Nyswander. It was convinced she would read it and cry out: 'Great God! I must see this!' But apparently, she was more dedicated to the field of addiction than to the addicts who suffer from it, because she would otherwise have taken the first plane out to the West Coast. The fact is that she never came out to see Synanon at all.

"And I was absolutely outraged. Her only contact with Synanon was a brief moment with Chuck when she met him in Washington at the President's conference on the problem of addiction.

"The strange thing is that you can read in Marie Nyswander's book that heroin was once considered a cure for the morphine habit and that for twelve years American doctors prescribed heroin to morphine addicts. And the fact is that morphine itself, many years before that was being prescribed as a cure for the opium habit! And if we had a crystal ball we could look into the future and find out what new narcotic will be prescribed to cure the methadone habit!

"Ideally," Zev continued, "every dope addict ought to have a chance at Synanon. Granted that many addicts are beyond redemption, and no institution on earth could build character into them, there is still no way of knowing for sure what an addict is, or is not capable of, until he has been brought into the Synanon program.

"And as for those poor sons of bitches who can't make it here, well, let them get out and go on a methadone program. But with no verbal disguises. Let it be known for what it is: a free-dope program. Let's be brutally honest about it. And let them have their free dope for the rest of their narcotized lives.

"But how to attract into Synanon all the dope addicts who could make it here—and perhaps brilliantly—but who somehow never get here—well, that's something I don't know. Did any of us come to Synanon of our own free will? No. We had to be utterly smashed before we stumbled into the place. The very idea of a dope addict doing anything intelligent voluntarily is totally absurd.

"Think of Ron Silva, for example. God knows where he would be today if a judge hadn't given him the choice of going to jail or to Synanon for ninety days. Look at him now. Years after his sentence has run out. Still in Synanon and now running our facility at Tomales Bay. And designing and superintending there the construction of a half-million dollar cultural center.

"He's got a little army of former dope addicts busying themselves soliciting expert help where they themselves lack the necessary skill and knowledge. They beg and borrow machinery. They hustle lumber and plate glass. They learn how to carpenter and lay brick and do landscape gardening. And when that half-million dollar building is finished, late this year, it will have cost a total cash outlay of six thousand dollars. Think of that! And then think of that methadone program, and that zombie carrying urine!

"It's the potential in people!" Zev cried. "And only God can know that potential. And when you put people on a narcotic for the rest of their lives, by fooling them into thinking that it isn't a narcotic, you're denying them the soul-searching experiences of discovering the outermost boundaries of their abilities. They will live and die without ever knowing their true potential. You will have killed that potential, instead of uncovering it. That's medically prescribed acedia. One of the seven deadly sins."

Urinalysis or methadone or jails or what have you, they are all varieties of containment to stop stupid and vicious children from behaving that way. And the very success of these containment methods means that it isn't necessary that these children be given a chance to grow up. So naturally they remain children, and maybe even get more stupid and more vicious. And the moment the methadone is removed, the moment the urinalysis is stopped, the moment the jail doors swing open, or the hospital doctor signs the discharge papers, these stupid and vicious children go right back to the streets to carry on exactly the way they were doing before. They haven't grown an inch.

"We've got something too precious here at Synanon to risk it on urinalysis," Jack Hurst, the president of the foundation, told me. "How the hell does a guy feel, standing before a urinal and aiming his piss into a bottle. And then carrying out this liquid evidence to some nurse or to some guy in a white smock. We're trying to give people dignity here. How would an ordinary law-abiding citizen feel if the secret police came around every morning to fingerprint him? Just to make sure that he wasn't a criminal.

"I feel the same about the Nalline tests of California. This is the only state that perpetuates that degrading business."

"I've heard a lot about Nalline," I said. "I remember some of your residents had to go downtown at regular intervals and go through that process."

"Nalline," Jack explained, "is a morphine antagonist that throws a person into almost immediate withdrawal symptoms and thus reveals whether the subject has been using or not. But it's not only the drug I object to, it's the whole spectacle which is as if designed to destroy a human being.

"They herd all these parolees into the office and of course some of them are clean and some of them are strung out. And you can imagine the emotions that are stirred up in these unstable characters when they are compelled to witness once more the symbolic rites of the needle and accept a shot of Nalline, itself a weak and ineffectual narcotic that can only whet a drug addict's appetite for more, reviving all his old passions, his struggles, his miseries.

"And then come scenes out of a nightmare, with those that fail the test being immediately handcuffed and shoved into a paddy wagon, charged with parole violation, and ordered back to jail to serve out old sentences. And some of them are suffering from the pangs of withdrawal and they are screaming and kicking. While inside, those who passed the test feel all the discomfort of a fix that left them unsatisfied and will nevertheless soon produce in them some of the malaise and nausea of withdrawal.

"No. Absolutely not. We've got something far too precious here at Synanon," Jack said, "to risk spoiling it in order to satisfy some scientists who have time and again demonstrated that they can't do what we're doing."

Anyone who spends any length of time at Synanon knows that there is indeed something here that is sort of a precious jewel or eternal flame or holy shrine that must be guarded against the desecrating touch of those who have not been initiated.

What it is may even be too mysterious for Chuck himself to fathom. Lois Folsom, who came to Synanon to solve an apparently insoluble alcoholic problem, said to me: "I don't think even Chuck knows what a fantastic thing he has going for him here. After all Chuck was already over his alcoholic addiction as a result of his A.A. experience, long before he developed Synanon. So he's never had the experience of falling into Synanon as I did, in a state of absolute despair. So how can he possibly know?"

How then does this precious something make itself manifest? Jack Hurst, who came to the club a shattered addict, quarrelsome, sarcastic, hostile, forever running off to shoot dope again and forever begging to be taken back, had this to say:

"I just didn't believe it. I had absolutely no faith in Synanon. How could I possibly believe that this thing would work with me? There were only eighteen in the place when I first came in. And nine of them were alcoholics who had been connected with A.A. And of the dope addicts there was only one who had been clean for six months. And yet there was Chuck convinced that Synanon was capable of miracles. When all you had to do was open your eyes and see that it just wasn't so.

"It's different now. And becomes more different with every day. Just take a look at the board near Barbara's desk. See the marriages that will take place this month. And the list of people scheduled to go on vacations. And downstairs the schedule of recreational programs. The ski trips. Golf. Horseback riding. Bowling. What a totally different impression it must make to a newcomer, to have before him the examples of hundreds of former addicts who have been here for five, six, seven, and more years. Plus all the addicts who have gone out into the world and are still living clean.

"None of that existed when I came in. This was a place without money, without property, without a past. And if it had any future it was totally invisible, locked up in Chuck's head. And I was scared and crazy.

"I could not look back upon a single pleasant day in my childhood," Jack told me. "My father drank himself into cirrhosis of the liver and died of it. My mother was not only a drinker like her husband, but a pill-head too, addicted to barbiturates, and she finally ended up in a mental institution.

"Both of them shared another lovely habit, a fondess for physical violence—at least where I was concerned. My mother was if anything more brutal than my father. But he must have had some affection for her, because when she would grab me by the hair and slug me, and I would get so mad that I would want to hit back at her, he always came to her assistance. Never to mine.

"Our home was a bedlam. Really it was God-awful. Never once did I bring a friend home. And when I wanted to visit kids on the outside I had to sneak off. And then risk a beating if I was caught going out, and certainly face one when I returned.

"My mother had a history of numerous abortions, which my father himself administered to her. But she finally had another child, when I was fourteen. A boy. But defective, as it turned out. When my brother was two years old he became convulsive and showed signs of some mental retardation. And I had to drop out of school in order to take care of him.

"Escape! That was the only thing I wanted. It was that desire, that violent need to get away that kept attracting me to the rebels in school and on the street. I admired the boys that goofed off. I envied the boys who smoked and drank. For pocket money I sold papers. And then I got myself a job. But my parents demanded all my earnings. I tried to compromise by giving them half. But they wanted it all. And when I ran off they called in the police to fetch me back because I was under age.

"The only thing I can thank them for is that they inculcated in me a hatred for alcohol. I suppose that if not for the picture they presented to me of the effects of drink—which scared the shit out of me—I might have followed in their footsteps. As it was, I turned to marijuana and to heroin. I certainly needed an out, one way or another.

"I got involved with girls. I got one pregnant and had to marry her. I rather liked her, so that wasn't so bad. But I certainly didn't love her. And it developed that unknown to herself as well as to her parents, she had had rheumatic fever as a child and had been left with a damaged heart. She almost died giving birth to my baby.

"And now there I was, a child myself, tied to a sick wife, and both of us tied to an infant. And all I was looking for was the fun I had missed when I myself was a child. I bought myself a motor-cycle and found in racing the deepest interest I had so far developed for anything. And the prestige of winning in the races was the only compensation I had out of life.

"Naturally I neglected my bride. But not so much that I didn't manage to get her pregnant again, although that was the last thing in the world that should have happened to her. She had to have a legal abortion. She knew that I was playing around with other girls, and in the hospital she said to me: 'It's all right, Jack. I don't care. I don't want to live anyhow.'

"When she died her parents blamed me for her death. There I was, already loaded with feelings of guilt, and now had to shoulder that one too. I drowned it all out with drugs.

"I took to living with a hustler. Took to smuggling dope out of Mexico. Took to burglarizing. There wasn't anything I wouldn't do in order to have the dope I needed. Because nothing but dope gave me oblivion. And only in oblivion did life become a ball. I loved it.

"No. Not altogether. Because underneath my narcosis I knew that I didn't really like myself. That I didn't really want to be a dope addict. That I didn't really enjoy being a pimp. That I didn't actually want to be a thief and a smuggler. And besides, under the influence of heroin I had to give up riding my motorcycle.

"I really wanted to clean myself up. But everytime I did, life became hell. Guilt and remorse would chew me up. All the terrible things I was doing, all the terrible things I had already done, like driving my wife to her death, letting her grandparents take over the raising of my child, all the crimes I had committed came back to haunt me. Until every part of me cried out for a return to drugs and forgetfulness.

"When I had to report to the Army I took along pills that were supposed to help me fight off the pangs of withdrawal. The result was that I went wild. Ran out of line, shoved my sergeant aside, fought the MP's, climbed roofs. I landed finally in the hospital with pneumonia, and in a fit of weeping confessed to the doctor that I needed morphine because I was an addict. And so, eventually, I was recommended for a discharge. And promptly went back to my old life.

"I was beginning to reach that point that most drug addicts must sooner or later come to, when they can no longer live with their drug, and no longer live without it. But meanwhile I had a brief spell of doing fine. In the great California housing boom I earned big money. Enough to get married again. To Terry—who is still my wife. Built myself, in my spare time and with my own hands, a thirty-thousand-dollar home. Had a son and daughter. Great!

"But at the same time I kept messing it all up with my need for drugs. Lost my home, spent so much money for dope that I couldn't buy food for my family. Got arrested for burglary and came out on a three-year probation. And then, finally, with everything around me caving in, got myself into Synanon and saved my life.

"And can you imagine me now standing by and seeing Synanon wrecked? Can you imagine me standing by and seeing anyone tamper with Synanon? To the slightest degree. Not on your life!

"I remember years ago when Synanon had still to see a check as big as five hundred dollars, when some guy comes around and offers us ten thousand dollars. Boy, did we roll out the red carpet for that angel. But it turned out that he was some kind of dietetic nut. Had some screwball theory that dope addiction was the result of what and how much an addict ate. And all we had to do for the ten grand was let him weigh everything that was eaten here and tabulate it. Count all the calories. Keep weighing everyone.

"The money tempted us. But Chuck said: 'Hell no! We don't want this guy mucking about, giving our people the idea that junkies only have to clean up their diet. Let him go out on the street where the real dope addicts are and count their calories! And cure them! And not get his operation confused with ours, so that we don't know which is which.'

"So we turned that big check down.

"I know that there are people who think we've changed now and that today Synanon is out for nothing but money. But listen to this: we turned down not just ten thousand dollars, but two years ago we actually turned down three hundred and sixty thousand dollars! And that was only the first part of a grant that would eventually have totaled a million and a half.

"The offer came to us from the Department of Health of New York, from their sub-committee on addictive diseases. And we said: 'No. No, thanks. But no.' I want to tell you that this firm NO of ours did not come easy. But we saw that this money would be wrong for us. Because New York was going to send us a lot of addicts. And New York would buy their beds and other needs and set them up as a separate section within our club. And assign certain case workers to the job of following the progress of this group. And certain supervisors to be in charge of the whole operation.

"Of course it was supposedly a test of *our* methods, but it was not the right test. It would have set up a division within the club. A division among the members, and a division of authority. And Chuck said right away: 'Synanon will of course have a class system, because that will be the natural reflection of the varying ability of different members. But it will never tolerate a caste system.'

"And that's what this program would have done: set up a caste system in Synanon.

"It would have done other things too. With all this easy money to spend, we would have been tempted to neglect our hustling, to become careless about our speaker's program, and I doubt if we would have ever pushed into our industrial operation, which has made us our own biggest cash donor. And wouldn't there have been a natural tendency in us to give more attention to the addicts who were bringing us in all this money, than to those who weren't bringing in a dime?

"It was a subtle kind of hook that once fixed in our gullet could never have been removed. I remember that at that very time when we rejected this offer we were so short of money that we couldn't distribute our usual WAM, even though the highest salary we paid anyone then was five dollars a week. But we just didn't have even that much to spare. But in spite of that we wrote a letter which has since become known as the Sam Grafton letter because Sam had a hand in composing it. But it was signed by Bill Crawford, who was then the director of our little branch in New York and who is equally responsible for its final form."

I have studied this letter. It illustrates Synanon's role in the American scene, as part of what Dan Garrett, the San Francisco lawyer who abandoned his lucrative law practice in order to become part of the Synanon movement, calls the "Third Sector," a phrase taken from De Tocqueville's study of our early republic, to describe a peculiarly American characteristic of people organizing themselves into groups to get something done exactly as they want it done and generally without government support and certainly without government interference.

The letter is worth quoting in full:

Dear Dr. Philp:

The recent offer of financial assistance to Synanon by the City of New York comes to us as an exciting affirmation of the value of the work our Foundation has been doing for the past eight years. We are most appreciative and grateful. This tender of public assistance on a massive scale is a genuine milestone on the long road we have traveled since first a few of us met in a room to give each other strength against drug addiction, criminal behavior and other aspects of the human condition.

The offer comes, however, at the very moment at which Synanon has concluded a long internal debate as to its own nature, its own future, and its role in what is obviously an emerging many-pronged national and local attack against such problems.

That Synanon needs money goes without saying. We have needed it from the first day; we have never had enough. But organizations have other problems besides the financial. Every organization affected with a public purpose must, we are sure, continuously study itself, assess its nature and its methods, and try to isolate the particular thing it has to offer that others do not. Obviously, Synanon is not alone in engaging in continuous agonizing self-appraisal. That is why we have both public and private schools, public colleges and private universities. They have chosen the private road and have not done so beause they have enough money. All of them could have easier experiences if they accepted public participation and continuous public subvention. Many have chosen not to do so, because of their feeling that they have more to offer, as experimental, dedicated private communities within the public world—whether their names be Harvard University, or Mount Sinai Hospital, or the Community Service Society of New York. All of these will gratefully accept contributions. But all of them cling to their private nature.

And so must we. We have asked for help, and we ask it now. But we must ask for it in the form of a general grant, which does not create particular classes of residents among us, or divide us into the publicly and privately supported. Complete mutuality within the doors of Synanon is not only our motto—it is our method. We must perpetuate it. The New York City contract may, perhaps have done us a great service by precipitating our own discussions of our nature and our goals, and we are grateful for that aspect of the offer, too.

Your offer is a good and generous one. It shows that a great city can think boldly and freely. Our regard for you is of the highest. We hope to retain yours. In deciding against the proposed contract, we are not in any way declaring that we do not need help, or voting against being helped. Through our open doors friends have come from the beginning. Parents of residents have come with baskets of food. A city policeman has come to investigate us, and has ended by leaving money for cigarettes on our mantel. Foundations have given us checks for thousands of dollars. We hope many more gifts will come. They are badly needed. A public agency that wished to help us with an outright grant would receive deep appreciation for joining hands with us, as other friends have done. In receiving such unconditional gifts at the door, we can remain what we are, with no price put upon our services, and no classifications set up among our membership—changes we fear because we believe they would send a tremor through that balance of confidence which is our only operating method.

In the multiplicity of agencies now forming up to fight addiction, we think it would be wrong, at this time, to risk changing the character of the one that alone has been successful. We wish all other efforts in this field well. We shall try to help them all by remaining ourselves.

Synanon never received any reply to this letter.

Actually neither Synanon's dedication, nor its principles, were so firmly embedded at the time of the receipt of this offer that this gift was not examined and re-examined, argued and reargued over many long hours. Those were difficult days. And the temptation was powerful. But Chuck himself reached the decision one morning and laughed out loud.

"We're turning it down, fellows. We're sending this money rolling out into the world to hunt up other money and bring it back to us multiplied many times. We're casting our bread upon the water so that it will come back increased a thousandfold.

"Let's play difficult to get. Let's make these people break down our doors and compel us to take their money. After all it's we who have the Synanon savvy. They don't. They never will. All they've got is the money. You'll see: the day is coming when they will shower us with it. Money will come pouring out of the walls. It will come in such quantities that we will have trouble scooping it up."

That day isn't yet. But already some of the big foundations send sizable checks, confident that in Synanon the money is being honestly and intelligently used. The Scaife family of Pittsburgh makes a generous contribution that grows with each year. The last check was for fifty thousand dollars. Kresge Foundation is coming into the picture. Groups of people with money join hands to underwrite Synanon's real estate purchases. Money is still short. Very short. But only because Synanon must plan ahead and because all the different directors, from San Diego, New York, Detroit, San Francisco, and so forth, are all making their own independent plans for expansion to meet the ever-increasing need.

The offer from New York has not yet been topped. Nor even equaled. But already the California Department of Rehabilitation is moving up to it with a hundred-thousand-dollar grant (which will most likely be expanded) and is beginning to feed into Synanon some fifteen thousand dollars a month for a program that is to demonstrate Synanon's ability to train the so-called untrainables, educate the so-called uneducables, and make employable the so-called unemployables.

Such cooperation between officialdom and Synanon is bound to increase as it becomes ever more difficult for the hidebound bureaucrat to keep denying and concealing the fact that Synanon has a way that other programs lack. Whatever that "way" may be. Whether it lies in the total confrontation of the Synanon games that Chuck described as forcing open all lines of communication and thus exposing all phoniness, or in the unremitting honesty that Reid stressed in his letter to the Office of Economic Opportunity, and which, he said, differentiates Synanon from so many of the other efforts now being made to help our problem people.

Or whether this Synanon savvy is nothing more than Synanon's determination to build character into their members, a type of containment that works while preserving each member's individuality and dignity, whereas other programs still goosestep along with the old system of containment, the containment that is built around the outside of people, in the form of stone walls and barbed wire, or compulsory Nalline and pee-in-the-bottle examinations which extinguish in people both their dignity and their individuality.

Or whether it lies in that mutuality that Bill Crawford emphasized and that caused Synanon to reject over a million dollars lest it "send a tremor through that balance of confidence which is our only operating method."

18

This field for helping people who need help (and who can best get that help by helping others) is of course as vast as the earth. So there is ample room for any number of imitation Synanons, which cannot possibly be competitive so long as they can accomplish what they propose to do. But for that they need the key. The savvy. The precious something.

Which isn't a secret at all, although how to use it most effectively requires a good deal of experience and practice. Years ago Dr. Cressey had already put that secret into writing, but had never seen it in actual use until he happened upon Synanon. He said so at a meeting in Sacramento.

And later the Synanon key was put forward again by Assemblyman John O'Connell when he was chairman of that California Assembly Interim Committee on Criminal Procedure (of whose fruitless efforts to get the Department of Corrections to cooperate with Synanon we have already spoken).

Several years before, the Department of Corrections had made its position on Synanon clear by pulling out of residence there some seven parolees whose subsequent fate under the supervision of the department was nothing anyone could be proud of. Not one of the seven stayed clean of narcotics or crime. Subsequent incarceration is recorded for all of them. A total, dismal, murderous failure.

Nevertheless, Dr. Forman, representing the Department of Corrections before the Interim Committee, defended this yanking back to addiction and crime and death on the grounds that Synanon was not equipped to handle these people because it did not have a proper professionally trained staff.

Mr. O'Connell's retort was to wonder what Dr. Forman had in mind by professional qualifications, since "we all seem to be at sea on this whole problem of treating addiction or fighting readdiction, and we seem to have an overwhelming number of professionals all over the country applying techniques that just haven't worked."

But apparently in the field of the treatment of addicts, professionals remain professionals even when they keep on perpetuating disaster and Synanon, with all its years of success, must remain suspect because it has no professionally trained staff.

"Isn't it we who are now the professionals?" Chuck has asked several times. But no. The diploma still counts. Ahead of results. Not the number of addicts you clean up, but the number of framed pieces of paper you have on your walls. That's where the totals are.

The fact that professionals—in spite of their diplomas—were failing all over the map did not disturb Dr. Forman one bit. He argued that Synanon's method had never been proven by a previous "pilot experimental program." Failure or success with human guinea pigs must be considered as secondary, when it comes to the primary necessity, which is the observance of strict scientific etiquette.

It was at this point that Mr. O'Connell brought up Dr. Cressey's key, which pointed out that so long as in our prisons (both state and federal) and in all our narcotic hospitals, the inmates acquire status by bragging of their past misdeeds—the moment they feel themselves out of the range of wardens, guards, and doctors—and so long as he who can tell the worst crimes is looked upon as a hero, just that long will our institutions fail.

"Whereas here at Synanon," Mr. O'Connell pointed out, "the highest status is conferred, by mutual agreement and by admiration of the co-residents, on that person who can claim that he has had the longest record of constructive conduct, to wit, being free and clear of addiction for the longest period of time, or of having studied certain books that he had never thought of studying before which stimulate his intellectual interests and also his interest in returning to society in a very constructive capacity.

"This seems to me to be the key distinction between the Synanon program and all the other programs that I have heard and read and learned about, *and this is only made possible because there are no guards or administrators or wardens or any of the group that constitutes the restrictive element that confines these people, confines their thinking and prevents this free expression on their own part toward a constructive outlook.*

"In other words, when you get into an institution, whether it's a hospital or a prison, you automatically have, built into it, the psychology or the attitude of *'it's we versus they.'* We are the inmates, *they* are the administrators. They could be the most Christian, the most tolerant, the most understanding, it's just in the very nature of things—by definition they are traditionally and classically and immediately set apart from each other, regardless of their own attitude, and the key to the operation here at Synanon seems to be that there are no such people here. That everybody works together and they have their bull sessions and their group discussions and all these other things together. *It isn't the staff on one side and the residents on the other, it is all the residents together."*

Not for one moment did Dr. Forman seem to get excited about a method that really worked in the field in which he was supposedly an expert with all the necessary professional qualifications. Not for a moment did it seem to occur to him that he ought to welcome this information about Synanon and rush to discover for himself if it were really true. No, he stuck to his position that "we don't have any data on Synanon," and "we don't know if it is kosher or not." And apparently felt quite satisfied with himself after this confession of ignorance and in no hurry whatsoever to clear it up.

Not for a moment did he express a feeling of exultation that perhaps a breakthrough had finally been discovered in a field where failure ran anywhere from ninety percent on up to a full one hundred percent. And when he was told about the importance of the *"we versus they"* type of institution, he had apparently not the faintest desire to follow up this suggestion or to find out how one might go about building an institution of that kind.

Because his kind of professional thinks it is only fair to keep on testing the addict to see if he is clean, but doesn't relish the idea of anyone returning the compliment by putting him or his institution to the test, to see if either is accomplishing anything.

It must be said, however, for Dr. Forman, that he fought vigorously and astutely to uphold the rights of the professionals to handle this matter in their own way. But apparently without realizing that he was thus giving genuine professionalism a black eye for which the true professionals who truly want to solve the problem and not just retain their hold on it will never owe him any thanks.

In order to free the addict from the hands of those professionals who are typified by Dr. Forman, the directors of Synanon had been on the lookout for an addict-parolee, who would consent to be their human guinea pig.

This was not easy. Because an addict who is on parole (that is to say living his jail sentence outside of the jail) is not really free. While in jail he had the usual difficulty of getting any drugs and so he was perforce clean, or very nearly so. But since nothing had been done to alter his character and his need for the drug, he probably came out in the same condition he went in: still unable to face life without his anesthesia.

But that ability is now the basic condition of his parole. He must live clean. And to make sure that he is doing what he hasn't been educated to do, his parole officer can swoop down on him at any moment and subject him to a Nalline test.

Ever since the Department of Corrections had decided that their parolees would not be allowed to reside at Synanon, the best method of remaining clean was thus denied them. Only the courts could break that ruling. And this would require a parolee who would be willing to face a judge in the Superior Court for a writ of Habeas Corpus. But parolees know only too well the iron whip hand that the Department of Corrections holds over them and which can so easily charge them with violation of parole and put them back into prison to serve out the rest of their term. And this time with no hope of another parole.

The situation at present is that parolees dread the Nalline test. At the same time they cannot stop themselves from using. Some of them therefore prepare for the test by concealing a loaded hypodermic about their person. And after the pupil of their eye has been measured and they are given their shot of Nalline, they must find a way to give themselves a shot of dope from their hidden source, perhaps shooting through their pants pocket, otherwise the Nalline will put them into withdrawal, and this will become visible in the dilation of their pupils.

Interviewed recently on radio by Lew Irwin, Reid Kimball described the sad procession of parolees who would come down to Synanon or else telephone in, in order to find out if anything had changed in this parole situation. Reid would hear again and again some story like this:

"Because I'm a parolee, and I'm dying out here. And I'm so sick of trying to beat the Nalline test. So sick of going to take it, and then having to shoot dope through my pants leg, you know. And eating pills, and getting drunk, and dodging and ducking, and then having maybe to go back anyhow. I'm really dying out here. Isn't there something you can do for me?"

And over the years Reid has had to tell these voices over and over again. "No. The department still won't let you come in here. They'll yank you back to prison if you do."

Reid said: "First, of course, I'd always ask each one if he or she wanted to be our guinea pig. But they all know what it might mean to incur the enmity of their parole officer, or that of the Department of Corrections, and it frightened them to death."

It was Herman, a Synanon graduate, who is now a successful businessman, but before his Synanon days had had a number of years of personal experience living in the gray misery of parole, it was Herman who finally brought in a man who was willing to take the risk: Gil Faucette.

Gil was in his early fifties. Ever since the age of eighteen, when he had married a woman addicted to opium smoking, he had depended on the use of drugs of one kind or another and had never known what it was to earn an honest penny. Gil still had eight years to go on a two-to-twenty-year sentence. Five times he had been out and four times had been found in violation of his parole, and had been thrown back into prison to cool off for a couple of years more.

Then, one day, while out on his fifth parole, he bumped into Herman, whom he had known in prison. He almost didn't recognize the man. He had never seen Herman looking so sturdy. Nor driving such a good car. And then, when Herman took Gil home with him, Gil stared at the large and beautiful home where Herman lived with his wife.

Herman introduced Gil to Rita and explained that she was also a Synanon graduate, and that the two of them had the distinction of having been married at the first wedding ceremony ever held at Synanon.

Naturally the whole evening was spent in explaining and discussing how and what Synanon had done for them, and how no other treatment had been able to do it for either of them. And of course the idea of Gil going to Synanon came up for discussion too. But it had to be explained to him that this was the one treatment that the Department of Corrections refused to approve. If he dared to do so, Gil would be held for parole violation, and he had still eight more years of his prison sentence to serve! The stakes were really too high.

Thus it was not until another occasion, when Gil found himself in a tight spot and was prepared to do something desperate, that Herman and Rita took him to their home again and talked to him all night. And convinced him that in spite of the heavy hand of the parole department hanging over him, his chances were better in Synanon than outside.

Early in the morning they took him over to Synanon and presented him to the directors as the man they were looking for: the man who would take the risk.

Gil said: "If you people can do for me what you did for Herman . . . I never knew his wife before but I hear she was even further out than Herman. If you can do for me, what you did for them, I want it."

The directors did not accept this offer right away They questioned Gil for an entire day to see if his resolve was firm, and if he fully understood the dangerous stand he was going to take. And not until they had satisfied themselves did they take Gil into Synanon.

"When that news spread around the club," Gil told me, "I can't tell you how many people came up to me, shook my hand, embraced me. Some of the girls kissed me. Seems like I was the hero of the hour."

In accordance with the rules of the parole system, Gil Faucette sent his parole officer a letter informing him that he had moved to new quarters. And that his address from now on would be the Synanon House in Santa Monica.

In return he received a letter from his parole officer. The letter said: "Pack your things. Bring all your personal belongings and report to your parole officer."

This was the turning point. Synanon's lawyer advised Gil not to reply. Instead Synanon filed a restraining order to prevent the department from forcibly removing Gil Faucette. Synanon demanded that the department should show cause why Gil Faucette should not remain where he was.

It came to a hearing before Judge Benjamin Landis, a hearing in no way different from all the other hearings and trials that Synanon has had to go through in courts and before zoning commissions, and so forth. Always the crowd of enthusiastic Synanon directors and graduates and sponsors and well-wishers pouring out their feelings and their convictions before an array of tight-minded civil servants maintaining a death grip on their rights. Giving never a thought as to where might lie the true interest of the addict, or that of society in general. Seeing nothing but their own personal interests.

So that Chuck was led to comment: "How many more people?

How many more employees and how many more parolees and inmates is the California Department of Corrections gobbling up every year. This is a very terrifying situation. I think it is definitely comparable to the rise of bureaucracies behind the Iron Curtain and in Nazi Germany. Now, this is what we are addressing ourselves to. We are supported by thousands and thousands of people . . . good citizens who wish to use their own time and their own money to do something about the social conditions in their culture, and we are being hampered at every step by public servants. Civil servants they call themselves, but are neither civil nor do they serve."

The basic argument offered by the parole officer against Faucette staying in Synanon was that it was four miles outside of this officer's officially assigned territory. The basic argument offered by Synanon was that the methods pursued by the parole department did not help addicts, but on the contrary returned them to their drugs.

In other words the department fought to uphold a ruling, while Synanon fought to uphold a human being. A reading of the three-hundred-page transcript keeps bringing up this difference again in the most glaring manner.

Two weeks after the hearing Judge Landis ruled in favor of Synanon. With the following comment charged with irony: "The suggested reason for requiring the petitioner to remove himself from Synanon House in favor of a hotel because it is closer to the office of his parole officer, does not appear of equal importance so far as the future welfare of the petitioner is concerned. *Society would hardly be benefited by the relapse into active drug addiction of the petitioner if the only incidental benefit of such a tragic occurrence would be that the relapse occurred within the supervisorial territory of the parole officer.*"

Among many other cogent remarks of Judge Landis is the following: "It is the opinion of the Court that the Department of Corrections had not given reasonable or adequate consideration to the usefulness of the Synanon House project to determine whether or not residence at Synanon would not be in the best interests of the parolee and in the best interests of the state. *The Court is frankly*

*unable to understand this lack of interest in such a proven tech-
nique for the rehabilitation of addicts."*

Did Judge Landis's ruling have any effects on the Department
of Corrections?

"Obviously not!" Reid said to me. "Consider this: the department
had Gil for twelve years and they were not only unable to straighten
him out, but kept making him worse and worse. While we've had
him now for only one year and he is unrecognizable. Even to himself. For the first time in his life he is usefully occupied. He's developing himself in every way. He is so proud of Synanon and so
grateful that he is determined to devote the rest of his life to the
Synanon movement.

"Now consider the attitude of the Department of Corrections. In
spite of Gil's improvement, they still insist that he should be turned
over to them, and are busy preparing their appeal before the Appel-
late Court. And what's more, they're doing it on government
funds.

"Think of the contradiction involved here. Our California Department of Corrections doing its best to keep a Californian from being
corrected! Appealing to the courts to help them stop a man from
getting better! And your taxes are paying for the legal expenses
involved! Think of that!"

Norman Herring, Synanon's counselor-at-law, a former alcoholic
who is just short of being blind, put the situation in a somewhat
different light. "Well the Department of Corrections damn well
has to put up a fight against Synanon! They must. It's a budgetary
matter. If Synanon is revealed as doing the correction job that the
Department of Corrections is supposed to be doing but isn't, then
why shouldn't the millions they take from the government be denied
to them and turned over to Synanon instead? You see, they've got
to fight us. Or they're out of business.

"Actually they already know that Synanon has something that
works, and that they don't have it. And some of their parole officers
are now coming down to our Saturday night open houses and
mingling with the boys and girls. But still on a kind of incognito

basis. But the executives in the department, they can't give in. They just can't. Don't you see that there's too much money involved? So they're pinning their hopes on an eventual reversal of the Landis ruling."

Norman laughed. "When I went up just recently to the Corona Rehabilitation Center to attend a convention being held there, I took Gil along to be my driver and my guide. His appearance startled them. To see this former addict walking around, no longer a worm crawling at their mercy, but a man, confident, alert, and better-dressed than most of the people attending the convention . . . I tell you that made quite an impression. It was a visible demonstration on home grounds so to speak of what they had been unable to do in the twelve years they had had control of him, and what Synanon had been able to do so quickly."

What is it that keeps creating these perpetual conflicts between Synanon and the Establishment? Is it just a budgetary matter, a fight for the allocation of funds and the power that goes with it, a power that attempts to hide its selfish greed under the mask of science? The following story may not smoke it out, but it will, I believe, demonstrate that there is something here that ought to be smoked out.

This is what happened: Several years ago the Kings County (Brooklyn) Supreme Court Probation Department, aware of the mess they were making of their attempts to handle their addiction problem, with an almost one hundred percent return of probationers to drugs, applied to the National Institute for Mental Health to give them money to finance a new program.

N.I.M.H. suggested that the probation department first accept a small preliminary grant to enable it to investigate existing programs all over the United States. A list of such programs to guide the efforts of the department was prepared by N.I.M.H., and it is significant that it contained no mention of Synanon, although the institute was well aware of Synanon's existence since they had only recently denied Synanon's application prepared by Dr. Yablonsky, and had instead sent out a delegation to investigate the place.

Dr. Markoff's opinion to the contrary notwithstanding, the N.I.M.H. very clearly did not consider the Synanon program worthy of the attention of the Kings County people. Or, in fact, worthy of any attention at all.

It was thus completely by chance that the Brooklyn delegation, while out in California, happened to hear about Synanon and decided to look into it, and were so stimulated by what they saw that they spent a few days at the club, and when they returned to New York, there was no doubt in the minds of these officials that Synanon was beyond comparison the most exciting program they had visited. And they lost no time in applying to the N.I.M.H. for their grant, specifying that they wished to create in Brooklyn a "Synanon-like" facility, and describing—as best they could, considering their short study—how such a program would be developed.

Realizing the difficulties involved, and their lack of experience, the Kings County Probation Department remained in touch with Synanon, initiating discussions of how they would go about the job and reaching toward the feasibility of turning over to Synanon the actual administration of their program just as soon as their application was approved by Washington and the money forthcoming. As far as the people at Synanon were concerned, they felt that no matter how these preliminary discussions might work out, once the Kings County application was granted for a Synanon-*like* program, the N.I.M.H. could not very well continue to deny aid to Synanon *itself*. Which only proves how naive Synanon could be at times about the Establishment and its bureaucratic centurions.

In a relatively short period of time the N.I.M.H. approved a grant of $390,000 to the Kings County Probation Department, the money to be expended over a period of three years. Whereupon the officials of the probation department called upon Chuck to come to New York and discuss the possibilities of Synanon's taking charge of the program. But the N.I.M.H. soon let it be known that this move did not meet with their approval, and in terms that were not too clear, they suggested that if Synanon wanted money they should apply for it on their own.

These developments put Kings County in a quandary. The court was turning out a constant stream of convicted addicts who needed care, the money for that care had already been allocated, and the nature of that care had already been decided on, and now they were forbidden to use the services of the only group who could get it started.

Their solution was to ask Chuck to permit them to send to Synanon some person who would stay there long enough to get to know the ropes. Chuck replied that the Synanon experience, the result of a number of years of trial and error, was something that no person could be expected to absorb in much less than two years. Of course, such a delay was more than Kings County could face, and they asked Chuck to make a hurry-up job of it.

Why Kings County officials chose for this crash course an ex-alcoholic is something that no one at Synanon has ever been able to figure out, unless there was some kind of dim reasoning that since Chuck had been an ex-alcoholic, the secret of imitating Synanon's success lay in the use of another former lush.

I have asked around Synanon for some information about this Ersatz-Chuck who had been selected to found an Ersatz-Synanon on the other side of the continent, but all I have been able to discover was that the decision was reached that the expediter's office, which at that time was a kind of funnel through which ran all the mail, all the messages, all the phone calls, all the directives from the various administrative offices, as well as all the applicants for admissions, would be the best place to put the Kings County man, for a quick bird's eye view of how a Synanon functioned.

And there he stayed for a month or two, and so inconspicuous that at the present time no one can even remember what he looked like. But back he went to Brooklyn to demonstrate immediately that he had learned nothing. Kings County had located an old estate on Staten Island, a place called Daytop Lodge, and there the Ersatz-Dederich was put in charge until found so lacking in what it takes that he had to be fired.

What now? The officials of the Kings County Probation Department would have been in a terrible fix without old ex-drug addicts who had had some Synanon experience and then had split or been expelled for one reason or another. Some of these discards were people so limited in their emotional development that they could never quite see the difference between Synanon and the usual jug into which they had been thrown so often, and when they wanted to split, ran away in the dead of the night, instead of leaving in broad daylight after shaking hands with everyone, and with bus fare in their pockets. They just couldn't understand that Synanon's door was always open, both to enter and to leave.

It was to such persons that Kings County had to entrust the operation of Daytop Lodge. They let the word spread that any drop-out from the Synanon program would be welcomed at their Staten Island facility, with every prospect of instant executive status and a liberal salary to go with it. The result was that a small number of promising Synanon people were actually lured out of California in order to get in on these questionable rewards. Which was Synanon's loss with little gain for Daytop, since such people were doomed to be washed out shortly for incompetence, and to find themselves eventually out on the streets again. Some later came back to Synanon and were readmitted.

However, as a result of circumstances which are confused and disputed, Synanon lost one of its more able members about this time, a young man named Dave Deitch, who upon leaving the club was almost immediately snatched up by Daytop and put in charge. In an article devoted to Synanon in the October 1967 issue of *Ramparts* magazine, Dave Deitch, now head of the expanded Daytop called Daytop Village, is willing to admit: "All of us owe Synanon a terrific, perhaps immeasurable debt . . ."

Synanon did not mind these developments as much as they might have because they lived in the illusion that the support that Kings County was being granted by N.I.M.H. for establishing their Synanon-*like* facility would now also be available to them. And in that rosy glow of rationality that afflicts people who haven't yet plumbed the depths of the bureaucratic mind, they dutifully filed another application.

Their application was denied.

Should one bother to look for an explanation for this generosity that the N.I.M.H. showed toward the imitation and the penuriousness it has repeatedly shown toward the original? Would that not be an utter waste of one's intelligence? It just so happened that about this time the real Synanon in California was already harboring more New Yorkers than its imitation in New York. In fact California's Synanon was doing such a good job for New York that it had actually emptied one whole community of its addicts, namely the Pelham Bay area. So that the grateful shopkeepers of the district, formerly mercilessly pilfered by these addicts, still to this day get together to throw an annual benefit for Synanon.

I do not see how one can escape the conclusion that Chuck reached and which I have already quoted: "This is a very terrifying situation. Good citizens who wish to use their own time and their own money to do something about the social conditions in their culture, are being hampered at every step by public servants. Civil servants they call themselves, but are neither civil nor do they serve."

19

Change is the essence of Synanon. Change and perpetual argument, debate, discussion about these changes.

Pete (whose name I have changed) said to me—just after I had written something about him: "Better leave me out. I'm handling some pretty big deals these days, and I often need important sums of money from the banks. What if they should deny me credit because of my past? Because they have read my name in your book?"

I understood. It was not an unreasonable request. So out goes my Pete episode.

Then pretty E. cornered me one day. "You wouldn't want to cause me any unnecessary pain, would you? Kerry and I are getting along so wonderfully. Why revive the past? It could trigger new doubts in Kerry's mind about his wisdom in marrying someone like me."

I understood pretty E. too. If Paul is entitled to his big money deals, surely E. is entitled to Kerry's love. So out goes my pretty E. story.

But Chuck raged against these efforts to conceal the truth. He thundered against these renewed attempts to build up false self-images. "Don't these idiots know what cured them? That it was being compelled to face the truth about themselves? And now, having moved up into the bourgeoisie by this method, they want to deny to others who are looking for salvation their own powerful example as living proof of what Synanon can do. Is that right? And how soon, with this kind of attitude, before they will once again have a needle in their arm?"

Chuck summoned pretty E. to his presence and lectured her. She heard herself compared to all the traitors of history. She wept and on her knees she promised to proclaim from the housetops what Synanon had been able to make of her who had been a drug addict, a prostitute, and a thief.

But no sooner had she informed me that I could tell the truth about her in this book than she began to hedge. "Of course you wouldn't want to publish anything in my story that might hurt innocent people, would you?"

"What do you mean by innocent people?"

"My children," she said. "My illegitimate children who are being raised by their adopted parents. They'll find out someday who their real mother is, and then think of the pain, think of the shame they would suffer."

And so it goes, until sometimes I wonder how much of the material I have gathered will ever see print. When I called up Brenda, who had cleaned up her alcoholism in Synanon, and asked her when I could come to see her and have her sign a release, I heard her obviously drunken voice answering the telephone: "I don't wanna be in your book, God damn you!"

I said something to her about this perhaps not being the best time to talk to her, which she cut short by yelling: "I'm drunk! You don't have to pussyfoot about it. But it's your fault. It's thinking about you and that God damn book of yours that started me drinking again."

She's lying of course. But that's how it is. With Synanon everything is fluid. It's the problem of Heraclitus over and over again: "What is reality if everything keeps changing?" No sooner have I written something about Synanon's business in art rugs imported from India, than I hear that the art-rug business is due to be cancelled. "We made money out of it," I was told, "but since it doesn't give our people a chance to talk about Synanon, what good is it?

Making money is only secondary with our sales crews. Spreading the gospel of Synanon comes first."

The problem is that I've forgotten just where I mentioned the art-rug business, and I'm not sure whether I should now take the trouble and time to go through the book in order to cut it out or not.

And then there's the ritual of the Saturday night open house that I mentioned I don't know how often. And the "clean" birthdays that were such an important part of that ritual. When I heard Chuck arguing that this ritual should be dropped, I was thrown into dismay. I saw myself painfully thumbing through the pages of my manuscript, rewriting and erasing in order to eliminate all those passages about those wonderful Saturday evenings at Synanon.

Then I shrugged. Why should I bother? Where had I picked up the notion that I was writing the definitive book about Synanon— as if the definitive book about anything as alive as Synanon could ever be written? Who could say that by the time my book appeared the Saturday evening open house might not have been restored?

Dan Spaccarelli, formerly of Synanon's automotive department, now a graduate, living and working on the outside, wrote to me from his hospital bed where he had just undergone an operation for ulcers: "Why did you let Chuck brush you off about registering Synanon as a trademark? What if some outfit were to come out with an underarm deodorant under the name of Synanon? Wouldn't we look ridiculous?"

The result of Spaccarelli's letter was that Chuck reversed himself and Synanon's lawyer was told to get busy and register the name as a trademark.

And Zev Putterman had this comment to make about another segment of my book: "Was it really necessary, Guy, for you to emphasize that Synanon's letter rejecting this or that official offer of money did not get any reply? Of course it didn't get any reply. How can any answer even be expected. Synanon letters are always written with such fucking finality that no answer is conceivable. Any dialogue between Synanon and any other organization is utterly ruled out because we have all the right answers and they have none.

"What you should write into your book is something about Synanon's Cassandra curse. The curse of being stuck with all the right answers? Why don't you do that?"

And it so happened that just a few days later I was a witness to Synanon's Cassandra curse illustrated in the most glaring way.

A very attractive woman with a warm expression and a bemused smile had come to Synanon to offer the club half a million dollars. She was connected with the Office of Economic Opportunity and more specifically with a drug addiction program that the O.E.O. had embarked upon, and she had one million dollars at her disposal with which to fund one or more programs in Los Angeles. And there she was, wanting to give one half of that million dollars to Synanon.

Jack Hurst said: "Great! The very moment you give us that money you're going to see something different in the handling of about five hundred kids whom we'll take in. Just watch us."

The woman explained: "Of course we'll immediately earmark that money for Synanon, so that you will know it will be yours eventually. Of course you can't expect to get it in a lump sum. It will be doled out to you at a certain flow-rate that will precisely match your intake of addicts. That's only good business practice, isn't it?"

Jack replied: "It may be good business practice with the job corps programs you've contracted with Litton Industries and with manufacturers of TV sets, and so forth. But in Synanon's case it is not. Because those are great big organizations who have vast funds at their disposal. But we have to operate on a shoestring. And it so happens that our present quarters are crammed. We're full up. In San Diego we have members sleeping in hallways. We're turning people away. We just can't take them in. We're giving them excuses. Any excuse. 'Come back in sixty days,' we tell them. Or 'Go out and dig up a thousand dollars for us, and then come back.' Our problem is always space. Space, space, space. And to even begin to think of taking in hundreds more, we would have to make a big down payment on some adequate property. And that means money. Cash."

The woman shook her head. "I'm afraid that would be out of the question in any case. Not only because that's not how we lay out our money, but also because we don't want any of our money to go for the purchase of property. You see, we're on an annual renewal basis, so we want all our money to be spent for current expenses. Nothing carried over into the following year. Which means rentals only."

Reid burst in: "But you gave Litton and other big companies the use of government buildings to operate in. Free!"

Jack said flatly: "Synanon no longer rents. Not anything. Our rental figure is already over twenty thousand dollars a month. For a year now we've made it a rule to rent nothing more. To limit ourselves to what we can buy. Some day we've got to get out of this rental hole."

"I'm sorry about that," the woman said, "but Washington issues us certain guidelines. . . ." She held up a sheaf of papers and shrugged. "Sorry. But these are orders."

"Well," Jack said, "you have your guidelines, and naturally we have ours. And *our* guidelines, it seems to me, are more important than *yours*, because you see, we can do something for these addicts, and these other organizations, they can't. All they can do is follow your guidelines. So what's the good?"

The woman shrugged: "Those are the regulations that Washington set up for us."

"Well you'll have to do something about it," Jack said. "Because you either want your money to be of some value in the dope addiction area, or you don't. It's that simple."

The woman insisted that she knew about Synanon and she did indeed want that half million to go to the club, and she would certainly get in touch with Washington to see whether this matter of renting versus buying could somehow be adjusted.

But in the course of her remarks it developed that what she had in mind was for Synanon to locate any new facility they acquired in a poverty area such as East Los Angeles. And not in

Santa Monica. Because the guidelines were explicit on that score: that drug addicts were to be treated in poverty areas. And Santa Monica was not such an area.

"In that case," Jack said, "the whole project is out of the window. As far as we are concerned. For three years Synanon battled all the authorities of Santa Monica in order to have the right to take our members out of the slums of Ocean Park and into a respectable neighborhood! And we're certainly not going to go back to the slums just to satisfy some bureaucrat sitting behind a desk in Washington."

The woman tried to argue, but Jack was very definite: "We will certainly not treat East Los Angeles addicts in East Los Angeles. That's out! We'll house them in Beverly Hills. Or in Malibu. Or in some other high quality area, but in no case will we house them in a slum. Do you mind if I ask you for an explanation? Where did I get the idea that you people who were trying to create the Great Society, where did I get the idea that you thought slums were bad places for people to be in? And that you were committed to wiping them out? Will you explain to me how that provision got into your guidelines, compelling us to go back to the slums?"

The woman smiled: "Those East Los Angeles slums do exist. That hasn't changed. And we do know that that area is swarming with addicts. So how do you expect to get those addicts to move into your program unless you go down to where they are? Do you see any other way?"

"You mean you don't see how we're going to get them into our program?" Jack exploded. "Well was it your idea that we would lure them into Synanon? That we would go down to East Los Angeles with a tambourine? Or spread sawdust and holy water? Hell no! We have absolutely no intention of getting those East Los Angeles boys into Synanon. None whatsoever! We'll do for them nothing more than we have ever done for addicts anywhere, whenever we have had space for them. Just hold our doors open. If *you* want to go down there and shoo them in, great! We'll be here to accept them. But that's all!"

The woman protested that the responsibility of bringing in the addicts would have to rest, of course, with whatever organization took up the contract.

Bill Crawford spoke up: "Well then this isn't for us. Can't you Washington people see that if we recruited these boys by holding out some kind of promise that they would feel that they had us under an obligation to cure them? And wouldn't their attitude then be: 'I double dare you!' Don't you see that we would be inviting all the resistance they could put up against our program? We'd look like the law to them. We'd look like policemen. We just wouldn't know how to go down to East Los Angeles and pick up five hundred dope addicts. That's totally foreign to our method. Totally. We wouldn't even know how to begin . . ."

Bill made a sudden turnabout. "Just a moment. I'd like to withdraw that. In part. We would know how to begin such a recruitment. In fact we could start out with a plan for recruiting one hundred and fifty East Los Angeles kids. Yes, we could do that right away. No problem at all."

Surprised the woman asked: "How would you go about that?"

"It's done already," Bill said. "Our open door policy has already taken care of it. We've got those hundred and fifty kids from East Los Angeles here right now. Start off our contract by paying for those hundred and fifty, and that will give us the money to acquire some property to house others from that same neighborhood. In fact we would use those same kids to persuade their parents to form a neighborhood association to funnel additional kids to us.

"That kind of a program, you know, is already working for us in Pelham Bay of New York City. The people there, the parents and the shopkeepers, they snapped to the fact that they were footing the bill for their sons' and their daughters' dope. These kids were stealing the money and the goods from them. So they organized to empty that neighborhood of drug addicts and send them all to Synanon. That organization is active all the time. The parents hold card parties and socials to collect money for us. They even got together to pay for a film and put it on TV. They hold a big annual party, a Synanon day. . . . That's something we would like to see started in East Los Angeles. . . ."

"That would be fine," the woman said. "But you understand we couldn't give you any money for the East Los Angeles boys you already have in Synanon. Our money is reserved for new programs. Already existing ones are excluded."

"Well, that's easily handled," Bill said. "We'll turn those hundred and fifty kids out! Back to their neighborhood! We'll just expel them. Then, if Washington wants them back in Synanon, why give us the money and we'll take them back in."

The woman smiled and shook her head.

"Why not?" Bill challenged her. "After all we've been taking care of them for your Great Society for years without a penny of your support. Nor any support from East Los Angeles. So why shouldn't you be willing to take it over now? You have the money . . ."

The woman still shook her head and still smiled.

Bill wouldn't let go. "Well, is my suggestion really so ridiculous? Now what if some disaster—and that's not at all farfetched, Synanon is right now only a couple of weeks ahead of bankruptcy; we're always operating on the edge of nothing—so what if some financial disaster now forced us to shut down part of our operation? What about that? Would you refuse to fund us so that we could at least continue with those East Los Angeles kids? Would you really?"

Still smiling and shrugging the woman said: "I'll see what can be done. I'll try my best. But we do have these guidelines, so I can't promise that I'll succeed."

Bill said: "Aren't those guidelines of yours just so much bureaucratic mucous. Something that ought to be wiped away?"

"I'd like to say this," Jack said. "If you discover that those guidelines are steel cables that can't be cut, then my suggestion is this: give that money back to Washington. Give it back to them. For God's sake don't give it to any other organization. That may sound awfully presumptuous of me, to give you this advice. But I'm leveling with you. Because I've seen all these other operations. I've known some of them intimately. And I've heard all about the government's job-corps operations. Believe me, they're all worthless. Worse than worthless.

"Their attitude is rotten. You can't take people from a culturally or economically deprived area and teach them a job. You're just laying it on like a mask. Smearing it on. And it will dry and crack off and fall away. So long as you haven't changed anything underneath. Not until you give these people a wholly new attitude towards life, will anything you teach them begin to penetrate. Until then it will just be something smeared on."

Reid said: "Let me add this to what Jack has just said. Because I think this is very important. Unless a program is total—and ours is —it can only do irreparable harm. Because it gives these youngsters the illusion that something is being done for them, when it isn't. And when they see the failure of it, it only confirms them in the opinion that their case is hopeless, that there is nothing that can be done for them. And it only takes one or two experiences of that kind and these kids don't care what they do. Believe me. I know. I was there. All of us here, we've been through that."

"I understand," the woman said. "But my job is to get a project started within a week. And if Synanon is going to insist that it must be all or nothing, then our conversation is over. We've got to find areas where we can compromise."

Bill Crawford said: "Well, suppose that we did find such an area for compromise. Would that mean that we would get the money? Or would it still have to go through Washington?"

"Oh, it would have to go through Washington," the woman said. "You would have to draw up a complete plan, in the form of a proposal. That's routine."

At some point in the conversation Chuck had stepped into the office. Introductions had been made, but Chuck remained silent. In the background. But at this juncture, he spoke up:

"My God! Another one of those proposals? Itemizing every bit of food and clothing? We're not going to go through that again, are we? Are we boys? Haven't we wasted enough time at that kind of thing? Why my files are loaded with stacks of papers we have written up over the years. Stacks that high. And not one dime to show for it."

The woman pointed out that the government did have the right to know precisely how the money was being spent. Whereupon Chuck said: "Well, you people go ahead. Fight it out." And he excused himself and left.

Jack burst out: "Wouldn't the simplest way be for you to give us the money, and then turn your watchdogs loose on us? We don't object to their nosing around to their heart's content, recording where every penny of your money goes. So long as they never try to tell us how to dispose of the money. So long as you let us carry on the way we know how."

Later, when the woman had left, Jack said to me: "She's really a good friend of ours. She admires our work. And she'll really try to get us that money. Whether she'll succeed or not, I don't know. But someday one of our good friends—and we've got a number of them in government—someday one of them is going to get us some of that money. They can't all fail, all the time. And like Chuck, I'm convinced that eventually we're going to be inundated with money. But the quesiton is when?

"I can remember way back," Jack continued, "when Chuck felt that once he had fifty addicts living clean, without bars, without threats, without phony medication, and all these former addicts visibly engaged in working productively to keep this plant in operation, that then the eyes of the world would be opened wide, and humanity would beat a path to our door. Bringing us all the money we needed. Because such a phenomenon was something the world had never seen before.

"But when that day finally came, and we had fifty addicts here, the world couldn't see us at all. So Chuck thought: 'What we need is something that will really sock them right between the eyes. Once we have a hundred addicts living clean and useful lives here, that will really wake them up.' So we just went on breaking our asses to expand our operation.

"But when we had those hundred addicts, the sources of money were just as oblivious of us as when we had fifty. But Chuck went right on dreaming. Figuring that two hundred addicts would do the trick for us. And then that it would be three hundred that would be the turning point. And so we just kept on struggling towards those higher goals. But nothing helped. And now, now when for the love of God we have eight hundred addicts here and more coming in all the time, the world still hasn't snapped to it. And we still haven't gotten a dime from any of the big anti-addiction sources.

"But of course this can't go on. It can't go on forever. There must come a point when the world will have to come to us, because we have the answers, and they don't."

This notion of Synanon having the curse of being stuck with all the right answers and the world having no use for them is what Marshall Cherkas finds most objectionable about the organization. Dr. Cherkas has long had a friendly interest in Synanon, but he finds this delusion of grandeur hard to take.

"This grandiosity," he said to me, "stems from Chuck himself, and seeps down through all the ranks of the club. With the result that each and every member, no matter how recently he may have blundered into the club, suddenly considers himself fully capable of lecturing me on psychology, group therapy, psychiatry, and why only Synanon can do the job."

I hesitated to argue this point with Marshall Cherkas because the Synanon pomposity has often had me gasping too, giving me the uneasy feeling of having been carried aloft in a hot-air balloon labeled Synanon, or else Chuck, or else the Game, and then left floating high above the clouds while the balloon disintegrates around me. And I find myself reaching out desperately for something to clutch.

This happened only recently, for example, when I had interviewed Estelle and she had told me the heartbreaking story of her many arrests, her endless cures, and how after many years of dope addiction and prostitution she had finally found her salvation in Synanon.

But no sooner did I have her story incorporated in a chapter of my book, then I learned that Estelle had disappeared.

"What happened?" I asked.

A shrug. "Who knows? She split."

"But why? How come? Just the other day she was talking of Synanon as if it were more precious than Fort Knox and the Eiffel Tower, both put together."

"Yes," I was told, "and not only that but right after Synanon had found a plastic surgeon for her who would donate his time and skill to removing her disfiguring tattoos. Right after the operation! We tried to get her to bear some of the fringe hospital charges, since her parents are rich, but Estelle refused to put herself in touch with them. So Synanon took over the whole bill. And the moment Estelle was on her feet, off she went. No message. No nothing."

I shook my head. I just couldn't understand it.

"That's a dope addict for you," I was told. "They'll burn you every time."

"But wasn't she going to games?" I asked.

"Oh sure, she was going to games."

That's when I give up. Synanon then becomes a thing of such unsubstantiality, and its very base, the game, a matter of so little strength, that the whole project seems to threaten to vanish before one's eyes, like morning mist.

And yet it doesn't. New people are pouring in, in quantities that far more than replace those who leave. And the club is busier than ever. A Black and White ball is set for Sunday night. Seventeen members sign up for a writing class which they petition me to lead.

And three hundred people gather to participate in a Seder led by Synanon's Israelite member, Shim Teitelbaum.

I was there and I can testify that it was a beautiful Seder. There was first Shim's explanatory speech, then the usual bitter herbs, the hard-boiled egg, the matzos and the grape juice (wine being forbidden in Synanon), and then the gefilte fish and the chicken. With almond macaroons to top it off.

And at the end Chuck gave a little talk.

He referred to Shim's remark about the empty chair, a tradition that Shim learned from his grandfather, symbolic of the welcome that awaits the unexpected guest. And Chuck observed that this beautiful gesture on the part of the Jewish people had a special relevancy here at Synanon where the door is open at all times.

"But our door swings both ways," Chuck pointed out. "It swings open when you wish to enter. And it swings open again, when you wish to leave. That is our hospitality. That is Synanon's empty chair. But our Seder," Chuck went on, "is more than the Jewish Seder. Because it is not exclusive. It does not just commemorate the rescue of one particular people. It commemorates the rescue of all people who need and want to be rescued.

"Look around you," Chuck said. "And what do you see under that black skullcap over there? It's Wilbur Beckham, the head of our San Diego facility. A Negro. You've never seen a black face like that under a yarmulke before. And over there is another face not often seen wearing a yarmulke. It belongs to Oscar Camaño, a Latin American. And there's Jimmy Middleton, half Indian. And over here is Reid Kimball, born a Mormon. And here I stand, born a Catholic. We have Jews and Protestants and every variety of believer and non-believer. All of us wearing the traditional skullcap. And celebrating a Seder the like of which is not to be found anywhere else in the world."

Grandiose? Without a doubt. But grandiosity had to underlie Synanon. Who else but a madman with a delusion of grandeur would have dreamed of architecturing a new society out of the most unstable people on earth: dope addicts. And forming them into the building blocks of this structure by the use of nothing more than words. No money. Just words. No employees. Just addicts.

That's not how they intend to do it in New York under the new Rockefeller program that has just gone into effect for the tens of thousands of drug addicts who roam the streets there. That program will have plenty of money. Eighty million dollars has already been allocated for the first year, and four hundred million is envisaged for the total three-to-five-year program.

And as for employees, they will have no end of them. Commissioner Pierce says: "We intend to control the movement of these patients with an average of one worker for every patient in the ward." For every two hundred addicts, eight recreation teachers, eight academic teachers, eight vocational teachers, eight counselors and two senior counselors. A total of 160 ward workers, not counting doctors and executives. All paid employees.

And despite all this pork barrel there is no intention in this program of dealing with anything else but one character disorder, namely that of dope addiction. While Synanon, without funds or employees, but driven by its own demonic forces, sees itself called upon to rescue all people who need and want to be rescued.

Dan Garrett, the San Francisco lawyer who abandoned his legal business in order to become a member of Synanon's board of directors, in his article *Synanon: the Communiversity*, had this to say about Synanon's far-reaching goals:

"It continues to escape the attention of most observers of Synanon (professionals especially) that Chuck has repeatedly said that Synanon is not primarily interested in curing drug addiction, but that this seems to occur as a side effect of something else which Synanon teaches. Synanon addresses itself to the problem of ignorance. This has nothing to do with intelligence, or a lack thereof. It has to do with a failure to achieve wisdom.

"The acting-out personality disorder (addiction to drugs is only one manifestation) is approached in Synanon as a problem of education for the individual involved. Whether this acting out takes the form of addiction to drugs, alcohol, habitual criminal behavior, or any form of sociopathic behavior is immaterial. Synanon does not consider such people as 'sick' or 'bad,' but simply as stupid.

"Synanon addresses itself to this problem with a total educational process which seems to reach all levels, and which is directed to the reshaping of the moral and intellectual qualities of its residents. The objective is not to bring the individual to the point where he can consciously exercise a choice not to shoot dope, drink, commit crimes, etc., but to reeducate him in a way which makes him the kind of a human being who would find it impossible to do such things."

Here is grandiosity to make one's head swim. It was by mere chance that Rex, a dope addict, blundered into Chuck's group and illuminated the power of the Synanon game. And it is on this most difficult of all behavioral problems that Synanon first sharpened its teeth. But its goal is to tackle all behavioral problems, and dope addiction, although the most thorny, is by far not the worst.

There are students of our time, for example Professor Pitirim Sorokin, who will prove to you with ease that our century, a century that has surpassed all previous times by its tremendous strides in wealth and knowledge, has also surpassed all previous periods of history in its violence and bloodshed.

Dope and alcohol may claim victims by the thousands and tens of thousands. But man's political and international conflicts claim their victims by the million and the tens of millions.

It is because of this vista upon the present and future of all mankind that I began this book with a pompous sentence that I hoped would give me the courage to devote a year and a half of my writing life to what is still largely nothing more than a dope addiction treatment center on the West Coast. I wrote:

"I've often thought that the story of Synanon—the story of that unique society of ex-dope addicts, ex-criminals, and ex-prostitutes— a society which these former felons now proudly hold up before the world as a model of sanity for all to copy (surely the most colossal piece of impudence in the history of man)—I've often thought this story worth recording."

And now that I'm about to end my chronicle I can see no reason to alter that sentence, except to add my feeling that someday Synanon's colossal piece of impudence may be put alongside other examples of blatant pomposity. Such as Copernicus shoving this earth out of the center of the universe. And Freud's obscene insistence on the sex life of infants. And Ben Franklin's suggestion that lightning might not be a display of God's wrath but just a very big electrical spark.

Does the Synanon game belong to such moments in the history of science?

Chuck certainly thinks so: "We regard all newcomers to Synanon as emotional and social first-grade students, whether they are illiterates or Ph.D.s or M.D.s, and we get both. They begin growing up again, but this time under firm paternal and family-type supervision. Whatever status they had on the streets is left at the door. The eminent surgeon will get dishpan hands and the craftiest thief—a much admired figure in prisons and narcotic hospitals—may specialize in removing stains from toilet bowls. Only when they have proven that they are worthy of promotion to more responsible tasks will they move on.

"There's no escape in Synanon through chemicals," Chuck adds. "Techniques of avoidance come to nothing. Dishonesty is anatomized in the Synanon game. The con-wise criminal finds himself thwarted at every turn, and the highly verbal professional can't find enough words to talk his way around things.

"I'm convinced that Jesus and his disciples played the game. Thirteen of them. That would be just about the right number. And I'm further convinced that the phrase in the Bible *Confess ye one to another* is further evidence of an ancient group situation requiring no priest, no witch doctor, no psychiatrist—just like our game. And I predict that in five years there will be a million people playing it. With unforeseeable results."

At this particular moment the total number playing the game is in the neighborhood of four thousand.

But of course that will change. As everything about Synanon is subject to change.

20

As important as the game itself, in the process of restoring an addict to sanity, is the structure that the game has built around itself. And this again was due to the happenstance of an addict coming into the game and drawing others in after him.

If the game had remained with alcoholics, it would not have required that the players be provided with a roof over their heads. It would not have been necessary to find food for them. And there might never have arisen the Synanon of today as a physical organization with properties and furnishings and people to occupy and run them.

At first, there were no scheduled jobs in Synanon. Everybody took turns at lending a hand, whether it was to the cooking of a meal or the washing up afterward. But this haphazard method soon had to give way to more defined programming. If a bakery would agree to give day-old bread, or a wholesaler would give Synanon all the bumped and bent and nicked cans of food, someone had to be put in charge of the collecting. And when the quantities of food increased, a place had to be found to store the excess. First in a corner, then in a basement, then in a warehouse. And then in warehouses. Plural.

Thus Synanon began to be a kind of a business and, therefore, had to introduce business methods. Mail had to be received and answered, so there had to be secretaries. Money had to be accounted for, so there were bookkeepers. Phones multiplied, so there had to be a switchboard. And when Synanon began to conduct a chain of gas stations, when Synanon began to sell advertising specialties, and for a time, rugs made in India, the business of Synanon became big enough to require the services of everyone in the club in some capacity or other. Often in two or three capacities.

All this because there was work that had to be done. And because Synanon has no employees. Only members. And, therefore, no payroll. Only your living. Plus a bit of WAM, or walk-around money, beginning with one dollar a week for members who have been there six months, and increasing slowly to five dollars a week, which for a long while was tops.

But the living of members improves as they step up their abilities and their responsibilities, and as various comforts and even luxuries become available, for example, a better apartment, a private car, household help provided by the Synanon service crew.

Thus what was originally merely a nest to house the game and the game players became a corporation whose executives took classes in business methods, in deportment, in salesmanship. Eventually, Synanon had to have specialized staffs to run a public relations department, a legal department, a department of archives. And as the game clubs for squares began to cluster around the various Synanon facilities in San Diego, in San Francisco, in Santa Monica, in Detroit, and in New York, Synanon began indeed to approach that "communiversity" that Dan Garrett had described, a community where education is total, so that no member merely exercises a conscious choice not to shoot dope, drink, or commit crimes, but where such behavior is virtually impossible.

Synanon is, therefore, something totally new. A test-tube sample of a world that could really co-exist. Bridging across every religious difference, every philosophical dispute, stretching across all the clefts that have split our earth in seemingly irreconcilable regions and peoples, a new monastic order free of enforced celibacy and other dogmatic confusions that have hitherto limited all the many attempts to unite man.

And it is because Synanon is such a rich and many-sided foreshadowing that the new member, whoever he may be, whether a drug addict or an alcoholic, a criminal or a prostitute, a mental or an emotional cripple, or all or several of these put together, or whether he is just a square who finds that the life he has been living has been too narrow and has not brought to him a sense of true joy or fulfillment, this new member makes one immediate discovery on joining, and that is that Synanon is totally unlike any other institution he has ever come in contact with.

Bill Burns gave me a little rundown on the kind of experience a new member goes through, first giving me a few words about his own history. About how he used to spend hour after hour and day after day, practicing before a mirror with a deck of cards. "Took me years, but I was determined to be so perfect that I could even deceive myself.

"Obviously I had a tremendous hatred, a tremendous contempt for the human race, or I would never have devoted so much of my life to learning how to cheat people. My conscience didn't bother me one bit. I had it all rationalized. I figured a guy who would bring himself and his money into the kind of gambling joint I ran, hell, his money was up for grabs. He wasn't entitled to a square deal, and I wasn't intending to give him one.

"All I did anyhow with his money was shoot it into my veins. So it wasn't doing me any good either. The way I threw money around, Guy, you'd have thought the stuff was going out of style.

"When I came to Synanon—for a long time none of the philosophy was reaching me. I guess I was held back for a year at least, because I was still busy hating people. Old patterns of thinking and feeling are difficult to erase. Why even now, wherever I am, if I see a man take a wallet out of his pocket, I can't help myself. I'm all eyes. I got to find out how much money he's got in it. Not that I want his dough. I don't want a dime of it. Not a dime. Not anymore. But there's that old impulse, popping up again, wanting to know how much money this sucker has got and already prepared to figure out how I can best cheat him out of it.

"It all goes back to those years of miseducation I gave myself, when I practiced how to cheat at cards. And I suppose that right now, in rooms here and there across our country, are young fellows, just as crazy as I used to be, sitting in front of a mirror with a deck of cards and dreaming of how they will soon be able to take away the money of the people they hate. God help them!"

Bill is now a kind of *ombudsman* for newcomers at the Santa Monica facility. He counsels them, listens to their complaints, sees to their comforts. An *ombudsman* is an official in Scandinavian countries at the disposal of troubled citizens who cannot find their way to justice amidst the labyrinth of modern government. And while American communities are debating the necessity of having an *ombudsman* for their citizens, you might say that Synanon is a community where almost everybody is an *ombudsman* for everyone else.

Bill said: "In every other institution the new member must feel that he has stepped out of the stream of life. An addict who goes to jail or is committed to a treatment center feels himself retired, put on a shelf, shoved out of this world, at least for a period of time. He tends to be resentful, lonely, miserable.

"But in Synanon the new member is as if plunged into a very torrent of life. In fact, we've got to go easy with the beginner who is confused by all the activity around him, bewildered by the constant stir, and is likely to become frightened and withdrawn unless we make an effort to introduce him to the full program very gradually. But right away he has a useful job. Nothing difficult. And short hours. But he's involved.

"We won't expose him to the games right away. Maybe just to the seminars, where the discussion is controlled by the chair. But, of course, eventually, we will get him into the games where the give and take gradually toughen him, enable him to pour out his anger and hostility, and discover that his own private misery is an affliction that everyone else has been through.

"And thus, bit by bit, he gets into the swing of it. Rises before seven, has his breakfast with the gang, and after that his morning meeting which consists of announcements, singing, jokes, the news of the day, and is usually loud and funny, and ends with the recital of the daily Synanon prayer, which is addressed not to God, but to himself.

> Please let me first and always examine myself.
> Let me be honest and truthful.
> Let me seek and assume responsibility.
> Let me understand rather than be understood.
> Let me trust and have faith in myself and
>   my fellow man.
> Let me love rather than be loved.
> Let me give rather than receive.

"Once the breakfast meeting is over, the members scatter to their jobs. Some have never had a job before, so now they learn to work for the first time in their lives. But they must also learn to play. And if there is one thing that delinquents generally have failed to achieve it is an ability to play. For that reason we have sheets on the bulletin board asking people to sign up for all sorts of sports, both as spectators and players. Our members also get tickets to plays, concerts, movies, museums. And we watch out to see that the tickets we get are not monopolized, and that deserving people all get their turn.

"And the club itself schedules no end of dances, entertainment, meetings of all kinds. And classes in all sorts of subjects. And once or twice a week the member will get to the warehouse, which is like a great department store, where he can pick up for free something he needs in the way of clothing, or a toilet article, or maybe a lamp.

"The sense of security and friendliness—as much as the game itself—gradually brings a newcomer out of his encapsulation. At the end of six months, he begins to have a sense of his own importance in the Synanon scheme of things. By the end of a year, he has already helped someone else, and finds that he has filled a void he may not even have recognized that he had: namely, the feeling of doing God's work. At the end of two years or more, he begins to realize that he is a part of something really big. And then he experiences, perhaps for the first time in his life, the pride of fulfillment. But he is still a year or more removed from the ability to handle large groups of people and take on the responsibilities that involve the making of administrative decisions.

"He has come a long, long way, but now he can begin to understand how far he still has to go before he can equal the contribution made by those Synanon members who, having committed their lives to the club, find themselves working backbreaking schedules of twelve and sixteen hours a day. And loving it."

Jack Hurst gave me an illustration of how time-consuming his job as president of Synanon is. Three times in the course of a single week, I had found Jack and his wife, Terry, Reid Kimball and Phil Altomare, and others, holding meetings on what to do about Bill Christian. For various reasons I had been unable to attend all these sessions and thus did not get a clear picture of the problem until Jack summed it up for me.

"You know, of course, that Bill Christian runs our kitchen in this plant," he began. "And that's a job that would drive Chef Milani crazy. And Bill Christian isn't doing a bad job of running it. In fact, I'd say he's doing an amazing job. But for Synanon, that's not enough.

"You know that any and every meal at Synanon is something of a miracle. And Bill has to get out close to a thousand meals a day, and more with each passing day, and he has to do it mostly with untrained help. For example: two of his people are Puerto Ricans who can't speak a word of English!

"So you see, we're asking a hell of a lot from Bill Christian. A hell of a lot. Our vegetables, for example, are generally half rotten. That's why they're dumped on us. Nothing wrong with one half, but the other half has to be combed out. And how Bill ever manages to get out a meat dish when he has available, say, fifteen pounds of liver, twelve chickens, and twenty pounds of hamburger,

I don't know. I wouldn't have the vaguest idea of how you could add all that up into something edible.

"So in one respect Bill Christian is our man, the man we need. Because Synanon is like Napoleon's army, it marches on its stomach. You know, there's no one with such a sense of insecurity as a dope addict, and nothing that erases that sense of insecurity so well as regular meals. In fact, for many an addict, that's about all that holds him to Synanon in the very early days when his emotions are all churning around in his gut and he still yearns for a shot of something to knock himself out with.

"But in another respect Bill Christian isn't ready for so big a job. When we keep having incidents in our kitchen, blowups, like when gas station boys come off from an eight-hour night shift and Bill Christian refuses to serve them a breakfast—hell, that's serious. That's very serious. Our gas stations are paying for a good share of Synanon's expenses. Those men working there are helping support Synanon. We can't have Bill Christian telling them that he can't give them a meal just because they happen to drop in at an odd hour.

"Synanon has to have food ready at all kinds of peculiar times. Late-night snacks, for example, when we have staff meetings that often last into the dawn of the next day. And meals for anywhere from five to seven hundred visitors who drop in on us every week. Most of them unannounced. And then special occasions. Maybe a V.I.P. or a wedding, or some celebration when we really put on a feed and eat from high off the hog. And whoever heads our kitchen has simply got to produce. We can't stand by and see our kitchen going to hell. It's got to run at all times. Like a well-oiled machine.

"And if Bill Christian can't run it one hundred percent perfect, then we've got to get someone who can. That's it!

"But let me tell you first about Bill Christian, so you'll understand something of the background of this problem. Almost seven years ago, he fell into Synanon. It was just after we had made our jump from Ocean Park to Santa Monica. I had been in for about two months, and I remember him coming in loaded out of sight. And I remember him kicking on the couch like everyone else, because in those days we didn't send our newcomers down to San Diego to kick, for the simple reason that we were still two years away from having a San Diego facility.

"Bill and I got along well together. I remember the two of us working on restoring beaten-up furniture, sandpapering and shellacking, and so forth. And Bill was doing great, except for one thing: his wife.

"In those days, Synanon was still groping around for the best method to handle wives and children. And we had not yet reached a hard and fast position, for example, on the question of families not sticking their noses into our house until at least three or four months after admission. Not so much as a phone call. And this wife of Bill's would get on that phone day after day, and she'd whine about how much she loved him, and how much she missed him, and how they were all crying for him, and asking questions about him, where he was, and was their daddy dead.

"And, of course, this would just about destroy Bill.

"We should have had sense enough to refuse to let Dolores call. But we didn't. And when her whining act wasn't working to smash her husband, she'd go into her scolding act. What kind of a man was he, she'd ask, to leave his wife and kiddies? Wasn't he ashamed of himself to be living in Synanon while she was struggling to feed his children?

"But no matter what act she put on, she always had a finale for him that would kick him right in the guts. She'd beg Bill to come back to her, telling him with tears in her voice, how lonely it was all by herself in bed at night.

"After every such phone call, Bill had to be pasted together again. Because he'd want to run home.

"But even worse than Dolores' phone calls were her letters, in which she'd always apologize for their being illegible because she couldn't prevent her tears from dropping on the ink and making stains.

"And that doesn't end all the tricks she had up her sleeve. Because Saturday nights she'd show up in person, weeping all over the place until there was nothing we could do but give Bill permission to leave Synanon for weekend visits home. For which he was far from ready.

"And still that dame kept fighting to get Bill out of Synanon altogether.

"Finally Chuck had them both in his office. He said to Bill: 'You've been clean now four months, haven't you?' And Bill agreed.

" 'Well, have you ever been clean that long before?' Chuck asked him. 'I mean while not in jail?'

"And Bill had to agree that he never had.

" 'Then Synanon is doing you some good,' Chuck pointed out. 'Because your wife, she was certainly never able to make you clean up, was she? So why don't you tell that broad to take her ass out of here and leave you alone until you've really made it?'

"Well, that was something Bill just couldn't do. Not to save his life. Not while Dolores was in tears and mumbling about her babies wanting their daddy.

"So finally Chuck turned to her: 'Well is that what you really want? A dope addict for a husband? A dope addict for the father of your children?'

"She kept insisting that Bill was clean now, while Chuck tried to make her understand that in this matter he knew a hell of a lot more than she did. 'I'll give him three days at home,' Chuck said, 'and your husband will have a needle in his arm.'

"And when she wouldn't desist, then Chuck said: 'Dolores, you're sicker than Bill. A lot sicker. Because if you were a normal broad you'd tell that stupid husband of yours that you're going to beat his brains out if he dares leave Synanon. That's what you'd say!'

"Well, Chuck was right. Dolores was sicker than Bill. We know that now. We know that from many experiences with wives and mothers. We know that a mother who will tolerate a son in her home while he is shooting drugs is awfully sick. Much sicker than her son. And as for a mother who tells us that she can't stand by and see her son suffering the torture of withdrawal, and goes out and buys him drugs—well, she's the sickest of them all. And we've run into many such mothers. Mothers who aren't ashamed to tell us: 'But you don't understand a mother's heart. A mother's heart can't stand by while her son is suffering such terrible pains.' And, of course, the son knows that, and exaggerates tenfold all the pangs of kicking. These are just a few of the things you learn at Synanon. And why we refuse to buy this kind of mother-love, and this kind of wifely affection either.

"So Bill left one Sunday and, of course, was back on drugs in no time at all. Until five years later, with his children now numbering three instead of two, and with his family now living almost all the time on welfare, and he himself shuttling back and forth in and out of jails, only then, when he was finally ground to a pulp, did he stumble back into Synanon.

"This time he had the guts to tell his wife that he was going to Synanon and she could like it or lump it. Of course, she went right back to her old tricks, her phone calls and her tear-stained letters, and the same whining about the kids having no shoes and about their being dispossessed, about the light and the gas being turned off—all of which was true. But not essentially different from what she had been enduring whenever Bill went to jail.

"Although Synanon now has a rule that we don't take in families until a member has been living clean with us for a year and a half at least, we once again made an exception in Bill's case. Bill was handling our kitchen and handling it well. And we didn't want to lose him. So we brought her in, along with the children, and set them all up in one of our Venice apartments.

"We thought we could control the situation by having them all together. But although she recognized that her behavior had given her husband five years of suffering and held him back from what might have been an important career in Synanon, with all the kudos that go to the wife and family of an important person here, her behavior hadn't improved one iota. She puled and she whined. She threw tantrums. She refused to wear a contraceptive and got herself pregnant again. She couldn't cope with her household, and for one reason or another, was always trotting from one doctor to another. We finally had to throw her in a hospital for a complete checkup.

"And, of course, all this bickering and doctoring was showing up in the kitchen. Whenever her behavior became too impossible, the kitchen went to pieces. The food was lousy or insufficient and on occasion not there at all. Bill's family trouble was radiating throughout the whole club.

"That's why we had those three meetings. To debate what we should do about Bill and his problem. Throw him out of the kitchen and put in another man? Or keep Bill, and put a boss over him? Or persuade him to get himself a divorce.

"It took a lot of discussion to solve this matter. But I think we finally hit on the key to the problem. The children! We said: 'Let's relieve this woman of her three children for a while. Let's send those kids up to Tomales Bay, where we have a school and where there are horses and cows, and swimming, and so forth, so that it will be almost a vacation for them, and let's see if Bill and his wife, left alone for a while, freed from household chores, will not recapture some affection for each other. There must be something there that's warm and solid if it has held them together for so long. So let's give it a chance to blossom again.'

"I think we've hit on it. I think it's already showing up. Dolores has become a changed person. And the kitchen is running like a top. But I want to make this clear, Guy. Let's say we had fired Bill from his kitchen job. He would not have been hurt. Not really. He and his family would have continued to have the shelter, the food, the clothing, the medical and dental attention—whatever they needed. There was never any question of injuring Bill in the area of his Synanon security. Or that of his family's. Never.

"All we wanted to do," Jack concluded, "was just clean up that mess in the kitchen. That's all. And I think we've done it."

But Chuck had this to say to me later. "Well, of course, every minute of that time had to be given to the Bill Christian situation. If necessary, the executive staff would have met not three times, but seven times. Or seven times seven. It's true that right now we're at a crucial moment when our first consideration ought to be the acquisition of important pieces of real estate, to house the flood of people who want to come in and can't because we have no space.

"But our main business is, and remains, love. That's what we're organized for. To give love. And love isn't love if it isn't total. And Jack, like any good business executive, is in there giving it all he's got.

"He's running an important organization. At the moment, we happen to be in the business of helping dope addicts stay off dope. We're manufacturing clean-man-days. And our factory is a roaring success. And Jack's the head of it. He never had much education in the formal sense, but he's learned a lot. And he has a big ego. That's the muscle that makes a man a success in business. And we've set him up accordingly. He drives to work in a fine car. His wife wears good clothes. He has a fine office with a fireplace. He has his secretary in an office to one side, and his board room for meetings to the other. And, of course, he has his bat boy. Why a United States Senator hasn't got it much better.

"But why not? Synanon is not a church. It is not a jail. It is not a hospital. It's a business! And our executives must live well.

"This country's trouble, in fact, the trouble in this world, is that we get caught up in the Jesus influence. When General Motors sets up an executive to sell Chevrolets on the West Coast, it never occurs to their board of directors to pinch pennies. They set their man up in a luxurious office, and give him a big salary. They begin by picking a man with a big ego, and then they make sure to nourish that ego.

"Synanon is equally consistent with reality. Synanon doesn't want the second-best for its people. We want tangible ego affirmations, and I have to arrange for that. People often say to me: Synanon should give the world an example of single-minded devotion to a cause, and eliminate some of these useless expenditures. But my answer is that Synanon refuses to model itself after the Salvation Army. We model ourself after General Motors.

"We're the only charitable organization in the country that does.

"Meanwhile Goodwill, for example, is being run by a man in a sweat shirt sitting at a broken-down table behind some packing cases. And he drives to work in a wheezy Essex that the cops chase off the Freeway. And some people think that's as it should be. And those are, of course, the same people who think that professors at Valley State College, for example, should be content with a bit of an office space in a huge bare room, with nothing but a tin desk to work on, and ugly classrooms to teach in. They seem to say: you educator fellows who devote your lives to one of the most important functions of civilization, you'll get your reward in heaven when you die, and meanwhile you can wear this cheap suit and drive around in this secondhand clunker.

"What is the result? There's a terrible need for top brains in the humanities. Why? Because there's a confusion between two words, the words *rewards* and *tools*. People don't seem to understand that the big house on the hill for the head of General Motors is not a reward but a tool. That house is where he entertains important people and feeds his own importance. And those servants and telephones and private planes, and so forth, that's all there to nourish that importance.

"But when it comes to handling a big charity we look around for old Bible prophets, men willing to live in a shanty, in sackcloth and ashes. Personally I wouldn't have the gall to think that I could imitate Jesus and run Synanon as if I were a saint or a prophet.

"Who the hell wants to be a colonel in the Salvation Army and get dressed up like a doorman, and stand on a street corner beating a drum? Synanon is full of young men loaded with piss and vinegar who want to become executives, or get on the board of directors, or maybe even take away my job as chairman of the board. Of course, I'm not going to let them. But they have the right to try. Because Synanon, unlike churches, jails, and hospitals, allows for constant upward mobility. Any man who is willing to make solicitude and good will a business can join Synanon and rise in it.

"That's why Synanon is known, and why Synanon literature secretively circulates in all the jails and treatment centers of the United States. It's human, you see. Not inhuman. That's why there's all this buzzing about Synanon everywhere, and why so many of those administration fellows who are scared for their jobs are so dead set against us. Prisoners never get along with the management of the prison. Never. But in Synanon, our members are united with management because they have this upward mobility: they can look forward to becoming part of management themselves.

"But note that when we speak of Synanon as a business organized to give love, we are speaking of only one aspect of Synanon, namely its structured, its formal, its rigid side, where we have people who give orders and people who obey those orders. But members of Synanon live only part of the day within that efficient boss-system. During another part of the day every member moves over to the completely unstructured side of Synanon. He moves into a game. It is as if he moved out of despotism and into anarchy. And his boss, who only minutes ago was bawling him out for slovenly work, can now be bawled out in turn. By his own underling. By the lowest menial on his staff. Who can pitch into him, call him an ass-hole and try to convince others that this executive is no better than an idiot.

"Of course, he isn't likely to convince anybody that he is doing anything but pouring out a lot of hostility. But that's important too. We want that hostility out. Not locked up inside people so that when the pressure rises they are like living bombs walking in our midst, ready to explode.

"If Synanon isn't already unique as a burgeoning General Motors manufacturing love, then it is certainly unique by this split structure that is by turns formal and informal. For just as we are the only people in the business of charity, so we are also the only people in the business of playing and spreading the Synanon game.

"When I look back and try to figure out how this development got started, I feel it as something that materialized out of a kind of pressure point where a universal intelligence impinged for a moment on our mundane thinking, and thus brought something new and different into our world.

"That was the time that Dr. Cohen was experimenting with the use of LSD on alcoholics, and I believe that a trip that I took then was responsible for altering my life and bringing me into contact with cosmic consciousness. Of course, these are all words that only poorly express what happened.

"But something did happen. And probably it was happening at that time to a lot of people. I mean many different people in many different places had a moment of startling intuition.

"But of all these people, which one was ready for this moment of inspiration? And of those who were ready, how many were actually capable of dropping everything else they were busy with and going to work on it? And how many who might have had the leisure to work at it had the ability to actualize it?

"But there I was, unemployed, and not only without money, but with no desire to make any. And with no ties to any person or to any organization that would have interfered with my giving it every minute of my time.

"And another thing. Very important. My willingness to launch myself into something absurd. Because you see it really made no sense at first. And how many people at that particular time and place knew the works of Emerson and were ready, as I was, to follow his command to 'grab cause and effect and bend them to your will'? In other words, rise above the limits of logic and reason?

"What was required for the founding of Synanon was social scientists. And there are none. Except in Synanon. Those people who call themselves social scientists today are nothing of the kind. They are really just observers who study already existing social forms. We introduce the x-factor, the unknown, into a social milieu and study what happens. If good, we keep it. If bad, we throw it out. While they remain mere lookers-on, refusing to mix unknowns and see if the mixture explodes and blows them through the transom.

"We take that risk. And that's why we, here at Synanon, are the only pure scientists in the social field. And naturally that brings us up against all kinds of opposition and criticism. We open gas stations. We go into the pen and pencil business. We open square game clubs. We may some day be in the moving picture business. I don't care what it is, Synanon will try it on for size. And study what happens.

"Right now we're moving deep into the field of the long-distance game. And I want to have a laboratory specially designed to hold twenty or thirty people comfortably for periods up to forty-eight hours. Which means swivel and rocker chairs made of steel and upholstered with the finest leather. We're already looking around for someone who will donate to us a couple dozen such chairs which retail as high as five hundred dollars apiece.

"We're already planning the audio-visual aids that will go with it. Because I want to keep complete records for a thorough study. We've run half a dozen such 'dissipations,' as we call these forty-eight-hour group interactions, and so far it has been only Betty and I who have been able to trigger these psychedelic trips which are accomplished without the use of LSD or any other drug.

"I found that we could demonstrate the casting out of devils. That we could exhibit instances of catalepsy and catatonia. There's really no need for LSD any longer. We have better ways of taking a trip. Not only our long-distance game, but our new weekend trips which we have begun to institute in Santa Monica and which will eventually spread to all our facilities. We are trying out many variations of these forty-eight-hour group interactions. Our latest is a combination of eight-hour games and four-hour periods of music and lectures. We find that over a weekend we can loosen up people psychically, shake them out of their hang-ups, bring them more tears and laughter than they have had in years, and lead them through expiation to forgiveness and to such love for their fellow man as many of them have never experienced in their lives.

"I think of these extended games and trips as powerful tools, like royal jelly in a beehive, capable of producing a new breed of human beings with greatly expanded potentialities, both intellectual and emotional.

"But my basic aim is to engineer a bridge for man so that he can link himself up, almost at will, to the cosmic consciousness and thus develop the most valuable part of man's brain: his intuitional intelligence. Throughout history man has depended on moments of inspiration to move him up the ladder of civilization. Surely this is man's most important faculty. And yet he still knows of no convenient or certain way of experiencing a truly creative moment that will bring something new and better into the world. In this area man still relies on chance. It is as if to make fire man would still have to spread his tinder and wait for lightning to strike.

"Right now I see our extended interactions as being at about the same point where our game was nearly ten years ago. But this time we are producing people who can spark the interaction faster than we did years ago. I can remember a time when, if I was not in a game, it wouldn't get going. And I had to play thousands of games before I could feel that there were enough experienced and capable players around so that the thing would roll on without me. But I doubt that the supply of skilled dissipationists will ever begin to meet the explosive demand that I already foresee in the near future."

Epilogue

Many years ago I read in the memoirs of Casanova how he watched one day the then famous painter Raphael Mengs working on a canvas. The painter surveyed his work, made a touch here, then a touch there, studied the picture again, made a few more touches, and then suddenly signed the canvas and was about to take it off the easel when he reconsidered and went back to his palette and his brushes for some more retouching.

"How do you decide when a painting is finished?" Casanova asked him.

"A painting is never finished," Mengs said. "But there comes a certain moment when the painter decides to stop working on it."

Such is the point I have now reached with respect to my saga of Synanon.

Otherwise I might go on working on it endlessly. Just recently, during the hippie craze, a bumper sticker done in psychedelic style with the motto *Synanon is Happening* began to appear on the club's own cars and the cars of friends.

It's this constant happening at Synanon that makes it so difficult for me to decide if my book is finished or not.

I have my notes on Celia, limping into my office and telling me about the circumstances of her life that led her to throw herself out of a twelfth-story window. And how she survived, with only her ankle joints destroyed. Her face unmarred, still beautiful.

She's gone now, Celia. Left one night for some reason that no

344

doubt even she would find difficult to explain. Perhaps a remnant of that same reason that had caused her to throw herself out of a twelfth-story window. And just as she must have immediately regretted her crazy decision to jump out into the void, so she no doubt must have immediately regretted leaving Synanon. For she called up at once and begged to be readmitted.

"But why, Celia? Why do you want back?" she was asked.

She could only weep and beg.

"Perhaps you need to make sure how you really feel," she was told. "Why don't you give yourself sixty days to think it over, and then call us up? You know your space here is badly wanted by people who have their minds already made up that they need our program. So think it over."

I don't know whether she thought it over or not. I don't know what decision she ever reached, if any. Perhaps somewhere in one of the offices of Synanon there is a letter or a message from Celia. Perhaps it got lost, snowed under the constantly rising demands on Synanon. I ought to look into it, but there are so many other stories I'm pursuing that I keep neglecting it.

One gets used to this tide of humanity that washes up on the Synanon shore and then flows back again into the sea, leaving a growing residue of people who will make it in the club. Of the others some will make it on the outside. Some won't. Some will return. Some will go to jail. Some will get lost. Some will die.

That's how it is. One gets used to it, without ever getting indifferent or callous. Just accepting it. The way Voltaire accepted the existence of God without understanding why God let so much rain fall into the oceans where it wasn't needed, while starving people on land were praying desperately for an end to the drought.

"We can't be all things to all men," Chuck will quote.

Perhaps I will go into the kitchen for a belated breakfast and a tall young man who is in charge will turn to me: "How about some soft-boiled eggs this morning, Guy?"

"Great," I say, and then when he has given the order to someone behind the counter, I ask him to introduce himself.

"I'm Steve Gilbert, the dinner cook. I work with Bill Christian."

"Where did you learn to cook?" I ask him.

"On a Florida chain gang."

"How did you happen to get involved with a chain gang?"

"For using," he says.

"Is cooking something they teach you on the chain gang?"

"It was on account of the heat," he explains. "I thought, if I keep on working out on the road under this burning sun, I'm sure as hell going to die. I was absolutely convinced of that. So one day there's this call for someone who knows how to cook. Right away I yelled out that I was a cook. I don't suppose at that time I could have boiled water without burning it. I just had to get out of that sun. That's all.

"Once in the kitchen I found an old cookbook lying around. And when no one was looking I read up on a few recipes, and to make sure that I wouldn't forget anything I tore out the pages and stuck them in my pocket, and now and then I'd sneak a look. Somehow I got by. There were a few complaints at first, but gradually I became a pretty good cook. And that's what I'm doing in Synanon."

"Better here than on the chain gang?" I ask him.

"Better," he says.

If it isn't one thing it's another. Perhaps Oscar Camaño calling me into his office, saying: "We're bringing Keith up from the prospects' bench. You said this was something you wanted to witness."

"How long has he been sitting there?"

"Since yesterday morning," Oscar informs me. "It's a kind of test to see how badly he wants back into the club. Just how much he'll take for the privilege of returning to Synanon, after running away. Taking along one of Synanon's best cameras."

As soon as Keith is ushered in, looking as miserable as he no doubt feels, Oscar attacks him violently: "A five-year member running off, sneaking out in the night to get himself loaded on heroin! Gone a month and already looking like a bum. Why do you want back in? Why? If we couldn't put our point across to you in five years, what makes you think we'll succeed in another five years?

"What a disgrace to Synanon! None of our members could understand it. They figured, if a five-year guy goes out and goes back on shit, what chance is there for me here? I'll never make it—I had to go around and clean that up. I've had to keep cleaning it up. Telling people that every village has its idiot. And Synanon too. Yes, we have our Keith."

Dino shakes his head: "We're not going to let this ass-hole back in, are we? Not when I got fifteen, twenty people calling me up every day, and I have to keep telling them we've got no empty beds, we haven't even got an empty couch. So why should we let this jerk who has demonstrated that Synanon can't do anything for him— why should we let him take up some of our space?"

June Marsh says: "This guy never really got himself involved in Synanon. I guess he figured just because he wasn't shooting dope that everything was coming to him—Keith, you've never done anything while here except take, take, take."

Oscar says: "I don't see how we can book that act of yours, Keith. Not once again. Keith, what are you going to do? What can we do with you?"

Keith finally speaks up in a dull voice: "Well, I can go to jail," he says, "if you won't have me."

"What about that expensive camera you stole from us?"

"I brought it back."

"If we decide to take you in again, Keith, you're going to have to work. Man, you're going to have to pull your weight around here. And we're going to be watching. Watching you every moment."

Reid declares: "That's not enough. I want to know what Keith is willing to do right now, so as to convince us that he means it. For example: Is he willing to have his melon shaved? Is he willing to get up tomorrow morning at the breakfast meeting and clean it up with the membership? And put it up to them? Beg them to let him back? Let the gang decide. After all it's their club he's messed up. And is he willing to go back to scrubbing the shitters?"

Keith agrees to everything. Nodding, yes, yes, in a barely audible voice.

"Okay," Oscar says to Dino. "Get him down to the basement and have his head shaved. And see that he gets right to work. At once!"

As Keith rises and follows Dino to the door, Oscar calls him back: "You mean we open our door to you again, and you just stroll in without a word of thanks? How about that?"

Keith mumbles: "Thanks."

A few minutes later I see a hardly recognizable bald-headed Keith sieving out cigarette butts from the sand of the refuse stands in the hall.

And still later Chuck says to me: "Well, of course, we had to let Keith back in. You know this guy was a member of the finest combat troops the United States has: the Rangers. He was fighting in Korea when someone sold him a bit of Ajax cleaning powder for heroin. He cooked it up and mainlined it, and thus became the victim of what is called a hot-shot. He was unconscious for two weeks, and one half of his body was paralyzed for a long time. He's still got brain damage. A guy like that has got to be in a hospital or a jail for the rest of his life. But in Synanon we turned him into a damn fine photographer. But what chance has he of making it in the outside world? None whatsoever.

"But what's wrong with that? Isn't Synanon big enough and important enough for Keith to devote his life to? Look at me. I'm in Synanon for life. And so are hundreds of others with me."

Or at lunch I will sit down with Anne Bancroft, who runs the legal department under Norman Herring, Synanon's almost blind attorney from Phoenix, who used to specialize in malpractice suits, and came to the club because of an inability to control his need for alcohol.

Anne had the same problem as her present boss.

"You know how Chuck described me when I came in?" Anne asks. "He assayed me at 'Ten pounds of alcohol, twenty pounds of hot air, and as for the rest it goes by the name of Anne Bancroft.' And have you any idea of how much that rest amounted to?"

"No," I admit.

"Seventeen pounds," she informs me. "Because all I weighed

when I came into Synanon was forty-seven pounds. For seven months I had been existing on nothing but alcohol."

"That's impossible!"

"First your body consumes all its fat," she explains. "Then all your muscle and other tissue. And then to spare your glands and other vital organs you begin to feed on your bones. I had chronic osteoporosis. Naturally I couldn't walk. I was lifted to the bedpan, and my doctor was convinced that at any moment this lifting would snap my spine, my bones were that thin and brittle. 'You have about ninety days to live,' he told me. And you know what? I didn't care."

"Why were you drinking so much?"

"A broken marriage. And drink was the socially most acceptable way out, short of committing suicide—which I had already tried three times without success."

"What made you think of Synanon?"

"Well, my husband—from whom I was already separated—was one of the sponsors who brought Synanon to San Francisco. And once, when I was visiting our oldest son, who was at college, I noticed this hypodermic, and afterwards I called up my husband and said to him: 'Did you know that Bud has diabetes? I'm sure he has, because I saw the hypodermic needle.'

"My husband knew more about the world than I did. He not only suspected heroin, but investigated and found out it was so, and got Bud into Synanon. Bud's been here for four years now. He's married to a Synanon girl. They have a baby, and I have the distinction of being the only Synanon grandmother. There are three generations of us here.

"It was my son Bud who kept after me to come into Synanon. Finally he said to me: 'Mother, you've just got to promise me one thing: try Synanon for thirty days. Don't stay a minute longer than that, if you don't want to.' So I promised. After all thirty days in Synanon didn't mean a thing to me. I had spent I don't know how many thirty days in different places, drying out from my alcoholism. I figured I could stay in Synanon thirty days standing on my head.

Besides I didn't think of it as really separating me from alcohol. I had never been in a place where I couldn't get alcohol. I don't care what hospital or rest home."

"How were you able to manage that?"

"Oh, there are always underpaid people around who will do anything you want them to do, if it's for money. Until I hit Synanon. There no one gets paid. Or rather where everyone is underpaid and doesn't give a damn. At least not too much of a damn."

"Did you ever try to get alcohol in Synanon?"

"No. Never tried. I had right away such a sense of being wanted. In Synanon. Even though I was such an awful mess of trouble for everyone. Just think: I had to be carried around like a baby. And even when I could begin to help myself, it was still months before the edema left me and I could wear shoes and learn to walk again. And now look at me. Why I run up and down those steps ten, twenty times a day."

"Would you say that the sense of being wanted cured you of your need for alcohol?"

"Cure?" Anne Bancroft exclaims. "Who said anything about cure. I'm not cured. Why right now, if I got just one sip of alochol, I don't know if I could stop until I passed out. That's why I'm never going to leave Synanon. Someone once asked me: 'What would you do if tomorrow morning you woke up and Synanon was gone?'— I said: 'Why don't you ask me what I would do if tomorrow morning the sun had vanished.'—This person then said: 'Then you're totally dependent on Synanon?'—And I said: 'Totally.' That's how it is."

Then, back in my office, it will be Jimmy Middleton, who is waiting to talk to me about the Detroit facility which he ran for quite a while.

"Am I glad to be back in Los Angeles sunshine!" he exclaims. "A Detroit winter is too much for me. But it was exciting there. Bumping into so many old friends."

"What do you mean old friends?"

"Well, I'm a Detroit boy, didn't you know that? But what a contrast! Used to be when I walked into the Detroit police headquarters, it was with my hands cuffed behind my back, and some cop shoving me forward. Not too gently either.

"Running a Synanon house, naturally brings you up against the police now and then. So there I am, walking in, dressed in a good suit, with a white shirt and neat tie, and everybody glad to see me. Nobody shoving me from behind. And Chief Inspector Turkely willing to sit down and bullshit with me. He'll talk about the time he was in charge of the 13th District, and several times had to handcuff me to a telegraph pole while he called up headquarters for a paddy wagon, which would be so slow coming and my position so tiring, that I'd sink down into the snow.

"And he'll look at me and wonder: 'God! I tried to rehabilitate you four or five times, Jimmy. How come I couldn't, and Synanon could?'

"I never bothered to explain to him that Synanon doesn't do it with handcuffs and prisons.

"Well, like I say, Guy, I was bumping into old acquaintances all over the place. Once I had business that took me out to the Women's House of Corrections, and the superintendent there used to be warden out in Jackson prison. We recognized each other right away. Hell, he ought to know me. I was in his care three or four times, for a total of seven years or more.

"And Hubert Locke, the assistant police commissioner, he too recognized me. The moment I stepped into his office he said: 'I remember you. I put you behind bars often enough.'

"Yes, Detroit was exciting," Jimmy concludes. "All but the weather."

That's how the days go by in Synanon, with me writing and running and despairing of ever catching up. One Synanon happening after another, one unfinished piece of business begun before another is concluded, so that I have no idea where to draw the line and write FINIS. I feel as if someone had handed me a towel and told me to dry myself while still under the running shower.

Chuck suggests that I listen to a recent tape of his that he feels has some importance, but Reid says: "We've got this girl here that wants to come in. A square. She's been playing the game for a few months. Now she wants to move in. Will you see her?"

"What for? What's wrong with her?"

Reid says: "I don't know. I suppose she has problems. But she's doing all right. I mean she works for a computer firm. Will soon be earning thirteen thousand a year. Says she is willing to keep on working on the outside while living here, and will turn over all her paychecks to Synanon."

Chuck says: "Well of course that settles it. She must be crazy. Anyone willing to give us thirteen thousand a year just for the privilege of living in our nuthouse must be insane. Okay, let's talk to her."

It's in Chuck's office, of course, that the Synanon thing keeps happening more often than anywhere else. Day and night Chuck is singlemindedly occupied with nothing but playing midwife to whatever it is that is trying to be born in Synanon. And the moment he senses that which is attempting to become manifest there, he lets it possess him, keeps talking about it to those around him, discusses it again and again, seeking the most effective words and locutions by which to make it vividly clear, until he is ready, finally, to present it to his staff in the way that it will be passed on to the membership.

And thus a new x-factor gets introduced into the Synanon milieu and is tested out in practice. "All we do here is guess," Chuck explains, "and then wait to see if we've guessed right."

The introduction of such an x-factor occurred recently with the purchase of the big Del Mar beach club. From New York, from Detroit, from San Francisco, and elsewhere, the Synanon directors gathered to hear Chuck address them.

"This will be Synanon's first great mutation," Chuck said to them. "I think that the metamorphosis that is now beginning here is going to proceed so rapidly and be so extensive, that five years from now it will be impossible to imagine what kind of an organization we were originally. We may, in half a decade, be so far removed from our present drug addict business that it will be difficult to believe that that is where we got our start.

"When we first saw dope addicts come into Synanon, eight and nine years ago, and we saw how they stopped wanting dope, we shouted that we, yes *we*, had cured them. And that was only natural because we were the only people around when it happened. So it must have been our work. But of course it wasn't. It wasn't really. Because no person in the world can cure a dope addict. I know that *I* can't. Such extreme aberrations simply will not yield on a person to person basis.

"How was it that we didn't see that, and that we continued to give ourselves credit for what was happening here? Well, that was because we kept on thinking administratively while actually we were moving and working in a completely different way.

"Administration, you see, is a process that can work wonders when it comes to building an automobile. Or when you've got a dam to construct. Administration will get a factory going for you, and it can handle traffic problems. But it can never stop a person from using dope. Never. If administration could do that then Congress long ago would have passed the necessary laws and allocated the necessary funds. And the job would have been done.

"But Congress can't. No legislature, no city council in the world can do that. The Prohibition Amendment demonstrated that, didn't it?

"Then how does Synanon manage? What happened in Synanon was that while we continued to think administratively we were actually building a new kind of society, a society that is an absorption machine. It was the squares forcing their way into Synanon that began to make us realize what we were accomplishing here. All other societies are exclusive. They rule out the young, or they rule out the old. They rule out men or else women. The sick or the well. The squares or the criminals. The rich or the poor. The educated or the uneducated. The black or the white. The believer or the atheist. The sane or the insane.

"But almost from the start it became clear that Synanon had to be inclusive. Had to open its doors to everyone. Until today we can say to every person on the surface of this earth: you belong to the human race? Then you're a member of Synanon. Whether you know it or not. So why don't you pay your dues?

"When you belong to such an inclusive society, and the playing of the game brings you into more and more intimate communication with everyone, you become part of an absorption machine. And it's this absorption machine that stops people from going to jail all the time, that stops them from forever scratching for dope, from craving constant alcoholization. While at the same time it deepens the happiness and the understanding of those who have no acting-out character problems.

"That is what is going to happen here more and more as Synanon breaks down all the old barriers between addicts and squares. Or between ex-addicts and ex-squares, because both groups, when they move into Synanon, must leave behind their past—and there will only be Synanon people here, some resident members, and others who will be non-resident members.

"Contrast for a moment the way the new Synanon life-style will automatically handle the problems of people, to the way the city of Boston administrates them as described in a recent *Manas* magazine article. There it is stated that in Boston, a full twenty-five percent of the population is suffering from some variety of mental aberration, some impediment or inability that cries out for help. And Boston is totally unable to cope with this condition. *Manas* cites the case of a family where the husband is an alcoholic, the wife uneducated and manic-depressive and completely defeated by the job of taking care of three children, one of whom is a hydrocephalic.

"What does Boston do about this? The city authorities have set up all sorts of agencies to look after every aspect of this situation. It's an almost total failure. One agency sends out a marriage counselor to work on the family. Another agency looks out for an asylum that will take in the hydrocephalic child. Still another agency sends out a psychologist to treat the manic-depressive symptoms of the mother, while a person from A.A. gets to work on the drunken husband, and a child expert moves in on the other two children.

"Of course all these separate activities can't do the job. They keep hacking away at it, of course, but it's like trying to sweep back the tide.

"Synanon's method will be completely different. It would not administrate such a situation. It would absorb it. It would take in such a family and introduce it to a completely new style of life, a life in which all those people would mingle with people who have succeeded on the outside, people who have had education and achieved a measure of success, but who are now exactly the same as the people of that family: that is to say paid-up members of the same club. All first-class citizens in Synanon. All living the same life-style.

"Of course Synanon will have to have vast amounts of real estate in order to accommodate all these people. And the purchase of a lot of similar highly sophisticated pieces of real estate as our Del Mar with its tennis courts and sauna baths, its swimming pool and dance floors will demand the close cooperation of our non-profit foundation with the American profit system, and I believe that combination is going to prove to be a Jim-dandy. Before this year is up Synanon may be the owner of ten million dollars' worth of such real estate. And in another five or ten years we may be the biggest property owners in this nation."

Of course everything that Chuck was saying was so highly exaggerated as to be unbelievable. Except that only recently Chuck had bought himself that palatial home in Beverly Hills that I've already described. He had put down ten thousand dollars to clinch the deal and had assumed a mortgage of eighty thousand dollars. But a few months later this ninety-thousand-dollar home with a valuation of two hundred thousand dollars was used as a down payment on the purchase of a complex of sixty-two large apartments, which were taken over by Synanon residents as fast as the old tenants moved out. And immediately on the heels of that real estate profit of one hundred and ten thousand dollars, Chuck had made another fifty grand in another deal; while up in San Francisco, Synanon put on a block party that was so popular that it brought in seventy-five thousand dollars, and this money, plus considerable support from

Synanon sponsors, had enabled the club to swing its first multi-million-dollar real estate deal: the acquisition of the Del Mar.

Obviously a man who can go around boasting: "This year I made more money for Synanon than all our industries combined. I became Synanon's biggest cash donor," such a man may very well be capable of making Synanon the largest owner of property in the United States within a very short time.

Even though at the moment, Synanon, having lost its milk connection, hasn't served its residents with any cottage cheese, butter, sour cream, ice cream, milk, or buttermilk for the last three months. Chuck shrugs that off: "Adults don't need milk. Maybe they're better off without it. Of course we have to buy milk for our kids. Naturally. But the rest of us can get along without it. The Japanese and the Chinese have been doing that for thousands of years with no ill effects. So why shouldn't we?"

Which only means that Synanon, forever growing richer while forever remaining as broke as before, will have to get along without milk products until good fortune brings them another milk connection.

It will emerge.

Of course. Because nothing stops Synanon. Not for very long. Not even the present tremor of concern that is sweeping through the club, because some of its best second-string executive talent is being lured away to New York by the high salaries that the imitation Synanons (richly funded by the four-hundred-million-dollar Rockefeller program) can now afford to pay to anyone who has some Synanon savvy, to anyone who can bring to them the knowledge of how to play the game.

"When you have a Flo, whom we saved from a ten-year rap," Chuck says, "and she can now go to New York and earn herself eight thousand dollars a year, and she runs to our free department store to pick up all the free clothing she can before lighting out, then I say we haven't lost a thing. And New York hasn't gained a thing. Because with that kind of greedy attitude Flo isn't going to be much good to them. Not really.

"And when you have another dope addict who never earned an honest penny in his life, and who had to come to Synanon to suck at Synanon's tit for seven years before turning into a man—but not enough of a man to know that you don't run off to a fifteen-thousand-dollar a year job without shaking hands with the people who gave you the knowledge and the training that now makes that job possible for you—then I say again Synanon has lost nothing whatsoever by his going. And New York hasn't gained anything. Not a thing.

"And the same with Larry, who drew a whole week's cigarette ration before skipping off the following morning. Of course Synanon still has a right to be proud of what it did for those dingbats. But can New York's program, by stealing our ideas and seducing our people, can they be proud of what they've done? Demoralizing these poor ex-addicts with bribes far beyond their capacity to resist? Is that how New York expects to cure dope addicts? Demoralizing their own staff before it puts them to work in the service of morality?

"Of course we knew—didn't we?—that this was coming. Six years ago Walker Winslow warned us about it. Remember? Remember his prediction that after spurning us the government would try to steal us? Steal our program and crap it up. He made that prediction on the basis of what happened to Dorothea Lynde Dix over a century ago. How she campaigned for years and finally woke up the United States to the horror of our prisons and insane asylums where our defectives were being kept worse than animals. And how after her work was done, her name was glorified but only in order to deceive the American people into thinking that everything had been reformed, when as a matter of fact, everything remained just the way it had been.

"What Synanon has to be afraid of is not that Tom, Dick, and Harry will go skipping off to land themselves cushy jobs. Why shouldn't they? More power to them. What we have to be afraid of is that behind the name of Synanon, a name that will eventually acquire a magic aura, the same old treadmill of crime, law courts, jails, and asylums will continue to operate as if they had all been changed into Synanons. Thus merely using our good name to flim-flam the public. That's where the danger lies."

Yes, that's a danger indeed. But not as great as it would be if Synanon were a program set forth in a manifesto. But Synanon is a program that wants to be born, and that is being born. And I know of nothing that can stop it.

A few weeks ago the leader of a branch of the hippie movement came down from Northern California to see Chuck. This leader, a man of wealth, had opened his ranch to hippies and eventually found his property overflowing with a disorganized group of electric guitar players, flower-children, bums and winos, crazed acid-heads, Buddhists and nudists, and other assorted seekers after God. All combining to make a shambles of his place, with mothers wandering off into the bushes and leaving naked children screaming for food, and drunks getting violent in the middle of the night, while ascetic Christ-children prayed for illumination.

Couldn't Synanon help him bring some order to his place? Couldn't Chuck lend him a couple of good Synanon-trained people to come up to his ranch and straighten things out a bit?

Of course Chuck refused. "No. No. It just can't be done that way. Synanon cannot be half one thing and half another. It's an either/or proposition. So why don't *you* join *us?* Then we'll move in and turn your ranch into a Synanon facility. And then it will be up to the bums either to conform or get lost."

The visitor couldn't make up his mind to take a step of such proportions.

"Why not?" Chuck asked. "After all Synanon is what the hippies are looking for. But don't know it!"

"Oh, we're all aware of Synanon," the rancher said. "Synanon is the most discussed topic of our place. Some of us are against it and some of us are for it, but most are in between, unable to make up their minds."

"In that case," Chuck said, "why don't *you* make up their minds for them? After all Synanon pioneered your hippie business. Long before any of your people thought of being flower-children and holding love-ins, when I was asked how you start a Synanon I said: 'Find yourself a dope addict and love him.' But you see, our love is total—not just a Sunday outing.

"Take your Diggers who are now getting all sorts of publicity because of their free store. Synanon opened its first free store eight years ago! And it's more than just a grocery business and a clothing store. Much more. When the Diggers give a man a loaf of bread or a dish of beans, do they see to it that he also has the teeth to chew it with? No, of course not. But Synanon does. Synanon wants to make sure that that loaf of bread will get down to that man's gut, well chewed. And for that we'll see to it that he gets the necessary dental care, or a set of crockery teeth if that is what he has to have.

"And we'll do more. We won't just send him away with a loaf of bread under his arm, we'll see to it that he has a place where he can eat that bread, and a place where he can digest it, like a clean room with a clean bunk to sleep in, and a clean bathroom to shower and crap in. And after we've helped him get some of the stupidity out of his head, we'll see to it that he has work to do so that he can feel good about taking our food and our space, and if he chooses he can go on and develop himself towards a career either inside Synanon or out.

"So to your Diggers I say, God bless them for doing the work that needs to be done. But you're eight years late. Eight years behind us. And you'll never catch up, you'll never catch up because you and your hippies don't think in terms of totality the way Synanon does. You think in terms of holiness, instead of wholeness. That W makes all the difference in the world.

"Like your Diggers, Synanon too is striving to make money obsolete, except as a statistical and commercial tool to facilitate the spread of the earth's goods, which is what money was invented for— but this attitude of ours towards the dollar doesn't make us forget the Golden Rule, which is to do unto others what you would they would do unto you.

"And how can you practice the Golden Rule when you're a hippie and are saying to society, in effect: 'I will take your automobile so

I can drive off to hippie land, and I will take along my electric guitar because that's the kind of music I like, and I will take along my LSD. But I refuse to have anything to do with chemical knowledge, I refuse to study chemistry or work in the chemical laboratory that makes LSD, nor will I work in a factory that makes automobiles or electric guitars. No, I'll just pick and choose from the established world what I happen to like, and then I'll tune in and turn on and drop out.

"Is that honest? Doesn't that make hippies panhandlers? Why of course it does. Synanon too accepts things from the larger society, such as cars and tape recorders, and so forth, things that Synanon doesn't itself make. But it does things in return. Things for the larger society, such as taking care of their dope addicts and their prostitutes and criminals. Besides involving itself in selling gas, servicing cars, teaching school, selling advertising specialties. Synanon is a hive of activity. If you turned over your property to us, we wouldn't wreck it. We'd build it up to where it would be worth twice what it's worth now. We've done that with almost every place we've occupied.

"Isn't it the absolute end of absurdity that hippies should loll around listening to a tape recorder that they cannot repair if it should break down? What's holy about getting loaded to your eyelashes and leaving your garbage to pile up and breed flies, while your plumbing goes out of whack and your girls get babies and the clap at the same time.

"Holiness is not what is needed in the world today. Because holiness is never anything but a partial answer, and the world of today is full of partial answers that have failed. The world today can't use another Congressional appropriation. It can't use another investigating committee. It can't use another slum-clearance program or another civil rights congress, or still another member admitted to the United Nations.

"The world of today needs wholeness. And as I look around the world I see no other program offering wholeness. None whatsoever. Except Synanon."

J14